Contents

Acknowledgements	1
Foreword	3
#1 Introduction	7
#2 How do People get Killed by "Unloaded" Guns?	9
#3 About Those Children…and Your Guns.	13
#4 No Such Thing as an Unloaded Firearm, Proper "Mindset."	17
#5 What is a Misfire/What is a Hang Fire?	19
#6 What is a Squib Load? Understand the Danger.	21
#7 Uncontrolled Bullets Anyone? Not on Your Life!	25
#8 Cease-Fire! What you do, Completely.	27
#9 Why Might dry Firing be Used?	29
#10 Weapon Safeties…Understand Them.	31
#11 Glaser Safety Slugs and Home Defense.	33
#12 The Aftermath of Defending Your Family/Home.	37
#13 Specific to MA Petition for Judicial Review.	41
#14 MA Change of Address Notification Forms and a Renewal tip.	45
#15 Concealed or Not Concealed, That is the Question…	49
#16 Gun Safety and Responsibility.	51
#17 What Should You Teach Your Child About Gun Safety?	53
#18 If you "Misplace" Your MA LTC or FID.	55
#19 "Reason" Letter for MA LTC.	57
#20 MA Misdemeanor? Been Denied Your Gun Permit/License?	63
#21 Shooting not Mandated? Why I do not Have you Shoot.	65
#22 MA "Stored & Kept"' and "Direct Control."	69
#23 Ten Cardinal Rules of Firearm Safety and Firearm Safety Test…	75
#24 Hollywood Bullets vs. Real Bullets.	79
#25 Can you Keep a Secret?	85
#26 MA Hunter Safety Class Information.	87

#27 Gun Laws to "Understand" in MA (with links).	91
#28 Is The Second Amendment Relevant? You bet Your Life!	95
#29 Answers to Firearm Safety Test #23.	99
#30 Graduated Licenses,(D-A) Under MA Law & "Green Card" Info.	101
#31 Frequently Asked Questions.	105
#32 Firearm Possession in MA.	113
#33 MA "Letters of Recommendation" & Gun License Help.	121
#34 MA CORI Report Info.	123
#35 Places you Cannot Carry Firearms in MA.	127
#36 Inheritance and Other Firearm Transactions, Form (E-FA10).	131
#37 Storage of Ammunition, Powder & Primers…	135
#38 Traffic Stops in MA.	139
#39 MA Application/"Interview" Process & Steps/Tips.	141
#40 The Right to Remain Silent has Changed, be Aware!	145
#41 Gun Law Changes in MA 8-13-2014.	147
#42 Legal Resident Aliens (Federal Law).	153
#43 MA Gun Registration Misconception.	155
#44 KSG 12ga Shotgun Demonstration.	157
#45 Gun Registration UNCONSTITUTIONAL.	159
#46 Firearms Confiscated in MA?	161
#47 26 States That Honor Your MA LTC.	165
#48 Nomenclature of Various Firearms-ATF.	167
#49 BATF Pays a Visit to MA Officials 4-20-18.	169
#50 Active Duty Service People in MA.	173
Children, Their Future Rights, are we Overlooking Them?	175
Zero Gun Sense = Uzi Submachine Gun Tragedy in Westfield MA.	177
UZI Tragedy in Westfield, Part 2.	179
Common Sense, The Meaning Has Flip Flopped.	181
Evil Guns? (by Ed Sinnott).	183
NRA and Relevance.	185

Constitutional Amendment for the Gun Control Crowd.	187
Bloomberg's Gun Control....	189
Warnings of Yesteryear for Today.	191
Liberal vs. Conservative.	193
I'm not Politically Correct...you Offended?	195
Humble Observation of a Beleaguered Tax Payer.	197
We the Problem – A Preamble to our Ignorance.	199
My Definition of a Politician.	201
Another Type of Solution.	203
Holiday Cheer?	205
APPENDIX A – RESOURCES	207
The U.S. Bill of Rights	207
The Department of Criminal Justice Information Services	207
Mass.gov Link to Gun Laws	208
Mass.gov Link to Approved Firearms Roster	208
Mass.gov Link to 527 CMR (BOARD OF FIRE PREVENTION REGULATIONS)	208
Massachusetts Gun Transaction Portal	208
The National Sport Shooting Foundation (NSSF)	209
The National Rifle Association (NRA)	209
Gun Owners Action League (GOAL)	210
The General Court of the Commonwealth of Massachusetts	211
Commonwealth Second Amendment Inc.	211
Massachusetts Hunter Education Program	212
Division of Fisheries and Wildlife MASSWILDLIFE	212
USA Carry	213
APPENDIX B – IMPORTANT FORMS	215
APPENDIX C – LETTER EXAMPLES	217
Reason Letter	217
Letter of Recommendation	218
Firearm Custody Letter in the Event of Confiscation	219
APPENDIX D - Massachusetts General Law (M.G.L.) Chapter 140 Firearm Sections	221
APPENDIX E - C.M.R. 527 Chapter 1 Excerpts	313
About the Author	315

Acknowledgements

I would like to dedicate this book to my wife Diane, for which none of this may have come about. Because of her insistence I brought the class to people, to fit their schedules. Since 2000 I have given the course in 86 towns and I am fast approaching 900 classes, all because of her!

I would also like to thank my editor John Petrolino, who answered to a comment I made about putting *Gun Sense* in the form of an E-book. I told him that I had thought about it off and on but that I did not have a clue as to how to go about it. John said that he would give it a shot and our partnership began! A very knowledgeable editor to say the least! John made this book possible.

This book is not only about Massachusetts gun laws, it covers a range of information that can keep anyone, from anywhere, up to speed where firearm safety is concerned and in using firearms, *Gun Sense* is a must. Pass it on to your family and friends. Be safe.

Sincerely,
Mark Shean

Foreword

Mark Shean's *Gun Sense* is in reality a series of numbered and un-numbered articles assembled into a book. In 2018, after taking Mark's License to Carry (LTC) class, he was talking about wanting to take his blog and turn it into an E-book. There was a desire to be able to reach a wider audience and make it easier for his students to follow along with him/review the material. Having had some experience in publishing, I volunteered to give his project a shot. One year later I'm writing this.

Mark Shean comes to readers with a combination of over 55 years of firearms, NRA LE Instructor and Nuclear security experience. Though originally from Maine, Mark has been teaching the Massachusetts gun law class since 2000. *Gun Sense* is not so much a book you read from the first page to the last (even though you could and should), as much as it is a guide to topics on gun safety, Massachusetts gun law, your general rights as an American, op-eds and so on and so forth, that can apply anywhere. The synergy of this work is that Mark just started writing these articles as the topics came to him. These are ideas that came to him in the order that they are presented here, over years. There are sections that are redundant and cover the same material over again, for a reason. In compiling the over 50 independent pieces, we have tried to lend some help in organization by referencing other Gun Sense chapters, which would give you more information on a certain subject. Chances are if you have a question when reading *Gun Sense* or taking Mark's class, the question will be answered by the time you finish reading the book or sitting in on the class.

Gun Sense is not affiliated with or endorsed by any group or persons mentioned within. While reference to organizations such as the Nation Rifle Association, Gun Owners Action League, National Sport Shooting Foundation, Commonwealth Second Amendment Inc., etc. are made and said groups cited...this book has not been endorsed or reviewed by any of them. This is Mark's work and his alone, except where notated.

Gun Sense is not to serve as a substitute for competent legal consultation. Mark is bringing forth his opinion on the subjects and sharing with you, the reader, what he has learned from his experiences. Any information should be checked and double checked. Also, *Gun Sense* is not to be in lieu of actual hands on firearm training. The safety topics covered and firearm handling information are all based on Mark's corporal experience. Further guidance and education on the subjects covered within this work should be followed up with by taking a class and or consulting a firearms instructor(s). There is no assumption of liability from the author, publisher or editor(s) concerning the use of any information contained in *Gun Sense* and the reader shall read at their own peril.

The good news is that Mark is a tangible and accessible guy. All you have to do is find his contact information at the end of this book in the **"About the Author"** section and if you have any questions, comments, concerns or general correspondence, Mark would be happy to field them. Also, if you are reading this book as a companion to his class, that is awesome and I think you'll find having this text handy while in class or before/after class will help reinforce the lessons he teaches. If you are reading this book and are thinking that you want some training, all the better. Reach out to Mark and he'd be happy to talk to you about a training session or teaching you the required class to obtain a Massachusetts Firearms Identification Card (FID) or License to Carry (LTC).

We have included Appendixes with helpful information and plenty of citations through the text. At the time of this writing, everything was accurate and up to date, but that does not mean it so shall remain. Concerning **Chapter 140 of Massachusetts General Law** and also **527 Code of Massachusetts Regulations**, be advised this is all subject to change, so always cross reference and ensure you have the up to date regulations. As with all citations and references in this text, they can and will change over time.

Happy reading and stay safe!

John Petrolino
Editor

"The American Revolution would never have happened had government 'gun control' already been in place, watch very closely all who want it. Ignorance of history can cost you your freedoms." - Mark Shean

"Firearm education will save lives, firearm ignorance can take lives." - Mark Shean

"Arms discourage and keep the plunderer in awe, they preserve order in the world as well as property...horrid mischief would ensue were the law-abiding citizen be deprived of the use of them." - Thomas Paine

Gun Sense #1 Introduction

Hello, I am no lawyer, I just try harder to keep up with the gun laws that affect people in MA than others do. So, if you do not agree with something here, by all means, research the answer for yourself. In this series I have written some numbered articles, 50 and counting, entitled *Gun Sense*. Many of these come directly from my experiences and touch on various aspects of firearm safety. *Gun Sense* is a useful reference extension beyond my class. We talk about some of these things in our firearm safety classes along with the laws. ***Gun Sense #32 Firearm Possession in MA.* & *Gun Sense #41 Gun Law Changes in MA 8-13-2014.*** are required by the state of Massachusetts for the Basic Firearm Safety Course, for those who would like to apply for a License to Carry (LTC) or Firearm Identification Card (FID).

With this class comes our support long afterward, consider us your safety net. If you have questions in the future, rest assured we will answer them through emails, GUARANTEED. If you have trouble with gaining your license we will point you in a direction to succeed and if for some reason it is beyond our scope, we can put you in touch with a group of lawyers that may take your case for free. This is a level of assistance I have offered all my clients since I started in 2000. It is not found anywhere else. A little research is all you need to confirm this.

We take your success in gaining a LTC or FID VERY seriously. My son Mark joined me on many classes, with 26 years of firearm knowledge/experience (to his credit), giving the same level of excellence and follow-through in every class that he will give.

In my opinion, gun owners who vote for any candidate(s) that are in favor of gun control, amounts to the same thing as turkeys voting in favor of Thanksgiving….get my meaning?

Gun Sense #2 How do People get Killed by "Unloaded" Guns?

How do people get killed by so called unloaded guns? Have you ever thought that this was possible? It is possible and happens sadly, on a fairly frequent basis. It is in the news from time to time, but it does not have to happen. People are quite often killed by "unloaded" guns. The reoccurring theme is, "I thought it was unloaded!" Foolish and sad.

It can go something like this....One day Jon buys a .38 caliber revolver at the local gun shop, he has always wanted to buy a handgun and this one just feels right in his hand. The price is right, so what the heck. Next Jon brings it out to a dirt pit in the woods behind his house with a friend. They run quite a few rounds through it and they have a good time. Jon puts it away in the house and forgets about it for a while....A couple of months go by and Jon has invited a group of friends over for a house party, no special occasion, just a get together.

When people get together like this, oftentimes the "toys" will come out of the woodwork. We may want to show something off that is kind of unusual, that is simple human nature. Guns easily fall into this category. People are particularly drawn to firearms, they appear to be excellent show and tell material. Jon gets the .38 caliber revolver out of his bedroom and takes it into the backyard where the grill and music are in full swing, the beer is flowing and the party is underway. "Hey," he says, "anyone want to check out my new handgun? Hey Scott, check it out, it's unloaded....and the safety is on, here take it Scott, take it!" Everyone in the backyard heard this, as Jon had to speak loudly over the music and now they are all looking directly at Scott, some egging him on to take the gun. The peer pressure is real and starting to effect the situation. Scott thinks: *What the heck, I will take a look at it, I've never held a real gun before, this could be cool.* Then Scott thinks, *Jon said it was unloaded, even said the safety is on, what could be the harm?* So he takes it from Jon.

Now, it is inevitable, that once a gun is in the hands of someone that has never had any sort of firearm training, the first thing they seem overwhelmingly, inexplicably, inclined to do, is to put their finger on the trigger. Next they want to test the theory that the safety is on and that the gun is unloaded, simultaneously. Scott points the gun playfully at someone in the group to test these two theories. Susan sees Scott pointing it at her and tells Scott not to do that! Scott laughs, "Its not even loaded, watch" he says and pulls the trigger, BANG! Susan drops to the ground with a hole in her chest, the gun hits the floor immediately afterward, dropped by a stunned and confused Scott! The first thing out of Scott's mouth is, "I thought it was unloaded!" Jon says, "Oh my God! I thought it was unloaded!" All this combined wisdom from Jon and Scott will never change the fact that Susan is now tragically dead, killed by an "unloaded" gun, she will be dead for a very long time. Jon evidently did not even understand the fact that a common revolver has no external safety. Jon and Scott will now have to pay the heavy legal consequences for this "accident." Susan's family and friends will never fully recover emotionally from the loss of Susan, ever.

How do you avoid a terrible scene like this? Firearm education is the first critical step. Common sense plays a huge roll. I like to think that we all have common sense, the key is to engage it before you act. That is the key, think about what you're doing before you do anything with a firearm. Take your common sense for a walk around the block once in a while and exercise it! You NEVER take anyone's word that a firearm is unloaded, EVER! THERE IS NO SUCH THING AS AN UNLOADED GUN! Treat them all as if they are LOADED! THAT IS THE "MINDSET" EVERYONE NEEDS TO EMPLOY for firearm safety! The only time your finger should EVER connect with the trigger of any firearm is when you intend to shoot the firearm, for no other reason. It is not a "resting" place for your finger! There is a trigger guard around the trigger (that little circle of steel). I don't call it a trigger guard...I do not think that is a serious enough description, I call it THE CIRCLE OF DEATH. When a finger enters that circle someone could die due to foolish actions. Keep your finger OUT of that circle of death if you're not going to actually shoot the firearm! If you're not going to actually shoot the gun, you never just ride the trigger with your finger, EVER!

Think about it this way...pretend that your very own mother comes home one day with a handgun, a revolver for instance. Now we all know that our mothers love us dearly and would never want to see any of their children ever get hurt. They would do anything in their power for their kids, most mothers are hard wired that way. With that in mind, your mother comes home with that handgun and wants you to see it, she is quite proud of it. "Look what I bought..." she says, "check it out." As she tries to hand it to you (I'm sure we can all picture our mothers doing something like this right?). Well for the sake of making my point, we will all pretend that she comes home and says exactly that. Should you take the gun from her and look at it? No, you should not. You should say to your very own dear mother, whom you know loves you, "Look Ma, could you please just show me that the gun is technically unloaded first?" And because she is your mother, she will not have any problem with that very simple request. She will quickly reach over and push forward the cylinder release button with the thumb of her right hand and at the same time she will deftly push the cylinder open from right to left with the middle finger of same right hand, openly exposing the now obviously, (technically) empty cylinder for your inspection. Now that you are satisfied that the gun is indeed technically unloaded you may take it from your mother to "check it out," observing muzzle discipline (pointed in a safe direction) and treating it just as if it were loaded (proper mindset).

The point that I am trying to make by using "dear ole Ma" in the example is this, If you are going to make your very own dear mother, whom you love, show you that the gun is unloaded before you will accept it from her, you will NEVER give anyone else privileges that you would not give your own mother! Not Joe Blow who you hardly even know, or the head of The NRA, nor anyone else in this entire world would you ever give that privilege! Understand? If someone is not willing to show you that a gun is unloaded, then you are not willing to take it from that person, period!

Remember, there is no such thing as an unloaded gun! Have I mentioned that yet? That is the mindset you must ALWAYS have to handle them safely! I know that there will be wise guys who will say, "How can I clean it if it is always loaded?" To them I say "I am talking about developing a mindset for a fully INTACT firearm, if it is broken down into parts for cleaning then clean it, if you pretend not to know the difference, why are you pretending? Grow up."

People who handle firearms the most can actually become more susceptible to accidents as they become lackadaisical around them, they become ripe for an accident. Always give firearms the respect they demand. Your first mistake could be someone else's last breath on Earth. Guns do not give fools a second chance very often.

Sometimes people with a high level of firearm experience can get lazy, over confident and are even more susceptible to accidents. When that happens, they are vulnerable for an accident to occur. I will go so far as to say they don't take firearms as seriously as they once did, they need to pause and regroup. They have become a distinct danger to themselves and others with that lackadaisical mindset. To make the point, even police can accidentally shoot themselves, for stats see these links:

Gun Injuries Soar as Police 'Experts' Blast Themselves and Colleagues by Mistake

http://www.dailymail.co.uk/news/article-535071/Gun-injuries-soar-police-experts-blast-colleagues-mistake.html#ixzz1ulAaBTqE

DEA Agent In Foot Shoot Suit

http://www.thesmokinggun.com/archive/0411061foot1.html

Gun Sense #3 About Those Children...and Your Guns.

How many of you have children? How many of you know someone with children? They are everywhere and because they are everywhere they can get into mischief just about any place. Where guns are concerned there can be no room for mischief.

I am originally from the state of Maine where the gun culture was quite a bit different from where I live now in Massachusetts. People seem savvier about firearms and firearm safety generally, in Maine. This is what I have observed in my experiences within both states. Growing up I had a lot of supervised exposure to firearms, that was the key and I learned early-on how to safely handle and use firearms, it was encouraged. Knowledge kept me safer than someone without firearm knowledge. If that makes sense to you, as I hope it should, than I will share a bit of advice designed to keep your little ones safer than they were moments before you started reading this. Children, we all want them safe.

When it comes to firearms I believe there is a wrong way (based on wishful thinking) and a right way, based initially, on very simple rudimentary education. You may think you are able to insulate your child from harm and from knowledge of firearms in your home, but what about when your child is old enough to visit and play with the next door neighbors' children in their home? How things are done in the house next door may be quite different than how you prefer to do things in respect to firearms. You cannot insulate your child from the world. Do you think it may be wiser to impart to your child the danger that can be and is associated with firearms?

Education, it is like a form of preventive maintenance. If you own a firearm and believe that by keeping the gun well-hidden and a secret, that the child will be safer....That line of thought is only good to a point, until the child, caught up in the spirit of exploration, inadvertently finds the gun while you are mowing the lawn or taking a nap, etc. I like to call this the Easter egg syndrome. Children are very curious about everything around them, their whole mission in life at a young age is to dig around looking for/at things. If you have kids you know exactly what I am talking about. If you don't yet have kids, when you do, you will see soon enough that I do not speak with a forked tongue. Would you rather the child find a gun while you are busy? I hope not.

I feel that the very best way is to take the mystery out of firearms when children (or adults) are concerned, is to show the child the unloaded firearm. Explain the danger. Let the child hold and look at it. Let him know he will be in big trouble if he ever touches it without your permission or supervision, but the main thing is to take the mystery out of it. Once you do that, you will have taken the right step towards a child that will be safer around firearms. That is the first correct step on a long trail of steps where firearm safety is concerned. You do not have to show the child where you keep the firearm. Let the child know that you are accessible, if he/she wants to see the gun in the future to come to you and that you will drop what you're doing to look at the firearm together. This accessibility is very important and should keep your child from going behind your back to look at the gun(s). But, you must keep your word about this at all times.

To be on the safe side, the ammo should be kept separate from guns and any unattended guns should, at a minimum, have trigger locks on them. Firearms should never be left lying around loaded. You're probably saying "that is just plain common sense! Do you think we are all idiots!?" Well folks, if it is such plain common sense, why are children involved in accidental and tragic shootings in the home? That is not common sense at work, that is irresponsible gun ownership and parenting. I am not talking about gang bangers who burglarize homes, steal guns and go out into the street intentionally and idiotically trying to murder one another, no. I am referring to young children finding a parent's loaded gun in a night stand, etc. and through curiosity, they accidentally shoot themselves or a sibling. Not only tragic, unacceptable!

You can begin teaching a child at the tender age of three or four, a very simple message from the NRA Eddie Eagle program. If they ever see a gun they: 1.Stop. 2. Don't Touch. 3. Run Away. 4. Tell a Grown Up. Children are very smart, don't short change them. They can easily learn this with gentle reinforcement and incentive, make a big deal out of it when they repeat those words to you when they find the toy gun you use as a training aid. Because it is a big deal, it could save a life one day. You should not take toy guns away, they are part of a healthy upbringing. Set one aside as the training aid for the child to learn the lesson by.

If you own guns or want to own guns, you owe it to yourself and your entire family to be proactively responsible in the safety of that ownership: for everybody's safety, for years of family enjoyment and being involved in a great American heritage, it's your birthright.

Read **Gun Sense #16 Gun Safety and Responsibility.** and **Gun Sense #17 What Should You Teach Your Child About Gun Safety?** for more information.

Gun Sense #4 No Such Thing as an Unloaded Firearm, Proper "Mindset."

I can hear them now; "What do you mean all guns are loaded all the time?! That's stupid! I have guns at home right now that are not loaded! Hell, I was at the gun store the other day, none of them guns behind the counter and on the wall rack were loaded!"

I say, yes they are. They are all loaded. Every gun at your house, every gun in that store and everywhere else, they are all loaded.

"You're Crazy! They Are Not!"

Listen, if you don't have the mindset that they are all loaded and ready to fire, you are a prime candidate for a firearm accident. You assume too much, take too much for granted, you're a danger to yourself and others.

Even people with a high level of firearm experience can get lazy, over confident and are even more susceptible to accidents. I will go so far as to say they don't take firearms as seriously as they once did, they need to pause and regroup. They have become a distinct danger to themselves and others with that lackadaisical mindset. To make the point, even police can accidentally shoot themselves. In case you had not a chance to look at them previously, check out the links from **Gun Sense #2 How do People get Killed by "Unloaded" Guns?**.

The NRA now says the first rule in firearm safety is: Always keep the gun pointed in a safe direction (muzzle discipline). That was not always so and I will never agree with that change. As a kid, I distinctly remember the first rule being: Treat all firearms as loaded at all times! It conveys a far sterner and implies a much stronger sense of urgency/danger to safe firearm handling. I still have my little red Jr. NRA Rifle Handbook from the mid-1960s to prove it. Even though I will agree that pointing the gun in a safe direction is a key to safety, if you treat every single gun you come into contact with as loaded, you had better point that muzzle in a safe direction! No exceptions! That will and should naturally, always follow suit. Just handling a gun and keeping the muzzle pointed in a safe direction does not lend to the situation the same grave responsibilities/danger as having the mindset of handling a loaded firearm will impart. I am talking about INTACT firearms, go ahead, double check for a clear action, disassemble and clean them....

All additional gun safety rules revert back to the number one rule: Treat them all as loaded. If you live by this you should never do anything unsafe with a firearm. That is why this is the most important rule. It governs all my actions with firearms, as it should yours. So, from this moment forward, for the rest of your life, all guns that you ever come into contact with will always, with no exceptions, be loaded (proper mindset) and treated accordingly.

There is a trigger guard around the trigger (that little circle of steel). I don't call it a trigger guard, I do not think that is a serious enough description, not even nearly serious enough. I call it THE CIRCLE OF DEATH. When a finger enters that circle someone could die. Keep your finger OUT of that circle of death at all times if you are not going to actually shoot the firearm! The trigger is NOT a casual resting place for your finger!

A safety on a firearm does not give you license to carelessly handle that firearm. You are the master safety on any/all firearms. NEVER trust anyone that tells you a gun is unloaded while trying to hand it to you! Make that person show you that it is technically unloaded before you will accept it from them. Then, you must still handle it exactly like it is loaded! EVERYONE must show you the gun is technically unloaded first, from your mother, to the gun shop owner, to the head of the NRA. Agreed? If all people did this, firearm accidents would damn near cease to exist, we can all live with that. If anyone has a problem with that, it is not your problem, but theirs, they obviously treat firearms far too nonchalantly, assume too much and are accidents waiting to happen.

Maybe you think that I am too hard line on this issue? No. Firearms are very unforgiving of careless/foolish people. Your first mistake could be your last breath on this Earth or maybe someone else's last breath due to your negligence. I do not believe there can be such a thing as too hard line in regards to firearm safety. Firearms do not give you second chances. Fun does not trump safety.

Gun Sense #5 What is a Misfire/What is a Hang Fire?

Some of you may already know what a misfire is. It is caused by a faulty primer at the back of a bullet casing, that when struck by the gun's firing pin will not detonate. Thus failing to send a spark into the main powder charge of the casing, which would have in turn, sent the bullet on its way down the gun's barrel.

So here is a little scenario: Let's say that you load six rounds into your revolver at the gun range, take careful aim at your target, BANG!, BANG!, BANG!, click! You know you have taken three shots of the six you loaded, so you don't necessarily have to be a NASA rocket scientist to realize that there should be at least three shots left. So what just happened is known as a misfire.

What should you do? Do not try to squeeze off another shot. When you hear that "click" instead of the usual "BANG," keep the barrel of your gun pointing DOWN RANGE. That will be your safest direction. Start a slow count to 10. When you reach 10 the danger will be over, unload the gun. You will notice that there will be an unfired round that falls from the cylinder. On closer inspection of the round you should notice a dent in the primer where it had been struck by the gun's firing pin. The primer was a dud, faulty from the factory. It happens from time to time. The main thing is to handle the situation properly and safely when it does happen.

You can now throw the dud away and resume your shooting practice. Your next question will probably be "Why did I have to count to 10 while pointing the gun down range?" It is a wise precaution that can protect you and others from what is known as a hang fire. A hang fire starts out as a misfire but can actually go off after a few seconds. The primer is faulty but not quite a dud, the spark gets hung up and that is where the danger lies. If while you are pointing the gun down range counting, the gun fires, it will startle you, but will do no harm because you handled it the correct/safe way.

Hang fires are rare, but they do exist and now you know how to safely guard against them. Misfires are far more common and should always be treated as if they could become a hang fire. A misfire and a hang fire are not the same thing. A hang fire cannot become a misfire.

If you want to see a misfire that becomes a hang fire then google: "Stupid people with guns" and look at the video of the guy wearing the orange hunting vest shooting the pump shotgun at bottles ten feet away (a real Davy Crocket). Only God will ever know why he looked down the barrel and it was only God that saved the fool.

NOTE: This is a very serious suggestion, when you go to the range with your family/friends, before you all start shooting, take five minutes out of your lives and discuss misfires, hang fires and squib loads. Make sure that you are ALL on the same page about this information. Don't assume people somehow automatically, magically, know this stuff. You will be surprised at how many do not fully understand it. Now, do you think this will give you some piece of mind as you're standing next to them shooting? It should. Read on to the next chapter about squib loads and pass all this information to your family and friends.

Gun Sense #6 What is a Squib Load? Understand the Danger.

The word "squib" is used in other applications, but for the purpose of this chapter the term is known and used in relation to firearms. A typical round of ammunition is made up of four components:

1. The outer casing or shell.
2. The primer.
3. The gunpowder.
4. The projectile or bullet.

This will only be a general outline of production...When these components are assembled at the factory in mass production, the primer goes into the casing, the casing moves to the next step where a measured charge of gunpowder is funneled into the casing, then the casing is moved to the next position where the bullet is seated. Next they are all boxed and sent to the store for you, the consumer.

In the event of a squib load, the casing goes through the same steps mentioned above, but when it gets to the position where the gunpowder is supposed to be funneled into the casing, there is a glitch or malfunction. The automated powder drop does not work properly and very little or no gunpowder is put into the casing (This is more apt to happen to people that reload their own bullets at home by not paying proper attention to detail). But for the purpose of this example we are at the ammunition factory. So now, with no gunpowder in the casing it is automatically moved to the next position where a bullet is seated. The ammunition is boxed up and sent to various locations for sale.

You enter the store, looking to buy a box of ammo, you buy a box of .38 caliber ammo for your revolver and off you go to the range. The round without the gunpowder just happens to be in that box, but you don't know that, how could you? You just want to do a little target practice. All the rounds look the same from the outside to you. You set up your targets, load the gun with six rounds (unknown to you one of them is the squib load) and you start shooting, BANG!, BANG!, pop! *What the heck was that* you think? What you just heard was an audible "pop," it was the primer detonating. With no gunpowder in the casing you do not hear the loud BANG that you would normally hear. DO NOT TAKE ANOTHER SHOT!

The primer (that "pop") can generate just enough pressure within the shell casing to push the bullet into the barrel of your gun. This creates a blockage in the barrel and can be a very dangerous situation if you attempt another shot. With such a blockage in the barrel, the next bullet you might fire, with all of the pressure generated going down the barrel (for a .38 caliber around 52,000 psi, or 26 tons!) you could easily kill yourself and others around you. The firearm is not rated to contain that kind of pressure and will violently come apart at the seams like a grenade. All that pressure needs to escape "yesterday" and it will take the path of least resistance, back at you, not good. All that energy will be transferred to the shrapnel going in every direction at 900 + feet per second in the case of a .38...much higher pressures and velocities with rifle cartridges!

NOTE: You may hear a "pop" sound, but not in all cases. A gun range can be a noisy place, you're wearing hearing protection (initially you may think it is a misfire, so treat it like one), but if you hear it, you know that "pop" sound is not typical (or now you should know). In all cases stop what you are doing. If you think it's a misfire count to ten anyway, unload the gun, check it twice. If a shell comes out minus the projectile you know it is a squib.

Now you can put a cleaning rod down the barrel. Chances are that you will not be able to push it through to the other side due to the bullet lodged in the barrel. Take the cleaning rod and tap the bullet gently out of the barrel. Once that is done you now have a rare, but harmless squib load souvenir, set it aside, reload and resume shooting. You may have just saved your own life and the lives of those nearby. It is the follow-up shot that makes this situation so dangerous and is what we must all avoid!

We must all be alert for abnormalities while shooting, it is all part of staying safe. My reason for telling you about squib loads, misfires and hang fires is not to make you paranoid. It is simply to give you the knowledge that will help keep you safe.

I have been shooting on formal range settings since the age of eight. I have been a member of many gun clubs, rifle and pistol teams, I also like to hunt. In my work as a Nuclear Security Officer since 1987, I have been required to qualify at the gun range many times with different types of weapons/ammo. My point is this, I personally, with all that shooting, have only encountered a squib load once (no hang fires yet), but I know that they do exist and now you will know how to handle one with confidence if it occurs.

NOTE: This is a very serious suggestion, when you go to the range with your family/friends, before you all start shooting, take five minutes out of your lives and discuss misfires, hang fires and squib loads. Make sure that you are ALL on the same page about this information. Don't assume people somehow automatically, magically, know this stuff. You will be surprised at how many do not fully understand it. Now, do you think this will give you some piece of mind as you're standing next to them shooting? It should. Review **Gun Sense #5 What is a Misfire/What is a Hang Fire?** Share this information with your family and friends.

Gun Sense #7 Uncontrolled Bullets Anyone? Not on Your Life!

If you are not some kind of control freak in your day to day personal life, that is probably a good thing, I mean, no one likes a control freak. They are overbearing, domineering, insensitive, rude, crude, socially unacceptable (probably your boss) and usually end up in divorce court. But when it comes to firearms we all have to be control freaks where bullets are concerned.

I have mentioned common sense before and I will bring it up again and again. Engage your common sense every time you handle a firearm, take common sense for a walk around the block and give it a bit of exercise. You do not need to be a ballistics or trajectory expert to know that bullets can go far and do damage beyond your field of vision if you are not careful. If you are setting up targets, think of your backstop, be it dirt, tires, wood, whatever. Be aware of what is behind those targets. If there are stones, for instance, large enough to cause a ricochet, move them out of the way...if you cannot move them, find another safe spot for your targets.

A short definition of a ricochet is: an uncontrolled bullet. Gun clubs have been closed down due to ricochets, pending investigations as to what may have caused it and how it will be avoided in the future before reopening. That is no fun for the membership. Another form of uncontrolled bullet is to indiscriminately shoot a bullet up into the air. This is very irresponsible and dangerous. If done at a rainbow pitch, a bullet as small as a .22 caliber rim fire can carry a mile or more before coming back to Earth and you have no idea where it will land (you will be held responsible for what it may do, you own it). That certainly fits the uncontrolled category.

Bullets are not meant to be shot at water. The speed of a bullet will cause it to glance off and it will carry clear across that pond and if you're unlucky, into someone's camp ground. Again, you are responsible and will be held responsible for your negligence, whether it be known or unknown to you as to the damage the bullet has done. So make a point to at least understand the caliber(s) you own and the capabilities of those calibers, which is the responsible and right thing to do when you own firearms. The only firearm that is meant for over the water shooting is a shotgun. The bird shot from a shotgun does not carry very far. A shotgun shell with birdshot, once fired, will lose its energy rapidly, the pellets will fall and sink at around 150 yards give or take. The utmost effective range is about a third of that distance.

If you intend to hunt you must always be diligent as to what is beyond your intended game. It is not as controlled as a shooting range. If you are deer hunting you may be carrying a rifle or shotgun, both with the capability of shooting a long distance with large game loads. If you see a deer, look beyond it for the color orange, that will be another hunter (he/she is on your side) and that means you do not take the shot. If you're really hungry go to McDonald's and get a burger, that deer will never be worth risking someone's life. You may say "Gee that's just common sense!" Well, if it is such damned common sense, why are hunters shooting each other out in the woods most years all across this country? Because they are not taking their common sense around the block and giving it a little exercise now and then, that is why. Common sense is simply thinking something through before acting.

Once you squeeze off that shot you cannot suddenly say "Oops, that was a mistake, gee whizz, come back here little bullet and let me do that differently." It is far too late for that, you will have to live with the consequences. Firearms are very unforgiving. The mistake you make could be someone else's last breath. My point here is to think BEFORE you shoot. If everyone did that we would all be much safer. Avoid uncontrolled bullets at ALL costs!

Gun Sense #8 Cease-Fire! What you do, Completely.

I know, I know, you're going to say that when you hear a command like "cease-fire" at a gun range, you stop shooting...of course you are correct, to a point. But what else do you do, and should you do? Well that is what I am here to let you in on. There are those of you that may already know, so please be patient. For safety's sake I cannot take it for granted that everyone knows this information...that would be irresponsible on my part. Always check the range rules and standard operating procedures of where you are shooting to know their policies, which may vary.

When we are at a gun range, we naturally will be inundated with loud gunfire, especially if there are more than just a couple of people there. We need to protect our hearing under this barrage of noise. If we ever damage part of our hearing it can never repair itself, we lose it forever, so we must protect our eardrums. In the course of doing this we don various forms of hearing protection, not only do we muffle the sharp sound of gunfire, we mostly block the lower sounds of human voices. Let's say there are seven people shooting at the same time on the range today. They are all concentrating on their targets, when suddenly a ten year old kid (or anyone) that has been watching his parent screams "CEASE-FIRE!" At that point in time you will not immediately know why he yelled "cease-fire," but you must obey the command instantly, it can be a life or death command.

The second you hear the command you must loudly repeat the command so that the people to the right and left of you hear it. They in turn loudly repeat the command. While all are repeating the cease-fire command, they should also be simultaneously unloading their firearms and placing them on their shooting benches, with the actions open. The reason that it is so important to repeat the command down the line is so that everyone on a loud firing line will hear it.

That little ten year old kid (or anyone else) is the boss at the second he yelled "cease-fire" and everyone had better comply. He may have seen someone coming out of the woods down range chasing a dog, who knows? But, never second guess a cease-fire command! When the issue is resolved, whatever it was, then an all clear will be called and the shooting may resume. Anyone has the right to call a cease-fire on a gun range if they feel there is an unsafe situation and everyone must repeat that command, for safety's sake.

Gun Sense #9 Why Might dry Firing be Used?

Dry firing, there are two camps on whether or not dry firing can or cannot do damage to a firearm. I lean to the side that says damage can be done to the internal workings of a firearm. I am not going to chance doing damage to any of my investments and that is exactly what firearms are, investments. The firing pins in firearms are designed to strike the primers of the ammunition being used in the chamber. If there is nothing for the firing pin to strike it can over extend, it was not designed to take that kind of punishment from the viewpoint of my camp.

There is a solution to this dilemma though. The solution is called snap caps. Snap caps are nothing more than artificial or fake bullets. They do not fire, they do not make noise, they come in most common caliber sizes, usually five or six to a pack and can be used over and over again. They are of a color that cannot be confused with real bullets, so you can tell immediately that they are not real ammunition. They can be manually functioned through semi-auto's and are easily used in revolvers. They are specifically designed to give the firing pin something to strike to avoid any possible damage to the firearm. Who ever invented snap caps must be in my camp on this issue. Remember that when you practice dry firing in the home, NEVER have any live ammo in the same room.

Why would you want to dry fire you might ask? Dry firing is a tool to practice the mechanics/fundamentals of shooting, mainly at home, prior to going to a range, without putting holes in your walls. The idea is that by practicing the elements of shooting while dry firing, you will produce better results on targets when you actually shoot at the range. The elements that we strive to become proficient with are:

1. Concentration - We cannot shoot well if our minds are wandering, we must stay focused.
2. Breath Control - We must know how to regulate our breathing so that we are not all over the target, this takes additional coaching and practice, as does every aspect of shooting.
3. Good Positioning - Whether this will be standing, kneeling, sitting, or prone, you will need to find what is most comfortable and effective for you in each position and practice it, muscle memory will develop over time.
4. Proper Grip - Again, this can simply mean what is most comfortable

and effective for you, depending on the size of your hands, the length of your arms, the type of firearm, be it handgun, rifle or shotgun. How to mount a rifle or shotgun to your shoulder consistently for consistent results...these are all considerations to be looked at and figured out.

5. Proper Trigger Squeeze - Learning where best to place your finger on the trigger, learning not to slap the trigger, your trigger work, along with every other element of shooting will begin to blend together becoming second nature eventually.

6. Proper Sight Alignment - They all boil down to this, the Holy Grail. Without every other element coming together correctly, your target will not look as good as it would when everything does come together correctly. The main theme throughout the entire breakdown of these mechanics/fundamentals of shooting is simply this, practice, practice, practice and some more practice.

Dry firing does not prepare you for muzzle blast or felt recoil. Explosions a few inches in front of our face is not a natural thing, it may cause us to flinch. Recoil may hurt slightly, which may cause us to anticipate recoil, which also causes us to flinch, we must learn to ignore these. It can be tough to do, especially for larger calibers. I recommend you start with a .22 cal. if you are new to firearms. With proper coaching you will learn to work through these shooting distractions. As your skills improve, the satisfaction that you receive will be reflected in the scores you produce on your targets. Dry firing is an aid in developing all these aspects of shooting. These skills do not come over night, but they will come and become second nature.

Gun Sense #10 Weapon Safeties…Understand Them.

Safeties and where they are placed on firearms vary from one maker to another and cover a huge variety of firearms. I am not going to go into each type of firearm, that would take far too much space and bore you (and me) to tears. I am going to generalize the subject by giving you some good advice and coupled with your own common sense (that I know you have), this should suffice if taken as seriously as death itself.

When you go to the store to buy a new firearm it will come with a manual telling you all about it, please be sure to read the manual before you go shoot the firearm. Make sure you understand everything about the gun. If you buy a second hand firearm from someone and it does not come with the manual, you can find the address of the gun maker on the barrel. You can write them and ask for a copy of the manual for the model you bought, the model number will be on the gun also. That is what I did decades before computers (showing my age), but now it is easier to go online to the gun maker and simply download the manual, free in most cases.

Some firearms do not have external safeties, revolvers are prime examples, keep your finger off the trigger and it cannot go bang! Glock semi-autos are another good example of no external safety, it has a series of internal safeties activated by the trigger, read the book. Some guns have only one safety, others have multiple safeties, some have none, internal or external, none what so ever, understand this. Now I am going to let you in on a secret; YOU are any firearms best safety. YOU are the master safety, you can NEVER trust a manmade safety on ANY firearm! Firearms are manmade and anything man makes can fail and does fail. Simply because a safety is on a firearm, do not think for a second that it gives you license to carelessly handle that firearm! Remember that #1 rule, TREAT EVERY FIREARM AS LOADED AT ALL TIMES! Because they are all loaded! That has to be our mindset. Weapons' safety is everyone's responsibility, especially yours. Practice safe weapons' handling until it becomes a habit.

There is a trigger guard around the trigger (that little circle of steel). I don't call it a trigger guard, I do not think that is a serious enough description, not nearly serious enough. I call it THE CIRCLE OF DEATH. I hope you call it this from now on...when a finger enters that circle someone could die, keep your finger OUT of that circle of death at all times if you are not going to actually shoot the firearm! Firearms will not give a fool a second chance. Please pass this information on to your family and friends.

Gun Sense #11 Glaser Safety Slugs and Home Defense.

You may want to consider this information if you are looking to buy a handgun for home defense or personal protection reasons, it is important to know. The study/science of Kinetics (motion) is way over my head, but I understand the general properties of how a bullet works and for this segment that is good enough for me. Glaser Safety Slugs are made by:

Corbon Ammunition

If you need to find a store that sells their ammo you can contact them. I do not own stock in this company or benefit in any way from their sales, I just want to pass on information that will help keep you safer concerning firearms.

For home defense you need to be concerned about over penetration. If you were ever forced to fire shots in your home, and I hope that you never do, but if you did, in defense of your family and or yourself, you need to understand the danger of over penetration. Conventional bullets such as ball ammo, lead cast ammo, jacketed hollow points, shotgun slugs or buckshot, all have their place in the world of firearms. I just do not think that place is in the home for personal defense. A bullet, once fired, delivers energy known as kinetic energy. If the bullet strikes a mass, travels through that mass, and continues on, it has not yet delivered all of its kinetic energy. The bullet will need to expel that energy somewhere else. This is what you want to avoid happening and keep over penetration to the utmost minimum, at all costs in your home.

The danger of over penetration is obvious. If you took a shot at an intruder and missed, the bullet could easily pass through the walls of your home, leave your house and enter the house next door, endangering your neighbors before its flight path ends. You do not want that sort of thing happening, it could as easily kill a person in that house next door. In protecting your family, you would not feel very good about injuring/killing a neighbor. That scenario does not need to happen.

Glaser Safety Slugs have a very unique design. They are filled with tiny compressed lead shot. The walls of the bullet that contains this lead shot are very thin and designed to fragment on impact. This fragmentation immediately disperses all of its kinetic energy on the target (intended or not), causing abrupt stopping power and a large cavity wound. If you miss your intended target and this could easily happen under the stress of the situation, the bullet will then strike a wall and fragment, dumping its energy on the wall and not delivering any lethal fragments through to people that may be in another room, very important. Chances are good that even if you miss the criminal intruder, he will not hang around letting you take pot shots at him.

The usefulness of these Glaser Safety Slugs should now be apparent, the down side to them (if any) would be their cost, they are about $4.00 per bullet. There is only five or six in a pack, so it will not break the bank and you will not use them for shooting tin cans at the range. They are for defensive use only, hopefully you will never have to use them.

Another thing that you may want to consider for a great home defense firearm is a pump shotgun of any gauge. A pump shotgun has a very distinctive sound when it is pumped to chamber a shotgun shell. This sound is universally known and carries with it an intimidation factor for the intruder in your home. If someone is not willing to exit your home after you warn them that you have a shotgun and especially after you make the sound of pumping the shotgun, then in all probability that person is either insane or has a death wish. In either case it would then become a form of natural selection weeding out the idiots. He will be of no great loss to mankind.

A 20 gauge is the shotgun I recommend, as it is easier for people of smaller stature to use and just as effective as a 12 gauge at close range.

You still need to be aware of the problem of over penetration with the use of a shotgun. Do not use shotgun slugs, they carry with them far too much kinetic energy. A shotgun slug will pass through the criminal, through your house, through the next two houses and kill someone in the third house down the lane, not good. Do not use buckshot for the same reason. Buckshot does not have as much over penetration as a shotgun slug but, they can still make it into a next door neighbor's home. Again, not good.

The best defensive load to use, in my opinion for a shotgun is #6 or #4 bird shot, with a full choke smooth bore barrel. The average bedroom is around 15 feet wide, if an intruder were to enter that room and you let loose with a load of #6 or #4 bird shot, you could put a hole the size of a silver dollar and two dimes in that criminal. The birdshot would deliver most all of its kinetic energy on impact, keeping the birdshot confined to your bedroom. It would make one heck of a debilitating wound, stopping the threat to you and your family. If you were to miss, the criminal probably would not stick around for you to try again. The birdshot would lose its energy before leaving your home, it would not carry very far and the chance of it killing someone in another room would be greatly minimized due to the way birdshot disperses as distance increases. If you're going to deal with a turkey, you should use bird shot.

I hope that you never find yourself in a situation where you have been forced to shoot at criminals invading your home, but if you are ever in that situation, it is your first duty and responsibility to protect your family and yourself. The police have a very important and dangerous job to preform, but they are not assigned to sit at the foot of your bed and guard you all night long, you are on your own when criminal(s) enter your home, it is up to you to defend your family (The Supreme Court has ruled that police have no obligation to protect the individual and they have no responsibility to protect you from madmen or murderers). That says it all in my book, we are on our own!

Someone just broke into your home? Be verbal, "I have a gun!" (The criminal may not believe that). "I have called the police!" In this day and age of cell phones the criminal has no reason not to believe this, it may be your best tool to get him to leave much sooner than he wanted to. Keep a cellphone charging in your bedroom, not in the kitchen where it will do you no good.

We should all have a plan to follow in case of a fire, right? We should also have some idea as to what to do in case of a criminal(s) invading our home. Even if that plan is as simple as quickly going to the kids room with a gun, a cell phone, house keys, a flashlight and staying there! If you can, start the ball rolling by calling the police's direct phone number, NOT 911* on a cell phone and telling them the situation, but be prepared to act in the interim. Do not go looking for the criminal, again, stay put! Let him steal everything in your house, so what, it is only stuff, you can replace stuff! If your car keys and house keys are together and you can set off your car alarm, do it, it may help pressure the criminal(s) to leave. This is not the movies where the good guy will go and catch the criminal(s), that is not your job, your job is to protect your family, not to catch the criminal(s), let the police do that. This is not some phony Hollywood script, this can be life or death for real!

When the police do come, do not meet them at the door with a gun in your hand, they will be hyped up and do not know who you are, so be careful. If you're in contact with the police by cell phone and the intruder is still in your home, direct the police to a window were you can throw the house keys to them. The police, generally speaking, are the cleanup crew, they come after the fact in most instances. Make sure that if you had to act, then the scene they come to clean up or sort out, does not include the bodies of any of your family members!

NOTE: Calling 911 on a cell phone can add an additional ten minutes to the police response time. A lot can happen in ten seconds, let alone ten minutes. Put your Fire department and Police department direct phone numbers in your cell phone under "Town" - as in Town Fire and Town Police so you have them together. Please read the next chapter, **Gun Sense #12 The Aftermath of Defending Your Family/Home** as a follow up.

Gun Sense #12 The Aftermath of Defending Your Family/Home.

On TV there is a lot of exciting action designed to keep you on the edge of your seat, but more importantly, for the TV executives to keep their ratings high. TV is fun to watch but it can give the wrong impression more often than not. That cannot be more true than when it comes to guns. TV entertainment never seems to go to the next level after a home invasion/shooting scenario. I talked about having a plan in ***Gun Sense #11 Glaser Safety Slugs and Home Defense*** and the important aspects thereof.

First of all, I hope that you are never put in a situation to have to shoot anyone defending your family in your home, sadly this situation can be forced onto you. That said, I will touch on the aftermath of your use of a firearm defending your family and home. Again, I mention the importance about having a plan should someone ever break in while you are home, I hope that you do have a plan. On TV or in the movies the criminal(s) kick in a door in the middle of the night and start going through the home. The good guy in the story takes his trusty firearm and calmly saunters through the house, he easily takes care of each criminal in turn. Of course the actor playing the good guy is supposed to win, it is written that way in the script. He will not be injured because they need him for a sequel. He is in no danger, it is all make believe and he knows that after the scene he will go home to his mansion complete with body guards, surveillance cameras and killer dogs to protect him from the public at large. You on the other hand could just as easily be killed if you try to go find the criminal(s).

Once you know that someone has broken into your home your plan should begin. If you have a child or children take your cell phone, flashlight and gun into their room and STAY PUT, but be ready to act. If you have no kids stay in your bedroom. If the bad guy(s) should come into the room where you and your family are, even after your loud verbal warning that the police are coming and that you have a gun, be damned sure and understand that he, or they are NOT the neighborhood welcome wagon delivering flowers and candy, he, or they, are there to rob, rape and/or murder you and your family! At that instance in time you have an obligation and a duty to protect your family with any means at your disposal. The police will not be there to do that for you....

By staying where you are, you increase your chances of survival, making the criminal invader come to you decreases their chance of survival. Should someone be foolish enough to kick in your bedroom door, try your very best to hit who you are shooting at, aim at the center of that door. Under the stress of the situation you may miss, you may not, people handle stress in different ways. Some people may become very focused and angry at the very thought of a home invader(s) endangering their family...females are hardwired to protect those children. Others may become jittery nervous wreaks, but in any case you must do something, so fire away. Aim for the largest target, his torso, the center of the doorway. Even if you miss, the chance is very good that the criminal(s) will not hang around to let you take pot shots at him/them, hopefully he/they get the message.

Never fire a warning shot, that gives away your position and gives the criminal the first chance to get you. You must survive, your family must survive. After, if the criminal is dead or badly wounded, when the police come, you may initially be arrested. The police will need to work out who the person is in relation to you, to make sure there was no bad motive on your part. After they figure out that this was/is a criminal, or there is a history of abuse linked to this person with you, etc., you will be released in short order, probably within hours.

Fast forward to the court date...The criminal that you killed in defense of your family and home also may have relatives, the chances are good that you took out one of their main sources of income (other than welfare) and they want restitution, to replace that income somehow. They want your home, to garnish your wages, whatever they can do to take away what you have...All because you stood your ground to save your family. They will have a lawyer, his job will be to make you look bad and try to make you say things you don't really mean in front of the jury. And he has the ability to do it, the courtroom is his playground, it's how he makes his bread and butter, he is at home there.

You on the other hand are light years away from being accustomed to a courtroom setting like this. You never wanted to be here, it was forced onto you by the actions of a criminal. The lawyer is going to do his very best to finish the job the criminal started and make you a victim. He will say things at you in a forceful way to make you nervous, as he talks at you, that's right, at you, he is really talking to the jury and everything he says is for their benefit. He may say something forcefully like "So you wanted to shoot Rufus didn't you!" You may nervously say something like "I had to! He had a knife and was coming at my wife and kids!" He will try to make you sound like you are a trigger happy nit wit to the jury, "So! You admit wanting to murder him!" And you continue "I, I, I, didn't know what else to do!" Now the jury is starting to look at you in a different light, the lawyer is planting a subliminal seed in their minds that does not bode well for you, he used the word murder for the jury's sake.

People have lost their homes in cases like this because they said things that made them sound guilty when in actuality they were only very nervous and upset. Your lawyer knows what can happen in court and should do what he can to prepare you for the coming onslaught. You should focus on one main thought, that you did nothing wrong...That you were only trying to stop the threat to your family and yourself.

When the lawyer for the plaintiff tries to make you rush your words in his attack, such as "You wanted to shoot Rufus didn't you!" Say "No, I only wanted to stop the threat to my family and myself. The fact that the criminal died was not my intention. The criminal forced me into this situation by unlawfully breaking into our home."

Don't use his name, use criminal, because that is what he was! You too can plant subliminal seeds in the minds of the jury....Their lawyer will come at you from all different angles to try to make you change your answer, just stick like glue to the fact that you were only trying to stop the threat to your family. Never vary, because it is the truth! The jury will side with the truth. That lawyer will eventually give up trying to incriminate you when he realizes he cannot make you budge from the truth of the matter.

I am not a lawyer, this is meant as a guide, to give you an idea as to what can happen next in court. Seek legal advice in the event that you did have to defend your home from a violent criminal attack, don't be a victim twice!

Gun Sense #13 Specific to MA Petition for Judicial Review.

The Commonwealth has now taken the Federal stance on misdemeanors. For now, read **Gun Sense #49 BATF Pays a Visit to MA Officials 4-20-18.** Litigation is moving forward against this new stance. Stay tuned!

For prior to 4-20-18, you can read below and this policy may change again in light of litigation.

In Massachusetts, if you go through the hoops that many towns in the state force you to jump through in order to exercise your right to self-defense and are not successful in gaining your LTC or FID, the police must by law, within 40 days, send to you a written notification stating the reason(s) that you are being denied. If you do not agree with the reason(s) stated than you have at your disposal a remedy in which to challenge the police's decision. The police may not be arbitrary, capricious or abuse their discretion in denying a gun license...the petitioner would need to show that he/she believed they were being so.

NOTE: A Judicial Review is also referred to as a complaint, so file a complaint as the plaintiff against the Chief that you want a judge to review and make a decision on. Do not leave the courthouse without insuring that the clerk has filed and docketed your case and ask the clerk to stamp your copy of the complaint with the date and the docket number. Although in some District Courts, the clerk will insist that the matter go before a Judge, if the affidavit is regular and complete on its face this should not be necessary. You would attach a copy of the denial from the police for the judge to look at, along with clear reasoning from you as to why you believe the Chief is wrong. Read **Gun Sense #39 MA Application/"Interview" Process & Steps/Tips** closely concerning this.

This remedy is called a Petition for Judicial Review. You would need to go to your area's District Court, to the clerk's office at the courthouse to file a petition for judicial review based on the letter that the police sent to deny you your permit. The law states that you would need to show that the refusal was "arbitrary, capricious, or an abuse of discretion," that wording is straight from the law. You would want to state that there is nothing in your police record that would rise to the level of denying you your Constitutional or God given right to self-defense. You would want to attach a copy of your record, you may obtain that from:

Criminal Record Check Services

https://www.mass.gov/criminal-record-check-services

Online Request CORI as an Individual

https://www.mass.gov/how-to/request-cori-as-an-individual

Mail in Criminal Offender Record Information (CORI) Personal Request Form

https://www.mass.gov/files/2017-06/adult-personal-criminal-record-request-form.pdf

The Department of Criminal Justice Information Services (Information in Appendix A)

Use this as evidence to strengthen your argument, also attach the letter from the police that denied you.

Once you file your petition (complaint), you maybe given a date and time to go before a judge, the police will send a representative. The judge is supposed to make a ruling based on FACTS. If the police are short on facts and long on hearsay, you should win. If you are not denied a gun permit but instead are given a restriction such as "for target and hunting only" or "for employment reasons only," then technically, if you accept it, you have no grounds for a Judicial Review because you have not been denied a permit. Please read **Gun Sense #19 "Reason" Letter for MA LTC** before you even go to submit an application for a permit, this may help you. In those cases it would be wise to contact your selectmen or your state Representative and lodge a complaint, have them work for you, that is their job, but you need to let them know.

Now, apart from the afore mentioned, if you had a gun permit in the past and would like to have it reinstated after losing it due to a past misdemeanor conviction, a new law in 2004 created a seven member review board with the authority to look at your case. Read **Gun Sense #20 MA Misdemeanor? Been Denied Your Gun Permit/License?**, the burden is on you to show why you should get your permit back. The review board can recommend reinstatement of the permit based on the circumstances that surround your case, of course each individual case is different. Many gun owners with certain criminal records may now get the licenses that they were denied prior to the new 2004 laws. The best way to keep your rights is to know your rights.

NOTE: The Commonwealth has now taken the Federal stance on misdemeanors. For now, read **Gun Sense #49 BATF Pays a Visit to MA Officials 4-20-18.** Litigation is moving forward against this new stance. Stay tuned!

Gun Sense #14 MA Change of Address Notification Forms and a Renewal tip.

This information is for those who live in Massachusetts and have either a Firearm Identification Card (FID) or a License to Carry permit (LTC). This information can save you from losing your gun permit and or paying a huge fine. Any FID cardholder or LTC licensee shall notify, in writing, the original licensing authority who issued said license, the Chief of police into whose jurisdiction the licensee moves and the executive director of the criminal history systems board of any change of address. Such notification shall be made by certified mail (with a return receipt for your protection) within 30 days of changing your address. Failure to do so shall be cause for revocation or suspension of said license.

Basically the state wants you to photocopy the front side of your gun permit three times. When you send in the state's Change of Address Notification form, you send it to three different places.

1. To the police Chief in your old city or town.
2. To the police Chief in your new city or town.
3. To the Firearms Record Bureau at:

Firearms Record Bureau

https://www.mass.gov/firearms-services

The Department of Criminal Justice Information Services (Information in Appendix A)

If you have any concerns about this please email me:

Contact Information in "About the Author" Section

You will attach to each notification form a copy of the front of your gun permit and mail them out. It is very important that you file away the return receipts when they come back to you, in a safe place. Later they may come in very handy as proof that you did what you were supposed to do. Police departments may misfile this information and not have it when you go to renew your permit in a new town later, so CYA. If you trust the state not to lose your information, God bless you. I don't trust the state to do anything efficiently except to create new tax burdens/fees.

Your local police stations should carry the Change of Address Notification forms if you need them, the Firearms Record Bureau in Chelsea, (617) 660-4600, could mail them to you **or they can be downloaded from the MA State Police website.** You DO NOT need to fill them out if you're only moving from one street in your town to another street within your town because you're still in your town.

NOTE: If someone says that you must notify when moving out of state ask them to point out the section in the law where that is stated please....The law does not mention out of state moves, in any way shape or form. You are not under ANY legal obligation to notify this state! Once you move to another state you will need to find out what that state requires, if anything, about gun licensing.

Just keep in mind that the Change of Address Notification forms have explicit directions on them for your convenience, read them.

NOTE: As far as where the criminals live and keep their guns, no one knows, but by God, you should feel all warm and fuzzy knowing all the people least likely to commit crimes (legal gun owners) are right under the thumb of big brother at all times. Makes me feel good all over and makes politicians feel that they have created something really special and important (impotent). Concerning the number of crimes this address notification form has prevented, there are no statistics readily available at this time and there never will be....

Renewal Tip: Your permit is good now for six years and expires on your birthday. You are supposed to get a reminder notice to renew, but don't hold your breath waiting for it to come. I have never seen one since 1970...I know some people that have and that have not gotten one. At least three months before it expires you should start the renewal process anyway, read **Gun Sense #39 MA Application/"Interview" Process & Steps/Tips**. If you have started that process prior to expiration and your birthday comes before you have received your new permit, you will be given a receipt. That receipt along with your old gun permit will be honored for as long as it takes the state to send you your new license. Please read **Gun Sense #41 Gun Law Changes in MA 8-13-2014**.

Here is the catch, if your permit expires and you never started the renewal process, you can/will lose your license/guns and (in some towns) you will need to go through the safety class/process again before you can get them back. You also may be fined, as ridiculous as a fee sounds it is true and can be enforced! Be aware that fines/penalties vary from a low to harsh range, err on the side of caution if in doubt. Hey, you keep these pinheads in office....

Please, mark it on your calendar three months out and try to pay attention. If you do not want to renew your license it is up to you to legally get rid of your firearm(s) prior to your license expiration so that you will not be in illegal possession of them. I know that life sometimes can get in the way, that is why I give you this reminder. If you took my class you will know where I stand on this issue....Sincerely.

Gun Sense #15 Concealed or Not Concealed, That is the Question…

This next little segment will illustrate the confusion that is out there in the law enforcement community and in general, on whether you can carry handguns out in the open or not. I do not blame law enforcement for this confusion, I blame the legislature for drafting archaic laws that could confuse Einstein!

I was in Plimoth Bay Outfitters in downtown Plymouth, Massachusetts and I could not help but overhear a conversation between a patron and one of the store keepers. They were discussing the purchase of a new pistol and the patron asked about whether it was required in this Commonwealth to carry concealed when in public? The storekeeper emphatically announced that if one was to carry in the open without a badge, that it was a felony and they would go to jail. The statement struck me as odd, as I had recently been on one of the interactive maps through **www.usacarry.com**, had read that Massachusetts was an open carry state and I had never found any law to the contrary.

Now I am not generally an advocate of open carry, I have always felt that it should be a surprise to those around me and especially my attacker that I am usually armed. Nonetheless, I have never found the statute that requires me to carry concealed. So I challenged the storekeeper for the source of their declaration. Although he was absolute in his resolve, he could not produce the Massachusetts General Law (M.G.L.). I decided to make some phone calls starting with my local police station and queried the on duty detective. He had no answer, although he was certain as well that it was an arrestable offense to carry open. Being onto something, I called a few more police departments all with the same result.

By this point I decided to bump the issue up to the State Police (they regulate the firearms laws for the state) and phoned the Bourne barracks first. The Trooper at the other end of my cell was pretty sure that open carry was prohibited and said he would arrest an individual carrying in the open, but could not find the specific M.G.L. that supported the statement. He recommended that I call the State Police Headquarters in Framingham. The nice woman at the State Police Headquarters did not have a clue what I was talking about, but kindly referred me to the Firearms Record Bureau in Boston. After playing a few rounds of phone tag with an attorney, he answered the long and sought query. There is no specific written statute or law that prohibits open carry in the Commonwealth of Massachusetts. That technically makes us live in an open carry state. HOWEVER, as the local authority has the power to grant and revoke a license to carry, the wise gun toter would check with their local police Chief before waltzing down Main Street with a .45 strapped to their thigh like Wyatt Earp...just to avoid unnecessary harassment and needless trips to the court house.

NOTE: Law enforcement perceptions/misconceptions are a funny thing, not in a laughing sort of way. In my class I tell people that it is a good practice to carry concealed because of the liberal culture here in Massachusetts, which for the most part is very much anti-gun and anti-Second Amendment. Even though you would ultimately win in court, because no one would be able to dig up the law against open carry, it would surely put you through headaches and monetary burdens that you could live without. Err on the side of caution and conceal that handgun unless you don't mind spending your days in a courtroom....

Gun Sense #16 Gun Safety and Responsibility.

From state to state, laws vary. My information regarding "Responsibility" is mainly centered in MA, though it may overlap with other states. There are many programs, brochures and sources of literature on gun safety available. The National Sport Shooting Foundation (NSSF) has valuable information and resources where you can find information on prudent gun storage and the responsibilities of gun owners. Instead of reiterating or recreating the wheel on this subject, I will direct you to their home page:

The National Sport Shooting Foundation

https://www.nssf.org/safety/

Contact Information (Information in Appendix A)

There you will find links to their Project Childsafe Program, "Own it? Respect it. Secure it" initiative, Safety Literature, Safety Videos, Suicide Prevention information and Wildfire Prevention information.

Please read **Gun Sense #3 About Those Children…and Your Guns** for more detailed information.

Gun Sense #17 What Should You Teach Your Child About Gun Safety?

If you have decided that your child is not ready to be taught in a gun's handling and use, teach him or her to follow these simple instructions from the NRA Eddie Eagle Program if they find a gun: 1.Stop. 2. Don't Touch. 3. Run Away. 4. Tell a Grown Up. This may be at a very rudimentary level, but it is far better than nothing at all. To counter the natural impulse to touch/pick up a gun, it is imperative that you impress these steps of the safety message upon your child. You can accomplish this by using a toy gun, tell your child to pretend that the toy gun is real, children are the masters of pretend. Set the gun down in the house somewhere in plain sight for your child to easily see. Now, when your child spots it, ask your child what he or she should do? When the child repeats to you at least the Stop, Don't Touch and Go Tell an Adult, parts of the lesson, make a very big deal out of it, because it is a very big deal. This is a lesson that should be reinforced every few days so that the child understands the importance of the lesson. This lesson could well avert a tragedy one day while your child is playing in a friend's home with another child that was never taught anything about guns.

Gun Owner's Responsibilities: Most states impose some form of legal duty on adults to take reasonable steps to deny access by children to dangerous substances or instruments. It is the individual gun owner's responsibility to understand and follow all laws regarding gun purchase, ownership, storage, transport, etc. Contact your state police and/or local police for information regarding such laws. In **Gun Sense #22 MA "Stored & Kept"' and "Direct Control"** you can read MA laws on storage. If you own a gun and do not know how to operate it, do not experiment with it. Seek competent assistance and instruction as soon as you can. An untrained adult can be as dangerous and in as much danger as a curious child!

A parent must, in every case, be absolutely sure that the firearms in your home are inaccessible to your children and that your children may only see them under your direct/strict supervision. There are states that mandate a basic firearm/law course and have certified state instructors teach the course, like myself.

The NRA program pertaining to children cited above is called "Eddie Eagle." For more information:

Eddie Eagle

https://eddieeagle.nra.org/

Contact Information (Information in Appendix A)

On the Eddie Eagle Homepage, you will find more information, resources and a fantastic film which is catered to younger children.

Please read **Gun Sense #3 About Those Children...and Your Guns**. for more detailed information.

Gun Sense #18 If you "Misplace" Your MA LTC or FID.

I hope this does not happen to you, but if you ever lose (as in opps, where is it?) your MA Firearm License: LTC or FID, you can get it replaced by going to the police station where you originally filled out the application for the license. The police will or should have on file proof that you got the license through them and take care of the problem by getting a replacement for you. And also call the Firearms Licensing Bureau at (617) 660-4600 to tell them that you have lost your firearm license, this is so they can notify the National Instant Check System (NICS) to be on alert in case someone tries to fraudulently use your lost license.

You should have a place where you keep important records and have on file the number that is on your LTC or FID so you can tell the police what the number is, as well as the people at:

Firearms Record Bureau

https://www.mass.gov/firearms-services

The Department of Criminal Justice Information Services (Information in Appendix A)

You will be issued a different number than the one you previously had. The original number will be red flagged.

It is also a very good idea to have on file a list of the serial numbers, manufacturer, model and caliber/mm/ga. on individual index cards for each gun that you own in case of theft. Put ONE gun on each card, in order to help the police identify your property, when and if it is recovered. Do not give them a list of every gun that you own, just the gun(s) stolen. They do not have a need to know what you own.

Gun Sense #19 "Reason" Letter for MA LTC.

I have gotten more and more feedback from people around Massachusetts that have taken my State Basic Firearm Safety course or took it somewhere else, but could not get any answer(s) from where they took it, asking me about what they should say when the police Chief of their town will not accept "Any Lawful Purpose" as good enough a reason for issuing the gun permit. He will issue them a restricted license for "target and hunting" only, but later, they are told, if they can prove some good reason to be issued an unrestricted license with a letter explaining why you think you need an unrestricted LTC, the Chief will consider it, but of course that can/will cost you another $100!

NOTE: My Reason Letter is included towards the middle of the chapter and in **APPENDIX C – LETTER EXAMPLES**. Please read the whole chapter.

In my opinion, this is meant to intimidate you and is an illegal scheme/scam to charge honest people $100 twice by the state. It does absolutely zero to prevent crime, hell, I think it is a crime! Call your Representative, (617) 722-2000, if this is happening to you. If your Representative is not willing to stop the scheme/scam, then he/she is a willing participant in the scheme/scam, vote them out of office!

I have helped people on a one on one basis in the past, but this now will simplify things for everyone (and myself). Again, I strongly urge you to call your so-called state reps to complain about this if an issue should arise. They might listen, but only if it is an election year….I am going to give you a template to use if your police Chief tries to intimidate you in your legal pursuit for your right to self-defense. The Second Amendment is not about "target and hunting," this is a restriction some police Chiefs coyly love to bluff you with/use.

One reason I decided to do this was because someone called me who had taken the class from someone else. That person knew someone who had taken the class from me. The place that had given him the class told him they could not help him, that they only give the required class and that was all. Shame on them! I believe in standing with my students or anyone else looking to exercise their gun rights as American citizens!

Police Department Firearm Policies in some MA Towns:

The below letter will be your guide as to how you can counter and hopefully satisfy the Chief demanding such a hoop for you to jump through. If this does not satisfy him, then he is not trying to be reasonable and nothing short of a Petition for Judicial Review will help if you are denied outright. In that case revert to **Gun Sense #13 Specific to MA Petition for Judicial Review**. If the Chief or his designee wants to give you a permit for "target and hunting only," even though you know your record or lack of a record does not warrant that decision, I advise that you politely tell them to deny you outright and to put the denial in writing as to why they will not give it to you for "Any Lawful Purpose." What the hell do they want for a reason? Any criminal intent!? See a great letter at the end of this chapter from a past client.

They may argue that you are not being denied...but you most certainly are being denied for the reason that you want it! Don't accept less in the form of an unwarranted restriction like "target and hunting."

NOTE: As of 8-13-2014 the class B license is now gone, please read **Gun Sense #41 Gun Law Changes in MA 8-13-2014**. Also, with that in mind, read **Gun Sense #30 Graduated Licenses,(D-A) Under MA Law & "Green Card" Info** for definitions of the licenses. They know what they are doing is wrong, don't allow it to happen.

Here is a letter designed to guide you:

Your Name
Your Address Line 1
Your Address Line 2
Your City, State Zip

Date

Chief of Police (*His/Her Name if you know it***)**
Police Department Name
Police Department Address Line 1
Police Department City, State Zip

Dear Chief of Police (*His/Her name if you know it***):**

I am currently applying for my LTC and would like it for "All Lawful Purposes," as this would cover any contingency/reason that I would ever need for its use. I am a devoted family man/woman to my wife/husband and children and as such, must think of their protection. I pray that I would never be forced into a situation by a criminal(s) that would put the lives of my family and or myself in jeopardy. So, while I hope for the best, I would like to be prepared for the worst, wherever I may lawfully do so.

I realize that there are bad people in the world that do not follow the laws of man nor God. As important as I know the jobs of policemen are, I am not naïve. I realize they cannot be everywhere at once, especially in our homes at night guarding us. Is anyone anywhere truly safe from a violent criminal act? Not if the news is correct. This is why I feel strongly that as the head of my household, the defense of my family is MY immediate duty and responsibility and it falls to me first and foremost.

Thank you sir for your understanding in this matter.

Cordially,

Your Signature

Your Name
CC: *Your Attorney's Name*

This letter will not cover all individual circumstances but can easily be molded to your liking. Send it certified with a carbon copy (CC) to your attorney and put a copy in your file. As I said before, it is merely a guide as to how to write down your humble reason(s) as you legally try to exercise your Second Amendment right to self-defense!

Always, Always, Always, keep copies of all of your gun related information, including the state certificate for the gun safety class, along with your letter, in case you need it for proof in the future should you be unreasonably denied or injured because of such denial! Your concern about crime is real. Most crime happens when the police are not around!

NOTE: Another game some towns put people through is letters from friends, even employers. Read **Gun Sense # 33, MA Letters of Recommendation, Gun License Help.**

Recently someone who had taken my class had followed my advice about how to handle a town that routinely would only give a restricted license to its peasants. The town he lives in is Wareham. You may want to read the following letter he sent me, with his permission I have included it here:

LETTER: Mark, I have been meaning to contact you and thank you for your help, but I wanted to wait until I had good news….yesterday I picked up my class A license at the Wareham PD; a full five months after my interview, and almost seven months after I applied!

The interview went well and in fact….went down just as you suggested it might. I was told that they would "probably start me off with just an FID…" I politely said, "No…not interested. If you want to reject my application do so in writing and I will appeal."

I was then told that "We're winning all the appeals…" I replied, "Well…you won't win this one. I am a picture of stability. I've been in the same job for forty years, the same address for 30 years, I pay all my taxes & bills, I owe nobody anything, I've never been in trouble or arrested, and I'm not going to be the only one in this town without a gun. If I don't qualify…then nobody here does and you'll have to defend virtually every permit you have given out to justify excluding me."

The officer then said "Well we didn't give you a license to drive without a permit….why would we give you a permit to carry a handgun when you have no experience?" I said "Well, I don't have a right to drive, but I do have a constitutional right to have a weapon….and since you brought it up, I've had a driver's license for 43 years, driven over one million miles, and not had one accident."

At the end I said "Look…I don't own any property that I can't just replace. I don't own anything that's worth hurting anyone or getting in trouble over…but I do have a wife and two daughters in a neighborhood that is becoming increasingly dangerous, and the police alone cannot guarantee their safety." His response…."Perfect."

So again….thanks a lot for your help Mark, particularly with preparing me for that interview. Thomas, Wareham MA. 9-15-2013

Gun Sense #20 MA Misdemeanor? Been Denied Your Gun Permit/License?

The Commonwealth has now taken the Federal stance on misdemeanors. For now, read **Gun Sense #49 BATF Pays a Visit to MA Officials 4-20-18**. Litigation is moving forward against this new stance. Stay tuned!

For prior to 4-20-18, you can read below and this policy may change again in light of litigation.

If you have been denied in your quest for a firearm permit (LTC) here in MA due to a past misdemeanor conviction(s), there is a process that you may initiate to try to counter the denial by your police Chief. You need to realize though that if the Firearms License Review Board, a seven member board, finds in your favor, that will be a good thing, but your police Chief will still be making the final determination. He will look at your application in a different light if the review board has found in your favor. That will lend weight to your cause and may sway him to issue you a license. Initially he may only issue you a license with a restriction like "target and hunting only" and the next time around in six years may issue the license you really want, so keep this in mind. This link will provide you with further information:

Firearms License Review Board Instructions, Petition and Address (Information in Appendix A)

Another option for you would be to apply for an FID card first. With an FID card there are only three reasons you can be denied. The reasons are:

1. If you have been a felon.
2. If you have been a substance abuser within the last five years.
3. If you were involuntarily placed in a mental institution within the last five years.

Under the law, no other reason/criteria for denial may be used when issuing an FID card. There are even exemptions to a couple of these (2 & 3) reasons. You can also follow these for more information:

Criminal Record Check Services

https://www.mass.gov/criminal-record-check-services

Online Request CORI as an Individual

https://www.mass.gov/how-to/request-cori-as-an-individual

Mail in Criminal Offender Record Information (CORI) Personal Request Form

https://www.mass.gov/files/2017-06/adult-personal-criminal-record-request-form.pdf

The Department of Criminal Justice Information Services (Information in Appendix A)

NOTE: There is a non-profit group of lawyers under the name of Commonwealth Second Amendment Inc (Comm2A) that may help if you have been denied an LTC due to an old conviction, a minor firearms conviction or even a minor drug offense that may have caused you to lose your LTC/FID. If they take your case, there may be no cost to you. Comm2A has multiple cases pending in federal court in an effort to ensure state firearms law treats all lawful residents fairly and equally. You can contact this group at:

Commonwealth Second Amendment Inc.

http://www.comm2a.org/

Contact Information (Information in Appendix A)

Gun Sense #21 Shooting not Mandated? Why I do not Have you Shoot.

NOTE: After you receive your license, I can give you a familiarization shooting class with the gun(s) you bought so that you feel comfortable with it/them. Just reach out to me:

Contact Information in "About the Author" Section

Why I do not have you shoot in the initial class? In a nutshell, it is a waste of your time and extra money, read on...

I have an educated, common sense theory as to why the state has not made shooting mandatory for the state certification (so far). The course is carefully titled "Basic Firearm Safety" with emphasis on the basic, it covers gun laws and safety aspects. You do not want to run afoul of the gun laws in MA, that is a point of the course. The main reason I believe that shooting is not required can be summed up in one very big word, liability. The police are extremely careful about who will receive that little plastic gun license, they do an extensive background check before they will hand it out. Someone may be a felon. No one has done a background check on the people I initially see, that certainly is NOT my job. I would not want to put guns into the hands of a felon who may only want to steal the firearm(s) and ammunition, endangering me or anyone else at a range. That is number one, my safety, call me selfish, OK....

There is a very foolish push by a panel of left wing academic so-called experts that would mandate you must shoot in this initial class to get your state certificate. In other words, to them, it's OK to endanger firearms instructors PRIOR to the background check! But no one is allowed the little plastic gun license prior to the background check, BRILLIANT! I pray I NEVER get as smart as these so-called academic experts....who must live in La La land.

Prime examples are two instructors, Chris Kyle and Chad Littlefield. Good instructors with good intensions, who were murdered by Eddie Ray Routh while instructing him in firearms at the Rough Creek Lodge in Glen Rose Texas. They set him up with a firearm, briefed him on safety, he picked the gun up then killed them both. Routh then stole the firearms and Chris Kyle's vehicle. He was apprehended the next day. There was NO background check done on Routh prior to this double murder, they did not know his real motives...they had no idea he was already a felon.

Another prime example:

Woman Shot Firearms Instructor in Face

http://www.washingtontimes.com/news/2015/jun/30/firearms-teacher-shot-woman-scheduled-for-lesson-a/

Accidents also come under the heading of liability. The state does not want to be sued for making shooting mandatory in case of an accident (so far). The Representatives we elect may never be bright enough to balance a budget (it's easy to spend someone else's money), but they are not crazy. Also the state would not want the appearance of discriminating against the disabled, etc.

These things are legal and political landmines that will always be avoided. The state is perfectly willing to let private instructors take any falls should there be an accident, i.e. the little boy in Westfield MA. I have something to say about that accident in the supplemental chapter **Zero Gun Sense = Uzi Sub-Machine gun Tragedy in Westfield MA.** The instructors who do infer that shooting is required in MA do so at their own risk and if they are careful/smart, they carry insurance, which of course will drive the price of the class up to significantly impact your wallet. The state wide average runs around $155 per person (a house call and/or discounts not included).

I do not believe, knowing what I have learned in a lifetime of shooting, that the extra cost is justified, this is where knowledge through experience comes in...If you already know how to shoot, it is a waste of your time and additional money paying for the instructors liability insurance, range, ammo, guns, lights, targets and other overhead etc. to take a few shots. On the other hand a complete novice will not even begin to retain any of the fundamentals. I know I cannot instill the fundamentals of shooting by waving a magic wand after a few rounds.

Well intentioned or not, the few shots taken are more about justifying their higher price for the course than anything else. I strongly advise that the novice would be far better served by joining a gun club, to learn from knowledgeable members who will gladly help. Or, by taking the time for a series of lessons from an instructor, which most clubs have, to get you started down the right path over time.

In my experience with this state course since 2000, I can say without a question that a majority of the people I come into contact with have had previous experience with firearms through one venue or another. Some had moved into the state and needed the course simply as a way to legally keep the guns they already own. Others, through life experience and/or military training. Still others because they had just come to figure out that the old FID card that said "indefinite" in their wallets was no longer indefinite, it had expired years ago, October 1998 to be exact and had to be brought up to speed.

Then there are those who take the class because they want to legally keep guns that have been inherited, for sentimental or other reasons. There are people that want their spouse to have some knowledge of the firearms they keep in the house as well as the laws surrounding the proper storage of those guns. Then there are people that learn certain laws loosened in 2004, that no longer keep them from getting their gun permits back, lost years ago over something minor.

After looking at all that, it is not quite as dire as "No one could possibly know anything about firearms or the proper use of them" until they talk to someone like me. I wouldn't flatter myself for a second by thinking that egotistical nonsense. For the types of circumstances surrounding the people I have just mentioned, people like me are useful in helping them understand the MA state firearm laws so that they may stay in sync with them, as well as introducing/reiterating specific safety aspects.

Discovering the varied levels of firearm experience that I have come into contact with from class to class, really does not surprise me. On the contrary, considering that firearms are an American birthright and are estimated to be numbered in the hundreds of millions throughout America, it would be foolish of anyone to think all people looking for a gun license are completely ignorant about firearms or incompetent in the handling of them. I cannot resist inserting a quote by one of America's greatest Founding Fathers (in my opinion) as it happens to punctuate what I have been saying about American citizens….

This is an excerpt from the very first session of Congress, made by our first President:

"Firearms stand next in importance to the Constitution itself. They are the people's liberty, teeth and keystone under independence, the rifle and the pistol are equally indispensable...more than 99% of them by their silence indicate that they are in safe sane hands. The very atmosphere of firearms everywhere restrains evil interference. When firearms go, all goes, we need them every hour." - George Washington

NOTE: The word "Keystone" is from 1630, it means: "The central supporting element of a whole." Synonyms include: principle, foundation, basis. It is obvious to me, the meaning is clear, firearms and American citizens have had and will continue to have a long standing relationship. You hear that all you socialist progressives? We will run many of you out of office over time, my preference would be to have them all tarred and feathered and run out on a rail or jailed for breaking their oath to uphold the Entire Constitution...charged as traitors!

Gun Sense #22 MA "Stored & Kept'" and "Direct Control."

I am not a lawyer, but this is my attempt to make certain that you will understand the two main criteria set down, at this time, on how we should handle firearms in Massachusetts. If you want to research anything here, it is encouraged and you should. I decided to try and translate this from lawyer's legalese to common English, so that we mere mortals could then vaguely understand it. I believe that they are vague in order for the courts to interpret them any which way they feel like interpreting them, depending on the circumstances.

One of the larger pieces of legislation passed in recent times, Chapter 180 of the acts of 1998, took effect on or about October 21, 1998.

NOTE: As of that date anyone having a Firearm Identification Card (FID) marked "indefinite" will no longer be honored and you will need to renew it every six years thereafter.

The following precautions are advised to avoid perceptions/misconceptions and or laws, leading to arrest, felony charges, confiscation of guns and suspension or revocation of your FID card or LTC.

This is taken from **Chapter 140 Massachusetts General Law (M.G.L.) Section 131L**. (a):

"It shall be unlawful to store or keep any firearm, rifle or shotgun including, but not limited to, large capacity weapons, or machine gun in any place unless such weapon is secured, in a locked container or equipped with a tamper-resistant mechanical, lock or other safety device, properly engaged so as to render such weapon inoperable by any person other than the owner or other lawfully authorized user."

NOTE: At this time, I cannot point to any law or regulation stating that a firearm must be stored unloaded. There is no statute in the M.G.L. or CMR giving regulation on this that I could find...nor could the clerk at the Massachusetts Law Library that was reached out to. In a state police newsletter discussing firearms safety, they "recommend" that firearms are stored unloaded. A section on the Mass.gov website concerning firearms also notes that firearms "should" be stored unloaded. Further, no case law specifically covering a properly stored or kept firearm, that happens to be loaded can be found by us or even the clerk we reached out to from the Massachusetts Law Library. If you are able to find a statute, regulation or case law concerning this, please let me know. You make the distinction/call you feel comfortable with and perhaps seek legal counsel.

NOTE: There is no definition under **Chapter 140 M.G.L.** for the term "secured in a locked container," container being the key word. So I decided to crack open a dictionary, *Webster's Encyclopedic Unabridged Dictionary of the English Language*, to come up with this nugget of information:

"Container: Anything that contains, or can contain something, as a carton, box, crate, can, etc."

NOTE: "etc." can cover a lot of things, such as a secured and locked house for instance. Under the definition of contain I found: "To keep under proper control." Also under the definition of House: "To remove from exposure; to put in a safe place; to stow securely." In short, a secured locked container is also a house! But, MA case law has determined that a house is not a secured container. Nor is a separate room locked, if the lock can be opened by a bobby pin! The room being opened with a bobby pin is straight out of a Massachusetts Supreme Court case, Commonwealth VS Stephen Parzick. On that vein, anything with time, can be compromised by a determined criminal, you can only do your best. At some point the criminal is responsible for his own actions and that starts the second he breaks in.

There are huge penalties/charges for improper storage of your firearm(s) and the associated ammunition, so again, use good judgement, don't try to split hairs, be proactive. Also if you own one of those nice gun safes with the little compartments for ammo built into it, it would not be illegal to store ammo in the same locked container that the gun(s) is/are in. Remember, nowhere in the law does it specifically say that you cannot store ammo with the guns, as long as they are secure. But be sure they are very secure, don't make it easy for the criminal.

IMPORTANT NOTE: This is not in the Massachusetts General Law (M.G.L.) under **Chapter 140**, but it is law, as far as storage of ammunition. This is within the Code of Massachusetts Regulations (C.M.R.) 527, Board of Fire Prevention Regulations as outlined in Chapter 148 M.G.L. Section 13. **527 C.M.R Chapter 1**, Section 1.12.8.39.1.1.4 : It states:

"Small arms ammunition, primers, smokeless propellants and black powder stored in original containers and stored in a locked cabinet, closet or box when not in use as provided in **Section 1.12.8.50**. Small arms ammunition, as used here, shall mean any shotgun, rifle, or pistol cartridge and any cartridge or propellant actuated devices, excluding military ammunition containing bursting charges or incendiary, tracer, spotting, or pyrotechnic projectiles."

You instructors out there, there is more to regulating guns/ammo than Chapter 140...in MA!

After checking with a representative with the state fire Marshall, he said that the code on storage refers to the bulk storage of ammunition.

A State police Lieutenant from Sandwich was charged with a felony, for improper storage of a firearm. He had left an unlocked, unloaded gun, in an unlocked dresser drawer along with a loaded magazine, in an unlocked house in 2008. I heard the charges in this case may have been swept under the rug....Err on the side of caution, you probably will not be so lucky, keep stored guns away from the ammo, be proactive.

Transporting Firearms FAQ:

Q: How do I transport a gun in my vehicle?
A: A person with an LTC may transport a handgun loaded or unloaded on his person or under his direct control in the vehicle. If the handgun is not under his direct control, it must be unloaded and in a locked case, locked trunk or other secure container.

All persons transporting large capacity rifles and shotguns shall transport them unloaded (they must be unloaded) and in a case, just in case you break down and need to carry the long gun away out in public view to avoid mass hysteria. If the long gun capacity is less than ten rounds, the case does not have to be locked. If the capacity is ten or more rounds, the case needs to be locked.

For more specific information see **Chapter 140 M.G.L. Section 131C.**

Q: Do I need to lock my non-large capacity rifles and shotguns in a case while transporting them in a vehicle?
A: No. They must be transported unloaded, but are not required to be in a locked case while transporting.

Q: Can I leave my gun in my car if I need to go into the store on my way home from the range or from hunting?
A: If your handgun or large capacity rifle or shotgun is transported in accordance with the provisions of **Chapter 140 M.G.L. Section 131C** (i.e. unloaded and in a locked case, locked trunk or other secure container) then the gun may be left unattended in the vehicle temporarily. Weapons transported in this manner will automatically be considered "stored or kept" in compliance with the safe storage requirements of **Section 131L.** Your car is not to be used as a 24/7 "gun safe"....

A person leaving a non-large capacity rifle or shotgun in an unattended vehicle is required to lock the rifle or shotgun in a case/container or in the trunk, or install a mechanical locking device on the weapon (i.e. cable or trigger lock). Don't leave it in plain sight....

NOTE: Direct Control, this means under your immediate control, within arm's reach. If you are watching television in the family room and your handgun/any gun, is loaded upstairs without being locked somehow, in the master bedroom, it is not considered under your direct control, that would be labeled as improper storage of a firearm. Again, the gun described in that situation would need to be in the Stored or Kept condition, otherwise it would be a felony. Of course Direct Control applies to rifles and shotguns to a lesser degree, normally they would be stored unless being used in a hunting or gun club activity. Certainly, most of us do not walk around our homes clutching a loaded shotgun, though legally you could (That's your call)....Handguns are carried far more frequently on your person and under your Direct Control for personal protection than long guns would be. When in public you need to ensure handguns are concealed so as not to be arrested on the perception made by most police who think they must be concealed and to avoid a public panic.

Please read **Gun Sense #15, Concealed or Not Concealed, That is the Question**....Long guns should be cased in public (by law), to protect your investment and to avoid sending the general public at large into a panicked frenzy of 911 calls. Remember, we are not in Maine, Texas, Alaska, Arizona or any other free state. This is the Twilight Zone...

NOTE: Be certain your handgun is concealed and you will avoid all kinds of irrational hysteria, the channel 7 news helicopter buzzing overhead, 300 swat team members closing in on you from all sides, costly lawyer's fees, five soccer moms screaming frantically on 10 TV stations "Think of the children!" etc. You should get the picture, I hope. Just remember, you are in Massachusetts. Avoid the headaches. As always, err on the side of caution...Be proactive.

Bear in mind also that there are places you cannot carry (see **Gun Sense # 35 Places you Cannot Carry Firearms in MA.**) and these include: Schools, houses of worship (without written permission), professional sport arenas, banks, hospitals, post offices, federal buildings, court houses, prisons, jails, police stations, airports (you may transport guns only with prior notification through your airline) and anywhere that may be posted "no guns allowed." Should you carry in a bar? Not if you are going to be drinking. If you are found to be drunk in possession of a gun, you will be prosecuted and lose your license, so use your head. When in doubt call ahead first to see if where you are going has an anti-gun, pro criminal policy. Above all else, please use good judgment.

For more important information concerning ammunition storage read **Gun Sense #37 Storage of Ammunition, Powder & Primers...**

Gun Sense #23 Ten Cardinal Rules of Firearm Safety and Firearm Safety Test With Relevance to MA.

These are the ten cardinal rules of firearm safety, you break any one of these and you or someone else could die, many have. Firearms are very unforgiving of mistakes or foolishness. The first mistake you make could be someone else's last breath on Earth.

1. Treat EVERY gun as if it were loaded AT ALL TIMES! This is a crucial mindset, there is no such thing as an unloaded gun!
2. MAKE SURE ANY gun you handle is pointed in a safe direction. Because it is loaded! Never assume otherwise!
3. NEVER point a gun that is loaded at anything/anyone you do not intend to destroy. Proper mindset, remember, they are ALL loaded!
4. Be aware that a round as small as a .22 LR bullet can travel up to a mile or more. You must know where the bullet will end up or DO NOT take the shot!
5. When target practicing ENSURE there is a backstop high enough and with no hard objects, to avoid ricochets.
6. ALWAYS ensure your firearm is UNLOADED and the action OPEN before ever handing the gun to anyone! Check it TWICE. That person must then handle it exactly as if it were loaded! People are killed by supposedly unloaded firearms every year!
7. While hunting, ALWAYS unload your gun before climbing up or over anything, jumping ditches or negotiating any obstacle in your way. Use good sense to avoid any accidental discharge.
8. While hunting ALWAYS be able to IDENTIFY your game first, OR DO NOT TAKE A SHOT! Also, look beyond your game before shooting, if you see blaze orange DO NOT SHOOT, the deer/whatever is NEVER that important!
9. NEVER shoot at or over open water with ANYTHING other than a shotgun loaded with bird-shot. Bullets from rifles and handguns will glance off water causing them to fly wildly. You can/will be held accountable for any negligence with a firearm.
10. Alcohol, Drugs and firearms are a deadly combination. NEVER consume ANYTHING that will even mildly impair your judgement or physical coordination when you are about to use a firearm!

NOTE: A mechanical safety on a firearm does NOT give you license to carelessly handle the firearm, anything man makes can break. YOU are the overriding master safety on ANY firearm that you handle!

Firearm Safety Test with relevance to MA.

1. A firearm is given to, or received from another individual with the action open whenever it is possible to do so? T F
2. Ammo must be stored in a locked container, in original boxes. T F
3. Can a handgun be carried loaded in a vehicle in compliance with Direct Control ? Y N
4. A firearm in the Stored or Kept condition may be temporarily left in a vehicle unattended? Y N
5. What condition is a firearm in, if it is not under your Direct Control?
6. Define Stored or Kept.
7. While transporting firearms not under your Direct Control can they be loaded? Y N
8. When firearms are kept in the home, is it a good idea to talk to children about gun safety at the earliest age possible? Y N
9. Are firearms that are not under your Direct Control in the home supposed to be unloaded and secured? Y N
10. Should you treat firearms as loaded at all times? Y N
11. Today's double and single action revolvers have external safeties? Y N
12. Should you exercise the same degree of firearm safety no matter what size caliber/type firearm you handle? Y N
13. Are a miss-fire and a hang-fire exactly the same thing? Y N
14. Should you ever take a firearm from someone if that person has not shown you it is technically unloaded first? Y N, Once taken how should it be handled? Explain.
15. How long should you wait in a miss-fire situation?
16. When hunting always identify your game and what is beyond before taking a shot. T F
17. Can you describe a squib load?
18. Should a mechanical safety on any firearm be trusted to work? Y N
19. Definition of Conviction: A finding or verdict of guilty, or a plea of guilty, whether or not final sentence is/was imposed. T F
20. Who bears the responsibility of firearm safety at all times?
21. You will need to sign an affidavit stating that none of your guns have been lost or stolen since your last application at each six year renewal. T F

22. You should always make and keep copies of anything you file with the police. Y N

23. Ammunition is to be in original containers and locked in a cabinet, closet or box when not in use. T F

Gun Sense #24 Hollywood Bullets vs. Real Bullets.

Hollywood has quite an influence on how people view things, right or wrong. People formulate notions based on what they see at the movies or on television. In my gun classes, I dispel some of these notions. I start by saying something like "I am now going to ruin some of the things that you believe to be real because you have seen it on TV all of your life." Remember, Hollywood is entertainment, nothing else.

For example, I am sure everyone has seen a James Bond flick, when he is scuba diving underneath some mad zillionaire's, super-sized yacht, complete with its own 18 hole golf course and naturally the madman who owns the yacht is out to rule the Earth (every villain worth his weight in enriched uranium wants to rule the Earth in these shows). Every mad zillionaire naturally has his own highly trained army of thugs to command. Well, here is James Bond trying to sneak up under the yacht and he is spotted by the madman's sonar array, which would put the British Navy's technology to shame. This army is now eagerly waiting for Bond, all heavily armed with every kind of gun known to man (and some I cannot recognize) up on deck.

As James gets closer they spot his bubble trail and all hell breaks loose as they start shooting hundreds of thousands (maybe millions) of bullets into the water! The camera pans below the surface to show how James is doing under this massive onslaught. The bullets are whizzing past him all around, leaving little bubble trails as they zip to the bottom of the sea killing flounder and other hapless bottom dwelling creatures fathoms below. Of course they all miss James. HOLD IT RIGHT THERE! Do bullets really act that way in water? Hollywood would have you think so...it makes for cool special effects and at the end of the movie you're not told otherwise in the credits, they might say that no flounder were hurt during the making of this movie to calm down PETA, but that's about all.

Bullets can travel at very high rates of speed as we all know, some types go faster than others. At speeds that can be between 1000 fps to 4000 fps they will all have one thing in common when they are shot down into water. The water will have the effect of hitting a hard object on the bullet, it will shatter or deform and lose all forward motion and kinetic energy within about eight inches and sink harmlessly to the bottom, where the bottom dwellers will suck it up and may eventually die of lead poisoning, if they are lucky enough to live so long (don't tell PETA). So if James is swimming at least ten inches under water he should be safe, I personally am a chicken and would be at least 12 inches under...Sorry if I ruined your movies/TV shows.

OK, we are now watching a spy movie, a sinister looking character in the shadows wearing a trench coat and black leather gloves, a hat pulled low barely showing his evil eyes, he reaches into his coat to extract a pistol, next he pulls out a black tube and starts threading it onto the business end of the gun. From the look of things we think that his goal will be to assassinate someone, we are correct. The assassin inches down a darkened hallway in an old hotel and carefully opens a door, inside someone is asleep on the bed, he takes careful aim and lets six shots rip into the victim, each shot is almost completely silent with only a "putt, putt, putt, putt, putt, putt..."sound that cannot even be heard by the people in the next room. He silently leaves the room and a long string of commercials suddenly begin for your viewing pleasure.

Wait just one minute! Is that what would happen in real life? You have seen that type of thing from Hollywood so often you probably believe it. For one thing what you call a silencer is really known as a suppressor, it dulls the sound a little but does not even come close to what is depicted in the movies. People in the other room would have instantly been awakened by the sound of gunfire. A suppressor works best with subsonic ammunition, which is ammo that travels under 1125 feet per second. If ammo is used at or above that speed, a suppressor is very loud indeed. Sorry about wreaking your Hollywood fluff.

Hollywood bullets are the best for ending the usefulness of cars for any bad guy trying to escape, one or two shots and BOOM, the car is blown to smithereens along with all inside! Sometimes the car will even put Olympic gymnasts to shame with spectacular flips and twists! On another note, we often will see bullets sparking off everything they hit, even off trees in the forest, like little fireworks all around the good guy as he runs for cover! This sparking feature is so the bad guys can see exactly where they are missing so that they can correct their aim (just a little theory of mine). HOLD IT RIGHT THERE! Do common everyday bullets have these super abilities? In Hollywood they do. In real life they do not, you can riddle a car and never do more than put holes in it with your garden variety citizen weaponry. As far as all those sparks, sorry, only Hollywood bullets put on these Fourth of July displays (another reason I want some). More movies etc. ruined for you, oh well.

Another Hollywood cool special effect deals with bullets and fire. We have all seen what happens when some good guy on TV throws a handful of bullets into a campfire (or other hot place). All around the fire are many bad guys sitting and planning their next atrocity against mankind, this is to ensure that you will have no sympathy for them when the fireworks start. Within a couple seconds, or jussssssst enough time for the good guy to find cover after the bullets hit the fire, all hell breaks loose, naturally. The bad guys are dropping like flies in every direction as if those bullets had eyeballs. HOLD IT RIGHT THERE! Do bullets really react to fire that way? Hollywood has been selling that scenario for a very long time and people believe it hook, line and sinker.

In actuality the only thing that would happen (after about 40 seconds) would be dull popping sounds, some sparks would rise from the fire and no one would be shot off any logs. The cartridge(s) will become hot and if there is nothing to direct the gasses behind the bullet (like the barrel of a firearm will do) it will merely separate a few inches from the shell casing harmlessly. Many military studies on the effects of fire on ammunition bear this fact out. So if the Fire Department ever comes to your burning home (and I hope this never happens to you) they may ask you a few quick questions:

1. Is anyone in the house? Hopefully, "no."
2. Are there any pets in the house? Again, hopefully "no."
3. Are there any loaded firearms in the house? Be very honest with this answer, they have a very dangerous job, they run into a burning building while everyone else is running out of it, the job is dangerous enough without adding the possibility of being shot into the mix. A loaded and chambered firearm getting hot from a fire will discharge a bullet just the same as if you pulled the trigger yourself. So hopefully the answer again is "no," because if it is yes they may all sit back and toast marshmallows instead of taking the chance of being shot. If there are no loaded guns in the house, they will fight the fire, knowing that any stored ammo will just be 'popping' away harmlessly. Again, sorry for ruining your movies.

Hollywood bullets for the bad guys vs. Hollywood bullets for the good guys. I would love to buy some of the good guy bullets, just one box would do. If you know where they are sold please let me know. No matter what kind of firearm you put them into you will never ever miss again! They have the added benefit of being able to self-perpetuate, constantly, from second to second...you will never run out, never needing to inconveniently reload! They make shooting look as easy as falling off a log. The bad guys on the other hand don't have it quite as good with their ammo, occasionally they might wound a good guy and once in a great while may even get lucky enough to kill a good guy (if no sequel is planned), but by all accounts this is extremely rare.

The bad guys don't always have the luxury of never ending bullets, but where they lack accuracy in hitting the good guys, they are pretty good at hitting rival bad guys, which makes it easier for the good guys to mop up the remaining bad guys. But for the most part, the good guy bullets have the advantage of going through virtually anything while the bad guy bullets won't even make it through an overturned kitchen table if there is a good guy behind it.

The Hollywood western bullets have a quirk more unique or prevalent to them, they always ricochet, every shot, it astounds me. Watch any spaghetti western for the most ricochets, even the direct hits ricochet! So if you don't want to depress your friends, avoid buying the Hollywood western era bullets, that way it won't look like you miss everything you shoot at. You definitely would not impress your friends with this kind of bullet.

The effects that Hollywood bullets have on the people they hit are amazing. In almost every case, when someone is unlucky enough to be written out of the script, they need to exit in a particularly memorable way. When a hapless bad guy catches a load of buckshot from a 12 gauge shotgun for instance, it will undoubtedly throw him back thirty feet, at least four feet off the ground and most probably put him through a brick wall, memorable enough? A single bullet for instance will instantaneously kill any bad guy it hits wherever it hits, no ifs ands or buts, unless of course it is a good guy, then it's merely a flesh wound. HOLD IT RIGHT THERE! Do bullets or buckshot really affect people in this way? Not exactly. In Hollywood they always do, for the added drama meant to keep you interested, they have to keep the action moving quickly along. Bullets are traveling so fast that the thing that actually happens is, that a person may not know what happened immediately, it takes time for the body to shut down. People are not as fragile as the movies depict them. They do not fly backwards or die instantly, unless it involves a head/heart shot and in many cases not even then. In war, soldiers have been documented as being hit multiple times, still fighting effectively, even rescuing others and living to talk about it.

If you can think of any other wonderful or quirky things that Hollywood bullets can do that I may not have mentioned please send us your comments for our entertainment.

All in all though, I would still like to have a box or two of the good guy Hollywood bullets, it would mean that I would no longer have to work on keeping my fundamentals sharp. What could be better than never ever missing again or never having to buy ammo ever again? Great for your budget. Of course if too many people had them there would no longer be any need for firearm instructors!

Gun Sense #25 Can you Keep a Secret?

Outside of your immediate family and/or a trusted close circle of good, like-minded friends, in this day and enlightened age, don't tell people what you have when it comes to firearms. I know that sometimes people may ask you if you own guns, the question, on the surface, may be quite innocent but it can sometimes lead to bad consequences. In this state and time in history, it is an inappropriate question and you should politely decline to discuss your personal business with someone that does not need to know that information.

Your like-minded friends should/will all be on the same page with you concerning their and your firearm information. Simply put, it is a matter of security. I know instances where a firearm(s) have been taken because of loose lips. In one case the home owner in question was big on cookouts and inviting large crowds of "friends" over. These "friends" would sometimes come with people that the home owner did not know. We will call the home owner Willy. Now Willy had quite a nice collection of guns and was very proud of them. He would make sure that everyone had a chance to admire them by bringing people into his house and showing the guns off. They were great show and tell material. This went on for a few summers. I had long since given up trying to convince Willy that show and tell was a bad practice. One day Willy came home to find that he had been burglarized and 21 various firearms had been taken. I think that more would have been taken but the crooks probably ran out of hands to carry them. So far only four have been recovered, that was more than ten years ago.

Associates that you really don't know very well can innocently mention to someone you don't know at all, that you are a gun owner. They in turn can casually pass that information on. It only takes one bad apple in that chain of people to use that information against you.

Someone who had taken my class a few years ago called me recently and told me a thief had broken into his car and taken a handgun that was secured with a cable lock, in a locked box out of sight under the seat. He said that he only occasionally left it in the car for reasons I will not mention. I asked him if he had any other valuables in the car that were taken. He said that his GPS was not touched or anything else, just the gun. Obviously he was specifically targeted for that gun. Possibly someone he knew had knowledge of the hiding place and brought the correct tool to steal it. I asked him to think hard about who he had talked to about the gun, to come up with a list of people. It probably was not a friend that took the gun. It was probably someone a friend had talked to about the gun, so he needs to talk to his circle of friends to narrow it down. I think it will lead him to that gun or at least a good suspect.

The main point that runs through this chapter is this, don't trust those you hardly know to protect your secrets from others. Keep your gun(s) as private as you reasonably can. Your gun(s) are not anyone's business but your own. If a firearm is stolen from you, report the theft to the police as soon as you find out. Keep a list of the serial numbers from each gun to aid the police in trying to recover your property. Don't unwittingly become an accomplice in the theft of your own firearms. That's my two cents.

Gun Sense #26 MA Hunter Safety Class Information.

As of 2005 a FID card or LTC no longer allows you to purchase a hunting license. But, if you happen to have a previous hunting license dated from 2007 or older, that would suffice for you to obtain a new hunting license, without your having to go through the hunter safety course. For more information call the MA Wildlife Department at (978) 772-0693 for upcoming classes or call Bass Pro Shops in Foxboro at (508) 216-2000, as they sometimes host the Hunter Safety classes in their store. Also, at Old Colony Sportsman's Club, they will host two classes per year in Pembroke.

Topics covered during the Basic Hunter Education course include: safe handling of hunting arms and ammunition, hunting laws and ethics, wildlife identification, wildlife management, care and handling of game, basic survival skills and first aid. The course also allows students 15 years or older to apply for a firearms license (FID) at their local police departments. These Certificates of Completion are also recognized in all the United States (too bad our gun licenses are not), Canada and Mexico for the purchase of a hunting or sporting license. The state requires this to be a 12 hour course. Hunter education information can be found:

Massachusetts Hunter Education Program

https://www.mass.gov/massachusetts-hunter-education-program

Contact Information (Information in Appendix A)

You can sign up to be notified by MA Fish and Wildlife when the course becomes available. This is done by going to this link in the hunter education program website:

Course Notifications

https://www.mass.gov/service-details/course-notifications

This will allow you to be notified when the course is available for registration. ANY QUESTIONS MUST BE DIRECTED TO MA Fish and Wildlife.

Contact Information (Information in Appendix A)

Previous graduates who have lost their certificates may obtain a duplicate by visiting:

Duplicate Certificates

https://www.mass.gov/forms/duplicate-certificates

The electronic Licensing Website started in 2011. Inquiries regarding purchases of electronic licenses and permits from "Mass Fish Hunt" should be directed to Active Outdoors, by calling toll free or emailing:

Mass Fish Hunt

https://www.ma.wildlifelicense.com/IS/Customer/InternetCustomerSearch

Contact Information (Information in Appendix A)

License buyers will still be able to purchase the traditional paper hunting, trapping and freshwater fishing licenses and stamps at license vendors throughout the state until the switch is made to an entirely electronic system. For a list of current hunting, trapping and freshwater fishing license vendors visit:

MassFishHunt License Agent Map

https://www.mass.gov/service-details/massfishhunt-license-agent-map

You can subscribe to be notified when a Massachusetts Trapper Education course is available, visit:

Request to be notified about Hunter Education courses in your area

https://form.jotform.com/82404977446971

If you are interested in the course, please call (508) 389-7830. Classes are filled first-come, first-served and enrollment cannot be processed via email.

Also, please be advised, that if you are taking the course, as mandated for first-time trappers and Problem Animal Control (PAC) Agents, in order to apply for a Massachusetts trap registration number, a state issued certificate from any US state is accepted to meet this requirement.

Thank you for your interest in the Mass Wildlife Hunter Education Program.

NOTE: Age 15 up to 18, the fee for FID is $25.00, as stated in **Chapter 140 M.G.L Section 129B**.

Gun Sense #27 Gun Laws to "Understand" in MA (with links).

First, if you would like a copy of your adult criminal record (if any) read *Gun Sense #34 MA CORI Report Info.* I think the fee is $25. You can use this report to clarify, in your own mind, if there are any possible road blocks that may stand in the way of getting a gun license.

I will list some laws that you as a gun license holder are required to know. I am not a lawyer, but the last time I checked I don't have to be to reproduce what is public information, which is at times vague, confusing and contradictory. There will not be any order to this information and I am not going to sprinkle case laws throughout to justify anything, it is what it is. I have included some citations to help send you where I may have gotten the information. I will just put down the facts as they stand at this time, not always verbatim. You may or may not be aware of this information, but like I said, as a license holder you're supposed to be aware of it and more. This list is not all inclusive, it is an example of what you need to know, the links provided help to show a more complete picture.

You can view more information on these laws at Mass.gov under **Chapter 140** by visiting:

Massachusetts Firearms Laws

https://www.mass.gov/lists/massachusetts-firearms-laws#firearms-

1. Change of address notification form. Any licensee shall notify, in writing, the licensing authority who issued said license, the Chief of police into whose jurisdiction the licensee moves, and the executive director of the criminal history systems board within 30 days of your move. You may pick up these forms at any local police dept. Failure to notify shall be cause for revocation or suspension of your gun license. Directions on the form are clear and easy to follow. While it is a given that the authorities do not have any knowledge of where the criminals live with their illegal firearms, it may not comfort you to know that not one crime will be prevented by the authorities knowing exactly where you live at all times. **Chapter 140 M.G.L. Section 131.**

2. Transfer/Sale of Firearm(s). A seller shall report all such transfers to the executive director of the criminal history systems board, according to the provisions set forth in section one....etc,etc,etc. In short, as of 8-13-2014 you will need to use the online portal in real time, through the MA State police website to transfer firearms with the E-FA10 transfer form. Failure to report the private sale of a firearm(s) may be cause for permanent revocation of your gun license and shall be punished by a fine of not less than $200 nor more than $1,000 for a first offense. A fine of not less than $1,000 nor more than $5,000 for a second offense. I'm not sure here how a second offense could come down the pike if you lost your gun license permanently for a first offense, so file this second penalty under "BEWARE" I guess. **Chapter 140 M.G.L. Section 129c.**

3. If you do not intentionally let your gun permit expire and was not otherwise disqualified from renewing it (you just forgot, life got in the way) and then when you go try to renew it, you will be subject to a civil fine. Be aware that fines/penalties vary from a low to harsh range, err on the side of caution if in doubt. That should keep honest people from trying to renew a simply expired license. Hey, you keep voting these so-called law makers back into office, deal with it. **Chapter 140 M.G.L. Section 129b** & **Section 131.**

4. Any law enforcement officer who discovers a person to be in possession of a firearm(s) after the person's license has expired or it has been revoked or suspended solely for failure to give notice of a change of address, said officer shall confiscate such firearm(s) and the expired or suspended license as well and said officer shall forward the license to the licensing authority by whom it was issued. The officer shall provide a written inventory to the owner of the firearm(s) confiscated and shall exercise due care in the handling, holding and storage of these items. Any confiscated weapon shall be returned to owner upon the renewal of the license within one year of such confiscation or the firearms will be disposed of through auction. Basically, your guns will be held hostage until you cough up the ransom money as punishment for your being forgetful. **Chapter 140 M.G.L. Section 129b.**

5. An LTC shall be valid for the purpose of owning, possessing, purchasing and transferring low/or large capacity rifles and shotguns, handguns. **Chapter 140 M.G.L. Section 131.**

6. Penalty for loan of money secured by weapons: Whoever loans money secured by mortgage, deposit or pledge of a firearm(s), shall be punished by a fine or by imprisonment for not more than one year, or by both. Banks and other institutional lenders are exempt and can do this. The

government and its big money lobbyists hate competition. **Chapter 140 M.G.L. Section 131b.**

7. Sale or possession of electrical weapons (stun guns). It is illegal and it carries a fine or by imprisonment in the house of correction for not less than six months nor more than two and one half years, or by both fine and imprisonment. A law enforcement officer may arrest without a warrant any person whom he has probable cause to believe has violated this section. Non-law enforcement (civilians) cannot own/have them (This may change soon due to a case pending in court). **Chapter 140 M.G.L. Section 131j.**

8. Citizens right to arrest: A private citizen may lawfully arrest someone who has in fact committed a felony. Felonies include the crimes of murder, rape, assault, or assault and battery with a dangerous weapon, robbery, and burglary. A felony is any crime punishable by death or imprisonment in State Prison. All other crimes are misdemeanors. The private citizen cannot use fatal force to affect an arrest or prevent escape of one who had committed a felony concerned with property only. The citizen can only use that amount of force necessary to bring the person under control when affecting the arrest. My suggestion, just be a good witness instead...unless you're defending your life or the life of another person. **COMMONWEALTH vs. LEONARD L. LUSSIER, 333 Mass. 83.**

9. The Castle statute (Doctrine): The statute provides to one that injures or kills another in a dwelling an affirmative defense under certain circumstances. (a) Person using defense is an occupant of dwelling. (b) Reasonable belief that another is about to inflict great bodily injury or death upon the occupant or other lawfully present person(s). (c) The threatening attacker is unlawfully in said dwelling. (d) That occupant used reasonable means to defend himself or others lawfully present. The statute also says, "There is no duty for the occupant to retreat from the person who is unlawfully in said dwelling." **Chapter 278 M.G.L. Section 8A.**

10. About BB guns, air guns and paintball guns: Adults do not need an LTC/FID to purchase a BB gun, air gun, or paint ball gun. Minors under 18 may not buy BB Guns, air guns or paint ball guns. No Person shall discharge any projectile from these guns, across any street, alley, public way, or railway right of way. No minor, unless a holder of a sporting license, shall discharge these guns unless accompanied by an adult. There is a fine of up to $100 and confiscation of BB gun or air gun. BB guns, air guns, and paint ball guns are dangerous weapons per Chapter 265 M.G.L. Crimes Against the Person. BB guns, air guns, paint ball guns, are firearms

by definition per Chapter 269 M.G.L. Section 10 (a.- j.), relating to possession on school grounds. BB pellets are not ammunition. **Chapter 269 M.G.L. Section 12B.**

11. Definition of Ammunition: Cartridges or cartridge cases, primers (igniter), bullets or propellant powder designed for use in any firearm. The term ammunition shall also mean tear gas cartridges, Chemical Mace or any device or instrument which contains or emits a liquid, gas, powder or any other substance designed to incapacitate. It is a crime to possess ammunition without an LTC or FID card, this is an arrestable violation. The Commonwealth, in the context of a prosecution under Chapter 269 M.G.L. Section 10 (h), does not bear the burden of proving that any particular ammunition is capable of being fired. Rather, the government must show only that the alleged ammunition is designed for that purpose. **Chapter 140 M.G.L. Section 121.**

12. Conviction: "A finding or verdict of guilty or a plea of guilty, whether or not final sentence is/was imposed." **Chapter 140 M.G.L. Section 121.**

Gun Sense #28 Is The Second Amendment Relevant? You bet Your Life!

Not my opinion, these are facts.

I am going to point out some court decisions that have come down on the side of the police. These cases were filed by people who were victims of violent crime or filed by the surviving members of families on behalf of a member killed by violent criminals. They have two things in common: 1. The police did not arrive in time, or at all, to save the victim(s), and 2. No one has ever won a decision in court against the police because someone died before they could respond. Here are a sample of four cases to highlight why the Second Amendment is vital. At the end I will give a brief summary as to why this is the way things will always remain. In these cases, pay close attention to what the court ruled.

This first case, (1) concerns two women in D.C. who called the police for help when they heard people breaking into a closed off section of their apartment building. They called many times over a one hour time frame before the criminals broke into where they were hiding. Over the next 14 hours they were repeatedly raped before the criminals decided to leave. The police never came. The criminals were never caught.

1. In Warren v. District of Columbia (1981), The D.C. Court of Appeals ruled, "official police personnel and the government employing them are not generally liable to victims of criminal acts for failure to provide adequate police protection...a government and its agents are under no general duty to provide public services, such as police protection, to any particular citizen."

This next decision, (2) from the court is simply chilling, but, in lock step with the thread that runs through all of these court decisions. For more on this case and other cases like those mentioned on this page go to:

The Police Have "No Affirmative Duty" To Protect Us

http://www.endtimesreport.com/NO_AFFIRMATIVE_DUTY.htm

2. In Bowers v. DeVito (1982), the Seventh Circuit Court of Appeals ruled,

"There is no constitutional right to be protected by the state against being murdered by criminals or madmen."

This next case, (3) involves a woman, Linda, who had a restraining order against her violent husband (she lived in the city of New York). She was killed by her husband. The city had then, as it has now, a ban on firearms, even for protection. Linda was a good little citizen (victim), followed the law, so, she did not own a gun….and died because of it.

3. Riss v. NYC, (1958). Justices rule police do not have a constitutional duty to protect someone. The ruling applies even for a woman who had obtained a court issued protective order against a violent husband, making an arrest mandatory for a violation. Linda's family lawyer stated; "What makes the City's position particularly difficult to understand is that, in conformity to the dictates of the law, Linda did not carry/own any weapon for self-defense. Thus by a rather bitter irony she was required to rely on the City of New York for protection which now denies all responsibility to her."

Is it starting to SINK IN YET?

And last, but certainly not least, # 4…pay close attention.

4. Castle Rock v. Gonzales, on June 27, 2005, the Supreme Court found that Jessica Gonzales, did not have a constitutional right to individual police protection even in the presence of a restraining order. Mrs. Gonzales' husband, with a track record of violence, stabbing Mrs. Gonzales and 3 children to death after abducting them, the police told her to wait and see if he brought the children back and made no move to locate the children. Mrs. Gonzales could not get the Supreme Court to change their 7-2 decision for one's individual protection.

It is a well settled fact of American law that the police have no legal duty to protect any individual citizen from crime, even if the citizen received death threats.

There have been over 10 various Supreme and lower court cases that the individual has never won and never will win. Notably, the Supreme Court stated this about the responsibility for the security of your family and loved ones security: "You, and only you, are responsible for your security and that of your family and loved ones." That was the essence of a U.S. Supreme Court decision in the early 1980's when they ruled that "The police do not have a duty to protect you as an individual, but to protect society as a whole."

I thought society was made up of individuals?

This is the rock bottom line folks, YOU ARE ON YOUR OWN! When you hear all the clowns (our own reps) screaming about gun control and banning law abiding citizens from owning guns, or cities forcing people to rely on the police for protection, don't buy it. Never give up your right to self-defense...maybe you should read number 3 over and over again, until it sinks in. As the Supreme Court says, "That we alone are responsible for our own safety," we can never allow anyone to negate our Second Amendment or God given rights to self-defense!

Summary: I know the courts will never allow a case to hold police responsible where someone died because they did not respond in time or at all, that would open the flood gates of litigation, bankrupting police departments all over the country. It is a common fact they get to the scene after the fact, to gather evidence. So stop being naive by thinking the police will get there in time, it is your responsibility and duty to defend yourself and your family at the very moment crime happens. The police are the clean-up crew, you make sure it will not be any of your family members that will be put into body bags.

I would much rather be judged by a jury of my peers, than be murdered and carried by six to the cemetery, because I FOOLISHLY put my trust in the government to protect me and mine.

And you should take note of this, even in light of the above mentioned facts, there are those in positions of authority all over the country that treat the people in their jurisdictions as if they were mere annoyances. Example, in San Diego County, Sheriff William Gore will not consider issuing a gun permit unless someone can show they have good cause for it first. This is his definition of good cause: "A set of circumstances that distinguishes the applicant from other members of the general public and causes him or her to be placed in harm's way," adding to this, "fear for one's personal safety is not, standing alone, considered by me as good cause."

NOTE: About Sheriff Gore, in my estimation, after reading this highly educated pinhead's convoluted reasoning, I can only come to one conclusion. He, and many other, politically appointed hacks must think, *What's the point of having authority if you can't abuse people with it by playing God with their safety?* I believe he and others, are callously putting the lives of people in danger because they want to and because they can. With that in mind, remember to read number 3 over and over until it sinks in.

"When injustice becomes law, resistance becomes duty." - Thomas Jefferson

Gun Sense #29 Answers to Firearm Safety Test #23.

These are the answers to the Firearm Safety Test in *Gun Sense #23 Ten Cardinal Rules of Firearm Safety and Firearm Safety Test With Relevance to MA.*

1. True. With the exception of black powder firearms...If there is no percussion cap on the nipple or flint in the jaws of the hammer, they are considered unloaded. Read *Gun Sense #2 How do People get Killed by "Unloaded" Guns?*
2. True
3. Yes.
4. No.
5. Stored or Kept condition. Read *Gun Sense #22 MA "Stored & Kept"' and "Direct Control."*
6. Secured in a locked container or fitted with a mechanical device that would render it useless. Read *Gun Sense #22 MA "Stored & Kept"' and "Direct Control."*
7. If it is a handgun under your direct control, Yes. If it is a rifle or shotgun, No. They must always be unloaded in your vehicle.
8. Yes. Please read *Gun Sense #3 About Those Children...and Your Guns, Gun Sense #16 Gun Safety and Responsibility* and *Gun Sense #17 What Should You Teach Your Child About Gun Safety?*
9. Yes.
10. Yes, you must have the mindset that they are always loaded. Read *Gun Sense #4 No Such Thing as an Unloaded Firearm, Proper "Mindset."*
11. No.
12. Yes, they all can kill you.
13. No. Read *Gun Sense #5 What is a Misfire/What is a Hang Fire?*
14. No. Never trust anyone on this issue. You will handle it just as if it were loaded! Read *Gun Sense #4 No Such Thing as an Unloaded Firearm, Proper "Mindset."*
15. Ten seconds. Read *Gun Sense #5 What is a Misfire/What is a Hang Fire?*
16. True. People say that this is just common sense, I say if it is such common sense why are there shooting accidents every year? A deer/etc. is not important enough to endanger a human, you must be absolutely sure. Be an ethical hunter, only hunt for what you have set out to hunt, do not shoot at anything that walks, crawls, flies or slithers just because you're in the woods with a gun.

17. A cartridge that was not loaded with enough gunpowder or no gunpowder. Read **Gun Sense #6 What is a Squib Load? Understand the Danger.**

18. No. Anything man makes can break, you are the master safety on any firearm that you handle. Read **Gun Sense #10 Weapon Safeties...Understand Them.**

19. True. Under MA law, when you fill out your application, they already know your record, if you have one, they expect you to tell them what they already know about you, be honest.

20. Yes. We all do, every one of us, nuff said.

21. As of 8-13-2014, this is True.

22. Yes. ALWAYS keep copies of anything you turn in to the police, especially relating to firearms.

23. Yes. Ammo is to be locked up and secure in original containers when not in use. See **527 C.M.R. Chapter 1**, Board of Fire Prevention Regulations under Chapter 148 M.G.L.

Thank you for taking this test, please pass it on so those you know will be more aware around firearms. Remember, they are ALL loaded, ALL the time (proper mindset). Read **Gun Sense #4 No Such Thing as an Unloaded Firearm, Proper "Mindset."**

Gun Sense #30 Graduated Licenses,(D-A) Under MA Law & "Green Card" Info.

Revisions as of 8-13-2014.

CLASS D: You need this license from age 15 to 17, to possess pepper spray, mace or other chemical incapacitating agents legal in the State of Massachusetts.

NOTE: As of 8-13-2014 once you are 18 or older you no longer need this license or a gun license to buy pepper spray (sometimes called mace). Read **Gun Sense #41 Gun Law Changes in MA 8-13-2014.**

CLASS C (Gone as of 8-13-2014)/FID: Possession of low capacity rifles and shotguns. Low capacity is defined as a shotgun with a loading capacity of five rounds or less and a rifle with a loading capacity of ten rounds or less. $25.00 for age 15-17. For all other residents $100.

CLASS B (Gone as of 8-13-2014): Law revision. Read **Gun Sense #41 Gun Law Changes in MA 8-13-2014.**

Class A: Known as a License to Carry (LTC), possession of high capacity handguns. High capacity is defined as a handgun with a loading capacity of more than ten rounds. This is the only license that allows an individual to carry a concealed weapon if authorized by the licensing authority in your town, $100.

NOTE: Authorization/requirements vary from town to town and Chief by Chief, due to the disservice of Arbitrary Discretion, again, contact your representatives to establish set uniform guidelines, end Arbitrary Discretion once and for all.

NOTE: The possession of electronic incapacitors (stun guns) is illegal. There is no license available and if caught with one in your possession you will be arrested, fined up to $10,000 and can be jailed for up to two and a half years in a house of correction. There is a case that has gone to the Supreme Court, from MA, that case may very well overturn the ban in MA (and anywhere else) on these stun guns soon.

"GREEN CARD" Information: I verified this information through the

Framingham State Police, who also verified it through the Firearms Record Bureau in Chelsea MA.

If you have a so-called green card you may apply for an LTC. You must still take the state approved firearm safety class before applying for either an FID or LTC.

1. Call the Firearm Records Bureau at (617) 660-4780, (prompt # 2) for a permit application, to apply for a non-resident alien license.
2. You can take the MA Firearm Safety class any time and hang on to the certification as proof you took the required course.

Permanent Legal Resident Alien: Read **Gun Sense #42 Legal Resident Aliens (Federal Law).**

Question: Can a LEGAL Resident Alien apply now for an LTC in Massachusetts?

Answer: Yes, a Legal Resident Alien (so-called "green card" holder) can apply for an LTC on the SAME BASIS as a citizen. It is the result of the federal court, Fletcher v. Haas decision, found here:

Civil Action No. 11-10644-DPW.

http://volokh.com/wp-content/uploads/2012/03/fletcher.pdf

If you run into a Police Department that refuses to process your application even though you are a Legal Resident Alien, please contact Comm2A (though the word is pretty much out and PD's seem to be processing such apps).

Permanent legal resident aliens (so-called "green card" holders) are treated the same as citizens with a license duration of six years and the $100 fee. The case was all about fairness for legal resident aliens and we scored a decisive win.

NOTE: A yearly license fee for Non-residents is $100 per year, which I believe is designed to discourage people from out-of-state.

For potential legal help, Commonwealth Second Amendment Inc. can be found here:

Commonwealth Second Amendment Inc.

http://www.comm2a.org/

Contact Information (Information in Appendix A)

SUMMAARY: On Friday, March 31, 2012, a Federal Court Judge granted our motion for summary judgment in Fletcher v. Haas, effectively overturning the state's prohibition on handgun possession by legal resident aliens.

In his 41 page ruling Federal Judge Douglas P. Woodlock concluded that: "The Massachusetts firearms regulatory regime, as applied to Fletcher and Pryal, does not pass constitutional muster regardless of whether intermediate scrutiny or strict scrutiny applies…" and continues: "Any classification based on the assumption that lawful permanent residents are categorically dangerous and that all American citizens by contrast are trustworthy lacks even a reasonable basis." In answer to the Commonwealth's assertion that the Second Amendment protects a right of citizenship, Judge Woodlock writes: "The defendants' reading of Heller requires a considerable analytical strain." The Comm2A staff will be working with individuals affected by this ruling to determine next steps and to insure that the court's ruling is correctly applied. If you are a foreign national residing in Massachusetts or know of one, please contact Comm2A for more information.

Gun Sense #31 Frequently Asked Questions.

I will list some questions here that I have encountered in my MA classes, with answers.

Q: Do you give the MA state class for the LTC/FID license?
A: Yes, I have given the class since 2000. My son joined me in 2013 and we travel all over the state giving the required class. Please go to my webpage for details: **http://mafirearmsafety.com**. There you can schedule your own class.

Q: A Massachusetts friend wants to store a firearm(s) in my safe, is that legal?
A: If he has a gun license and you have a gun license, yes you can. But the licenses have to cover the gun. If it is a handgun you both must have a LTC.

Q: What does "unrestricted" mean in applying for LTC?
A: It means for any Lawful purpose in how you utilize your firearm(s).

Q: In Massachusetts is it illegal to ride in a vehicle with a loaded weapon, with a LTC and have children in the car?
A: No, the pistol must be under your Direct Control as outlined in **Gun Sense #22 MA "Stored & Kept"' and "Direct Control."** But, you cannot take it onto school property, read **Gun Sense # 35 Places you Cannot Carry Firearms in MA.** It is illegal in the state of Massachusetts to have a loaded long gun in your vehicle.

Q: In MA, if I apply for a license to carry, would my son, being a police officer, influence the decision in MA?
A: No, It should have nothing to do with your son being a police officer or who you know, instead it has everything to do with your past, as far as court records go, or lack thereof. Please read **Gun Sense #39 MA Application/"Interview" Process & Steps/Tips.**

Q: My friend has a MA LTC but I do not, can I shoot his gun?
A: Yes, you can shoot his gun under his direct supervision. Read **Gun Sense #22 MA "Stored & Kept"' and "Direct Control."**

Q: Can I win an appeal on LTC in MA if I had a restraining order 20 years

105

ago?
A: It should not be denied if you had a restraining order 20 years ago or two years ago, please read **Gun Sense #39 MA Application/"Interview" Process & Steps/Tips.**

Q: When should you follow up on your LTC application?
A: The average time it takes to be processed is about four months, give the police a call then to check the status of your LTC.

Q: Can a LEGAL Resident Alien apply now for an LTC in Massachusetts?
A: Yes, a Legal Resident Alien (so-called "green card" holder) can apply for an LTC on the SAME BASIS as a citizen. It is the result of the federal court, Fletcher v. Haas decision, found here:

Civil Action No. 11-10644-DPW.

http://volokh.com/wp-content/uploads/2012/03/fletcher.pdf

Read **Gun Sense #30 Graduated Licenses,(D-A) Under MA Law & "Green Card" Info.**

Q: In MA is carrying a concealed weapon driving through school zone legal/OK?
A: Yes, in any state it is OK, if it were illegal that would amount to a complete gun ban. Democrats in office would love that…At least the oath breakers would anyway.

Q: What do you do if you applied for a LTC and get no response after 40 days? How long will it take?
A: After 40 days it is just a waiting game, on average it takes four months before you get the license, be patient.

Q: If I am denied a MA LTC can I apply for an FID card?
A: Before any open ended question like this can be reasonably answered, I would need more details like WHAT were the reason(s) given in the denial letter from the police? I am knowledgeable about whether a denial is valid or not and how to proceed if it is not valid, but I don't read minds….

Q: I was asked for three reasons to get a LTC, what should I say?

A: The best reason would be "Any Lawful Purpose," on the application. Ask if they accept that, if not, put for "Personal Protection," don't restrict yourself by saying anything else like for Employment or Hunting. But if they want to make you explain yourself with three reasons read **Gun Sense #19 "Reason" Letter for MA LTC.** and **Gun Sense #39 MA Application/"Interview" Process & Steps/Tips.**

Q: Can you get a gun permit with a misdemeanor in Massachusetts?
A: Please read **Gun Sense #20 MA Misdemeanor? Been Denied Your Gun Permit/License?**

Q: What guns are approved to own in MA?
A: A list of the approved firearms can be found at (this list is subject to change):

List of MA Approved Firearms

https://www.mass.gov/lists/approved-firearms-rosters

Q: What do I do about a lost MA LTC?
A: Read **Gun Sense #18 If you "Misplace" Your MA LTC or FID.**

Q: When I get pulled over, do I have to tell the police I am carrying in MA?
A: No, please read **Gun Sense #38 Traffic Stops in MA.**

Q: Which states honor the Florida Firearm multi state license?
A: See my Florida supplemental article on my webpage:

Florida CCW Info

http://mafirearmsafety.com/utah-ccw-info/

Q: How do I check the status of my LTC application?
A: After 40 days contact the police by email and ask. Save that email and any response. Be aware though that the average wait is four months….Read **Gun Sense #39 MA Application/"Interview" Process & Steps/Tips.**

Q: What is a Squib Load?
A: Please read **Gun Sense #6 What is a Squib Load? Understand the Danger.**

Q: What is favorable Reason for gun rights request?
A: I wrote one, please read **Gun Sense #19 "Reason" Letter for MA LTC.**

Q: Is there a template for a character reference letter for LTC in MA?
A: I wrote one, please read **Gun Sense # 33 MA "Letters of Recommendation" & Gun License Help.**

Q: What is a hang fire or a misfire?
A: Please read **Gun Sense #5 What is a Misfire/ What is a Hang Fire?**

Q: I am moving in the same town, what do I need to do for my LTC in Massachusetts?
A: Please read **Gun Sense #14 MA Change of Address Notification Forms and a Renewal tip.**

Q: Can you carry a gun in a bar in MA?
A: Read **Gun Sense #35 Places you Cannot Carry Firearms in MA.**

Q: Is there a firearm safety test online for Massachusetts?
A: I wrote a test that is specific to MA. Please read it at **Gun Sense #23 Ten Cardinal Rules of Firearm Safety and Firearm Safety Test With Relevance to MA.** The answers are in **Gun Sense #29 Answers to Firearm Safety Test #23.** Don't cheat...!

Q: Is a person with a MA LTC permitted to carry in a hospital?
A: Read **Gun Sense #35 Places you Cannot Carry Firearms in MA.**

Q: What should I expect in a firearms permit interview?
A: Read **Gun Sense #39 MA Application/"Interview" Process & Steps/Tips.**

Q: Where can I not carry in MA?
A: Read **Gun Sense #35, Places you Cannot Carry Firearms in MA.**

Q: Can a LEGAL Resident Alien apply for an LTC in Massachusetts?

A: Yes, a Legal Resident Alien (so-called 'green card' holder) can apply for an LTC on the SAME BASIS as a citizen. It is the result of the federal court, Fletcher v. Haas decision, found here:

Civil Action No. 11-10644-DPW.

http://volokh.com/wp-content/uploads/2012/03/fletcher.pdf

Q: How long do I have to wait once I submit my firearm license application to the police?
A: Generally speaking, you should receive your carry permit on average four months from the time you turn in the application. This may still vary from town to town depending on staffing. Some towns will hold applications until they accumulate a certain number of them before sending them to Boston to be processed, this can add a little time to your wait.

Q: How does the denial process work?
A: You are sent a notification. If you do not receive a written notification, with reasons for denial from the police within 40 days from the day you applied then you are not being denied, it is still within the four to six week window so just be patient and it will come.

Q: If I am denied what recourse do I have?
A: Part one, that depends on the reasons given for the denial. If you do not think the reasons given have legitimate grounds then I suggest you read **Gun Sense #13, Petition for Judicial Review, Specific to MA**. A denial can be overturned by a judge without the use of a lawyer. Part two, if you are denied for a past misdemeanor read **Gun Sense #20, Misdemeanor, Been Denied Your Gun Permit/License in MA**. Some loosening of the laws occurred in 2004, this could mean you are no longer banned from getting a gun license in MA under certain circumstances.

Q: Do I have to notify the authorities if I change my address while in possession of a gun license?
A: If you move out of state no. If you move from one town to another in MA, yes. If you move from one street, to another street in the same town, no. Read **Gun Sense #14, Change of Address Notification Forms- and a Renewal tip, MA** for detailed important information.

Q: What do I put on my application for a reason to get my gun license?
A: These three words, "Any Lawful Purpose." This should suffice for reasonable to the police, as it covers any contingency in your use of a firearm under the law. But, if for some reason your police department inexplicably will not accept that, use these three words: "For Personal Protection" as your second option. If your police department also wants you to write a letter to the Chief explaining your reason for wanting a gun permit then read **Gun Sense #19, Reason Letter for MA LTC.** If you're now feeling a bit intimidated, I wrote a template letter to help guide you, tweak it.

Q: Can I carry a loaded handgun in a motor vehicle?
A: Yes, provided you have a LTC and it is under your direct control. Read **Gun Sense #22 MA "Stored & Kept"' and "Direct Control."**

Q: Can I leave a firearm unattended in my motor vehicle?
A: Yes, please read **Gun Sense #22 MA "Stored & Kept"' and "Direct Control."**

Q: Where can I find a gun club to join?
A: MA has an abundance of gun clubs, many feature fishing as well, some specialize in other kinds of outdoor hunting/shooting sports. Here is a good link to find a club near you:

Mass Gun Clubs

http://massgunclubs.org/mass_gun_clubs.htm

Q: Can I bring someone shooting at a range on my license if he/she has no gun license?
A: Yes, but you are responsible for safety as you supervise someone else shooting.

Q: How much is charged by the state for an FID card?
A: As of July 12, 2011, the cost for someone under the age of 18 will be $25 and $100 dollars 18 or over. An LTC or FID are free if you are 70 or older (should be 65)....

Q: Not having a license, can I shoot on a friend's property with his gun if he has a license but is not present while I shoot?
A: No, he needs to be present to supervise you shoot.

Q: If I found myself in a situation where a criminal has broken into my home, I fear for my life and the lives of my family, should I fire a warning shot or shoot to wound a threatening criminal?
A: Every situation can be unique, never fire a warning shot (that's a Hollywood move), it just shows an attacker where you are and if he has a gun he will not return the favor by firing a warning shot. Do not shoot to wound, shoot to stop the threat. Under stress you lose your fine motor skills and use your gross motor skills. If you try to wound the criminal you will not stop the threat to you, he can still fight back, aim for the largest portion of the attacker and fire until the threat has been stopped.

Gun Sense #32 Firearm Possession in MA.

A Synopsis of State Laws on Purchase, Possession and Carrying of Firearms in Massachusetts.

WARNING: State firearms laws are subject to frequent change. This summary is not to be considered as legal advice or a restatement of law. To determine the applicability of these laws to specific situations which you may encounter, you are strongly urged to consult an attorney.

POSSESSION: Either a Firearm Identification card (FID) or a License to Carry (LTC) is required to own or possess a handgun, rifle, shotgun or ammunition. An investigation of the applicant by the local Chief of police or his delegate is required before issuance of an FID. There is a $100 fee for the FID/LTC and they are valid for six years, unless revoked or suspended for cause, at the will of the licensing authority. When you renew, prior to your birthday you will receive a receipt that will keep your old license in force until the state sends you your new license, however long that may take. Persons over 70 shall be exempt from all renewal license fees.

An applicant is entitled to an FID unless he has been convicted of a felony within the last five years, has been confined or treated for drug addiction or habitual drunkenness within the last five years or has been confined to any hospital or institution for mental illness, unless he has an affidavit from a physician stating that he is not disabled in a manner which should prevent his possessing a handgun, rifle or shotgun. All aliens and minors under the age of 15 are prohibited from obtaining an FID card, but a minor between the ages of 15 and 18 may obtain an FID card with the written permission of his or her parent or guardian.

The licensing authority may petition the court with a non-statutory reason to deny the FID but the court would need to agree. Notice of approval or denial must be given to the applicant within 40 days. If denied, the applicant may appeal to the District Court for judicial review, read **Gun Sense #13, Specific to MA Petition for Judicial Review.**

Any person who inherits a rifle, shotgun or handgun is required to obtain an FID or LTC, within 180 days if he intends to retain possession of the firearm(s), read **Gun Sense #36 Inheritance and Other Firearm Transactions, Form (E-FA10).**

For MA Firearm Transaction List go to:

Massachusetts Gun Transaction Portal

https://mircs.chs.state.ma.us/fa10/action/home?app_context=home&app_action=presentHome#https://mircs.chs.state.ma.us/fa10/action/home?app_context=home&app_action=presentHome

The Department of Criminal Justice Information Services (Information in Appendix A)

A new resident moving into the state who owns firearms has 180 days in which to obtain an FID or a LTC, to make the possession legal in Massachusetts. A person may possess but not carry during this 180 day period. An alien may obtain an "alien permit to possess" from the state Commissioner of Public Safety, which will allow him to possess a rifle or shotgun. These permit cards are valid for one year and are issued only to aliens with a U.S. Immigration card.

EXEMPTIONS from the FID and licensing requirements are provided for:

1. The temporary holding or firing of a handgun under the supervision of a person with a LTC, the holding or firing of a rifle or shotgun under the supervision of a person with an FID or "where such holding or firing is for a lawful purpose."
2. The use of a rifle or shotgun for hunting or target shooting by a minor under age of 15, provided he is under the immediate supervision of a person holding an FID or a LTC.
3. Possession by a chartered veteran's organization and possession by their members when on ceremonial duties.
4. Possession by museums and institutional collections open to the public provided such firearms are unloaded and secured.
5. Possession by federally- licensed manufacturers and dealers and their employees when necessary for manufacture, display, storage or testing.

PURCHASE: To purchase a rifle, shotgun, handgun or ammunition the buyer must have an FID, LTC or proof of exempt status (police or military) and be at least 18 years old. It is a crime (felony) to sell, give away, loan or otherwise transfer any firearm or ammunition to anyone who is not properly licensed or otherwise authorized to possess or receive such firearm or ammunition. Read **Gun Sense #36 Inheritance and Other Firearm Transactions, Form (E-FA10).**

A private individual is permitted to sell up to four firearms in a linear (365 day period) year, more if sold directly to a licensed gun dealer. He must be properly licensed to possess these firearms and the purchaser must be properly licensed to buy them. The seller must file a report of the sale with the Commissioner immediately online via the E-FA-10 form. This report must be on the proper forms provided by the Commissioner and give all required details regarding the seller, purchaser and the firearm being transferred, including the caliber, make and serial number along with the FID or LTC numbers of both buyer and seller. This is form, E-F.A.-10 is the "Firearms Sale/Rental/Lease Transaction Form." The portal should be found online at:

Massachusetts Gun Transaction Portal

https://mircs.chs.state.ma.us/fa10/action/home?app_context=home&app_action=presentHome#https://mircs.chs.state.ma.us/fa10/action/home?app_context=home&app_action=presentHome

CARRY: A person may not carry a loaded rifle or shotgun on any public way. The LTC allows the holder to purchase, possess or carry an unlimited number of handguns. A license may be issued to an applicant who satisfies the requirements for obtaining a LTC, who appears to the Chief of police to be "a suitable person to be so licensed" and who has "good reason to fear injury to his person or property." In addition, the applicant must never have been convicted of a felony, must be 21 years of age, or 15 (with parent's permission) for an FID and be a US citizen. A license also may be issued for "any lawful purpose" including the carrying of firearms or for the reason of "target and hunting only."

An applicant must be notified of a denial within 40 days of submitting an application for a LTC. In the event a license is denied, revoked or no reply has been given within 40 days of submitting an application, the aggrieved may within 45 days file a petition for judicial review in the District Court. Read **Gun Sense #13 Specific to MA Petition for Judicial Review.**

CHANGE OF ADDRESS: Any license holder who moves his residence to another jurisdiction within the state must, within 30 days, notify the Chief of police who issued the license, the Chief of police in the jurisdiction where he is moving and the Commissioner of Public Safety. Failure to provide such change of address notification is unlawful and may void the license. You can find the form "Change of Address Notification For License To Carry Firearms and Firearms Identification Card" at your local police department. Pick up four of them, one is for your file. Read **Gun Sense #14 MA Change of Address Notification Forms and a Renewal tip.**

TRANSPORTATION IN A VEHICLE: A resident may transport a rifle or shotgun provided it is unloaded and he has at least an FID. A resident may transport a handgun only if he has a LTC. It is illegal to store a firearm in a vehicle as a permanent solution, 24-7, however they can be temporarily stored there on an as needed basis, read **Gun Sense #22 MA "Stored & Kept"' and "Direct Control."** for more information.

NON-RESIDENTS: A non-resident may possess a rifle or shotgun in MA:

1. While hunting and in possession of a valid hunting license.
2. While on a firing or shooting range.
3. While traveling in or through MA if the rifle or shotgun is unloaded and enclosed in a case.
4. While at a firearms show organized by a "regularly existing gun collector's club or association."
5. If he has a license or permit to possess any firearm in his home state. To transport or possess a handgun, a non-resident must obtain a temporary LTC good for one year, from the Firearms Record Bureau. To access the instructions and application visit:

Apply for a Firearms License

https://www.mass.gov/how-to/apply-for-a-firearms-license

The Department of Criminal Justice Information Services (Information in Appendix A)

TEMPORARY LICENSES: The Colonel of state police may issue a temporary license to carry a handgun to a non-resident, alien or resident who does not live within the jurisdiction of a local licensing authority.

1. A temporary license must clearly indicate it is a LTC. The fee for a temporary license is $100.00.
2. Temporary licenses are good for one year and renewable at the discretion of the Colonel of state police. Unlike a regular LTC, temporary licenses may not be used to purchase firearms.
3. A non-resident with a license to carry a handgun issued by his home state* may carry a pistol or revolver in MA for the purpose of taking part in a competition or exhibition of handguns, for hunting provided he has a valid hunting license issued by MA or the state of his destination.

*Provided that the home state has the same requirements as MA for obtaining a LTC.

ANTIQUES AND REPLICAS: An antique firearm is defined as any handgun, rifle or shotgun manufactured in or before 1898 or any replica thereof which is not designed for firing fixed ammunition or which uses fixed ammunition no longer manufactured in the United States and is no longer readily available commercially. An FID card is not required to possess antique and replica firearms in the home or place of business. A LTC is required when antique and replica handguns are being carried outside the home or place of business. An LTC or FID is also required to carry antique and replica rifles and shotguns outside the home or place of business.

MACHINE GUNS: A machine gun "is a weapon of any description, from which a number of shots or bullets may be rapidly or automatically discharged by one continuous activation of the trigger and includes a sub-machine gun." It is unlawful to possess a machine gun without a special license. Application is made to the local police Chief who, in his discretion, may issue a license to any applicant "who is a suitable person to be so licensed," and is a firearm instructor certified by the criminal justice training council for instructing police personnel or is a bona fide collector of firearms. A LTC is a prerequisite.

MISCELLANEOUS PROVISIONS:

1. Although persons in the military and other peace officers are exempt from the above requirements, this exemption is applicable only when they are performing their official duties or when duly authorized to possess weapons. It is not applicable for any private or sporting use of such rifles, shotguns or handguns.
2. Air guns and BB guns are regulated by the above provisions.
3. It is unlawful to possess, sell, or transfer any firearm whose shape does not resemble a handgun or short-barreled rifle or shotgun, or that is not detectable by x-ray or metal detector.
4. It is unlawful to remove, deface or alter in any manner the serial or identification number of a firearm, or knowingly to receive such a firearm. Possession of a firearm with an altered or defaced number creates a legal presumption that the possessor committed the offense.
5. Discharge of any firearm within 150 feet of a public way or 500 feet of a building in use is prohibited, except with the consent of the owner or legal occupant, in defense of life and property, or at licensed shooting galleries, target, test, trap or skeet ranges with the permission of the owner or legal occupant.
6. In the event of theft, loss or recovery of any firearm, the owner is required to notify the executive director of the Criminal History Systems Board and the licensing authority in the city or town where the owner resides.
7. Any person in possession of any firearm is required to exhibit his FID, receipt for FID card fee, LTC or hunting license to a law enforcement officer upon demand. If the person fails to display the appropriate document, they may be required to surrender their firearm, although they may recover it if they produce the license within 30 days.
8. The Governor shall appoint a seven member gun control advisory board. Their duties include compiling and publishing a roster of large capacity rifles, shotguns, handguns and feeding devices.
9. Any handgun or large capacity firearm sold without a safety device approved by the Colonel of state police "shall be defective and the sale of such weapon shall constitute a breach of warranty... and an unfair or deceptive trade act or practice." This creates a civil cause of action.
10. All firearms must be stored or kept, secured in a locked container or equipped with a lock or other safety device. A firearm is not considered stored or kept if carried by or under the direct control of the owner or other lawfully authorized user. A violation of this provision is evidence of wanton or reckless conduct in any criminal or civil proceeding if a person

under 18 gains access to a firearm. A violation of this provision is also criminally punishable by a fine of up to $10,000.00 and or imprisonment up to 10 years (Please read **Gun Sense #22 MA *"Stored & Kept"* and *"Direct Control."*).

11. In a domestic relations restraining order (201-A) the court shall also order the defendant to surrender any firearm, ammunition and cards/licenses, if it makes a determination that the defendant presents a likelihood of abuse to the plaintiff.

ADDITIONAL PROVISIONS IN BOSTON: In Boston, under a vague law, it is unlawful to possess, display, transfer or receive:

1. Any shotgun with a revolving cylinder and or a capacity exceeding six rounds.
2. A semiautomatic rifle with a fixed magazine capacity exceeding 10 rounds.
3. Any SKS, AK47, UZI, AR-15, Steyr AUG, FN-FAL and FN-FNC rifle.
4. Any semiautomatic pistol which is a modification of a proscribed rifle or shotgun with a shorter barrel or no stock and any magazine or belt which holds more than 10 rounds.
5. An "assault weapons roster board" may add additional firearms to the list of so-called "assault weapons." Such firearms must have been registered with the Boston Police Commissioner within 90 days of the effective date of the law (12/9/89) or they are unlawful. An owner, in Boston, of a firearm added to the roster of assault weapons must obtain a license to possess it within 90 days of its addition or it becomes unlawful. The provision does not apply to possession by non-residents of Boston at a sporting or shooting club or by persons who possess the requisite state license to carry. It also does not apply to persons taking part in competition, at a collectors' exhibit, meeting or traveling to or from such event or while in transit through Boston for the purpose of hunting by licensed hunter, provided that in all cases the "assault weapon" is unloaded and packaged and the person has a Massachusetts FID card or has a license or permit to carry or possess firearms issued by another state.

Massachusetts has a mandatory sentence of one to one and a half years imprisonment for anyone convicted of illegally possessing a firearm loaded or unloaded. It is legal to possess Chemical Mace or pepper spray without an FID, LTC or class D license as long as you are 18 or older. It is illegal to possess a stun gun or Taser, there is no license available.

Gun Sense #33 MA "Letters of Recommendation" & Gun License Help.

There are some towns in MA that may require two to five letters of recommendation when you apply for a LTC. As mentioned, this is on a town-by-town basis, many towns do not ask for these letters even though they can. If you are applying for an FID card this will not be asked of you and is stated on the application that it is not required. If you are asked to produce letters of recommendation, my advice to your friends is to keep it short and to the point. Only people not related to you can write these. This is an example/template to follow:

John Doe
John's Address Line 1
John's Address Line 2
John's City, State Zip
John's Phone Number

Date

Chief of Police (His/Her Name if you know it)
Police Department Name
Police Department Address Line 1
Police Department City, State Zip

Dear Chief of Police (*His/Her name if you know it*):

I have known *Your Name* for *X* number of years and have no reason to believe he/she should not attain a gun license. He/she has always been level headed in my view. Any questions please feel free to call me.

Thank you,

John Doe Signature

John Doe

The reason it should be kept short and sweet...in my opinion it has no legitimate purpose, as I am certain many towns have already surmised. When towns ask for letters from friends, it would follow that friends will write nice things about you. What would the police possibly glean from these nice letters? Nothing. It is just a hoop that some towns want you to jump through simply because they can. I do not believe the police even glance at these letters. Your friends can not possibly know what the police already know about your legal record (if any), so it is a pointless and time consuming exercise.

If you were a criminal in prison, you would probably be asked for names of those who might want to come visit you. This has relevance...if you were to escape, the authorities would now have a wider base of information in their search for you. You on the other hand are a law abiding citizen, the police already know this to be true, due to the lack of any criminal record...you should not need to jump through hoops. Treating you badly does nothing to prevent a single crime. Don't be discouraged or intimidated, play this game if you must, you will still get your license. Another hoop some towns/cities put people through is demanding a Reason Letter, please Read **Gun Sense #19 "Reason" Letter for MA LTC** for help in dealing with this game.

Gun Sense #34 MA CORI Report Info.

This is information that I think people need to know if they want a better chance for getting a gun license in MA. If you did not hear this in your firearm safety class, you have been inadvertently set up for failure, probably by someone who did not know enough to bring it up.

A Criminal Offender Record Information (CORI) report can be a good tool to use when checking into your legal background or lack of. But, just understand that it does not necessarily go as deep as the police are able to go when looking at suitability of an applicant. You can attach it to your application if you want to, but it is not a requirement.

There are a range of questions about being convicted for certain things. The application is not looking for parking tickets/moving violations, bankruptcy or mortgage foreclosures. It is absolutely imperative, that if you have been in front of a judge at some point in your life for some other reason, even if ultimately nothing came of it, you need to mention it, it is on your record and they want you to repeat what they already know about you. If something was dismissed make sure you emphasize that it was "dismissed," "continued without a finding" or "expired."

If you leave something out because you don't think it was important, because maybe it was a "continued without a finding" (CWOAF) or maybe it is an expired 209-A restraining order. Perhaps a long ago, long gone probation when you were a teen...it may not be important to you anymore, but if you leave it out the police consider it a "lie by omission" and it can lead to a denial of your gun license. It may be something that happened when you were a teen and you think to yourself that those records are sealed, think again. When it comes to a gun license they break the seals. Just because something may have happened in your past, it does not necessarily mean that you will not get a license, but if you don't mention it, that is what may stop you short in your quest. They have your record and they want you to repeat it, consider it a serious test of honesty. If there is nothing in your past, good, just check NO on each question.

How do I get a copy of my CORI report?

You can request a copy of your CORI online using the web-based iCORI service:

Criminal Record Check Services

https://www.mass.gov/criminal-record-check-services

Online Request CORI as an Individual

https://www.mass.gov/how-to/request-cori-as-an-individual

The Department of Criminal Justice Information Services (Information in Appendix A)

1. Go to the Massachusetts iCORI Service and click on the "Register as an Individual" link.
2. Answer "Yes" to the question "Would you like to request your own Personal CORI?"
3. Enter your personal information, including a username, password and e-mail address.
4. Verify your information, then follow additional instructions and submit your registration.
5. Check your e-mail for the iCORI Account Activation notice; follow the instructions to activate your account.
6. After you have registered, enter your username and password at Massachusetts iCORI Service.
7. Click on "Add Request," select the purpose of the request and enter the subject information.
8. Click on "Add & Checkout" and follow the instructions for submitting your payment.9. View your CORI online (in PDF format) or download your CORI to your computer.

For more information about using the iCORI service:

iCORI Training Documents

https://www.mass.gov/service-details/icori-training-documents

To get a copy of your Massachusetts CORI report by mail, you must send a Personal CORI Request Form to the Department of Criminal Justice Information Services (DCJIS):

Mail in Criminal Offender Record Information (CORI) Personal Request Form

https://www.mass.gov/files/2017-06/adult-personal-criminal-record-request-form.pdf

The Department of Criminal Justice Information Services (Information in Appendix A)

After you complete the form, you must:

1. Sign the form in front of a notary public.
2. Include a $25 check or money order payable to the Commonwealth of Massachusetts.
3. Include a business size, self-addressed stamped envelope.
4. Mail the notarized form, $25 payment and self-addressed stamped envelope to:

The Department of Criminal Justice Information Services (Information in Appendix A)

ATTN: CORI Unit

Your CORI report will be mailed to you in about two weeks. If you go online and pay for your CORI report you can get it almost immediately and just print it out. FYI, please read **Gun Sense #20 MA Misdemeanor? Been Denied Your Gun Permit/License?** and **Gun Sense #39 MA Application/"Interview" Process & Steps/Tips.**

Gun Sense #35 Places you Cannot Carry Firearms in MA.

Q: Are there any places in the Commonwealth of Massachusetts that I cannot lawfully carry a firearm?
A: Yes. Some of the more common places include:

1) State and Federal Courthouses.
2) Post Offices.
3) Police Stations.
4) Prisons and Jails.
5) Virtually all other Federal Buildings and some State Buildings where metal detectors are in use.
6) Schools and school grounds. Do not bring a gun onto school grounds without written permission (good luck getting that). School grounds include parking lots, driveways and the grounds outside the building. You can pass by on the public roads while in legal possession of a firearm(s).

NOTE: While all law abiding citizens are prohibited from carrying on school grounds, history shows us time after time, this has not prevented psychopaths from murdering our children there (or anyone anywhere else), in fact it has helped to enable criminals to easily commit these atrocities in so-called "gun free" zones. Foolish legislation for places not under static law enforcement protection....there is a lot of blood on the hands of the asses that made the "Gun Free" zones.

Other Places where law or policy can curtail carry:

1) Public Library's, (maybe a policy).
2) Private party sporting events, concerts, places where a search at the entrance takes place, a sign posted or policy. Anonymously Call ahead to find out.
3) Any House of Worship without permission (maybe a policy).
4) Medical property, Hospitals/Clinics etc. (maybe a policy, usually is).
5) Anyplace where there is a "No Guns Allowed" sign posted on private property. If you are not sure about a Hotel/Motel's firearm policy you can call ahead anonymously and ask (maybe a policy, maybe not, at the owners discretion).

6) Airports. For a brief and painful stint as a TSA employee, for one very long year at Logan, I had the opportunity to inspect numerous firearms declared in checked baggage. There is set protocol/regulations in place that allow this, they are posted on airline websites. Notify the airline in advance of your intention to bring a firearm(s). Do NOT show up the day of your flight with a gun asking if you can bring it with you! You would be carried away by six huge State Troopers and may never be heard from again…

7) Bars/Restaurants. Use your head when it comes to drinking at these places. If you're bound and determined to get smashed, leave the gun at home. If you're caught intoxicated while in possession of a firearm, you will lose your license to carry. Just as if you're caught intoxicated while driving a vehicle you will lose your driver's license. Here is the difference, in MA you will get your driver's license back long before you will get your gun license back, if ever…..keep that in mind.

Q: How do I transport a gun in my vehicle?
A: A person with a LTC may transport a handgun loaded or unloaded on his person or under his direct control in the vehicle. If the handgun is not under his direct control, it must be unloaded and in a locked case, locked trunk or other secure container. For more specific information see **Chapter 140 M.G.L. Section 131C**. Read **Gun Sense #22 MA "Stored & Kept"' and "Direct Control."**

Q: Do I need to lock my non-large capacity rifles and shotguns in a case while transporting them in a vehicle?
A: No. They must be transported unloaded, but are not required to be in a locked case while transporting. Large capacity rifles and shotguns, meaning 10 or more rounds, must be in a locked case while transporting.

Q: Can I leave my gun in my car if I need to go into the store on my way home from the range or from hunting?
A: If your handgun or large capacity rifle or shotgun is transported in accordance with the provisions of **Chapter 140 M.G.L. Section 131C** i.e. unloaded and in a locked case, locked trunk or other secure container, then the gun may be left temporarily unattended in the vehicle. Weapons transported in this manner will automatically be considered "stored or kept" in compliance with the safe storage requirements of **Section 131L**.

A person leaving a non-large capacity rifle or shotgun in an unattended vehicle is required to store it unloaded. You are required to lock the rifle or shotgun in a case/container, in the trunk of the vehicle or install a mechanical locking device on the weapon (i.e. cable or trigger lock).

Gun Sense #36 Inheritance and Other Firearm Transactions, Form (E-FA10).

When a gun owner dies, the "heir or legatee" is not immediately in illegal possession if they do not have a license. When faced with this situation it is best to consult a competent attorney for advice on how to proceed. **Chapter 140 M.G.L. Section 129C** gives a 180 day exemption. By the end of 180 days, the person in charge of the estate should have either done one of three things:

1. Transfer the firearms to a dealer.
2. Transfer the firearms to a person who has the appropriate FID/LTC.
3. Applied for an extension of the time period to the Chief of police

If the deceased had a MA license: It appears that an E-FA-10 could be filled out during this 180 day period, with the deceased person's information as the seller and the new owner as the buyer. The executor/executrix should sign [his or her name] for the estate of [deceased's name].

If it has been longer than 180 days or the deceased did not have a current LTC, then the sales must go through a licensed dealer.

If the inheritor is out of state, then have the executor/executrix ship the guns to a licensed dealer in that state.

Inherited guns still need to be transferred with the MA E-FA-10 form!

Inheriting Across State Lines: If a MA resident with an LTC/FID inherits guns from a deceased person out of state, they may go directly and pick up those guns (provided it is lawful for them to possess those guns in that state as a non-resident and in MA. <u>Consultation with a competent firearms attorney should be done prior to an interstate transaction</u>). Although the federal government prohibits private transfers across state lines, it does make an exception for "direct bequest or interstate succession." This is especially handy when we are talking about a person inheriting handguns that may not be "MA compliant." Inherited guns still need to be transferred on an E-FA-10 form.

The electronic E-FA-10 will be used in place of the paper firearms transaction forms as of 8-13-2014. E-FA-10 used by MA residents to report firearms transactions to the Firearms Records Bureau (FRB), as required by **Chapter 140 M.G.L. Section(s) 128A** and **128B**. E-FA-10 is an internet-based application that allows residents of the Commonwealth to safely and securely submit firearms transfer records electronically from any internet-enabled computer.

In order to utilize the E-FA-10 system, you will need your firearms license number and personal identification number (PIN). The ONLY way you will be able to complete your firearm transaction will be with your state provided Personal Identification Number (PIN). If you did not receive a PIN or can't find it, call the Firearms Records Bureau at (617) 660-4600 Monday through Friday between 9am and 6pm.

Please put your PIN in your phone, file and with a magic marker on the back of your LTC/or FID. To get to the firearm transaction list go to:

Massachusetts Gun Transaction Portal

https://mircs.chs.state.ma.us/fa10/action/home?app_context=home&app_action=presentTrans

At that site you can also generate a firearms license validation to prove your license before you buy any firearm.

Again, for any other questions you don't see your answer to on this page, Contact:

The Department of Criminal Justice Information Services (Information in Appendix A)

No person to person interstate transactions are allowed using these forms, for other than, "direct bequest or interstate succession." You could consult a Gun Dealer.

NOTE: In MA, the E-FA-10 form is not a gun registration form, it is a transfer of ownership form, from the gun store to you or from you to another person. By law it can NOT be used to determine what you own unless a firearm is part of a criminal investigation. FIREARMS RECORDS are EXEMPTED from the PUBLIC RECORDS statute. Chapter 4 M.G.L. Section 7 (clause twenty-six)(j). Here is the statute that defines this:

"Firearms Records Bureau may not disseminate firearms records "to any person, firm, corporation, entity or agency except criminal justice agencies as defined in chapter six and except to the extent such information relates solely to the person making the request and is necessary to the official interests of the entity making the request." Chapter 66 M.G.L. Section 10(d)."

Read **Gun Sense #43 MA Gun Registration Misconception** and **Gun Sense #45 Gun Registration UNCONSTITUTIONAL** for more information.

To find out if the firearm you are wishing to transfer is legal, visit:

List of MA Approved Firearms

https://www.mass.gov/lists/approved-firearms-rosters

Anything NOT mentioned obviously is NOT approved...but that does not necessarily mean they cannot be legally owned.

Gun Sense #37 Storage of Ammunition, Powder & Primers…

As outlined as law in Chapter 148 M.G.L. Section 13, the following exemptions for permits and licenses are set forth in **527 Code of Massachusetts Regulations (C.M.R.) Chapter 1** concerning ammunition etc. of the following materials and quantities:

Small arms ammunition of rim fire ammunition [private use]:

Less than 10,000 rounds no permit required, no license required.
Greater than or equal to 10,000-30,000 rounds permit required, no license required.
Greater than 30,000 rounds no permit required, license required.

Small arms ammunition of center fire ammunition [private use]:

Less than 10,000 rounds no permit required, no license required.
Greater than or equal to 10,000-50,000 rounds permit required, no license required.
Greater than 50,000 rounds no permit required, license required.

Small arms ammunition of shotgun ammunition [private use]:

Less than 5,000 rounds no permit required, no license required.
Greater than or equal to 5,000-50,000 rounds permit required, no license required.
Greater than 50,000 rounds no permit required, license required.

Small arms ammunition primers [private use]:

Less than 10,000 caps or other small arms primers no permit required, no license required.
Greater than or equal to 10,000 caps or other small arms primers no permit required, license required.

Small arms ammunition primers [commercial use]:

Less than 100,000 caps or other small arms primers permit required, no license required.

Greater than or equal to 100,000 caps or other small arms primers no permit required, license required.

Smokeless propellants [private and commercial]:

Note: Persons under 18 years of age may not keep or store smokeless propellants.
Note: Not more than two pounds of such propellant shall be stored in a multiple family dwelling or a building of public access.

Less than 16 lbs. no permit required, no license required.

Smokeless propellants [private]:

Greater than or equal to 16 lbs. through 47 lbs. permit required, no license required.

Smokeless propellants [commercial]:

Greater than 48 lbs. no permit required, license required.
Greater than or equal to 25 lbs. to less than 99 lbs. permit required, no license required.
Greater than or equal to 100 lbs. no permit required, license required.

Black powder [private and commercial]:

Note: Persons under 18 years of age may not keep or store any amount of black powder.

Less than 2 lbs. no permit required, no license required.

Black powder [private]:

Less than 5 lbs. a permit is required, no license is required.

Black powder [commercial]:

Greater than or equal to 5 lbs. no permit required, license required.
See Section 1.12.8.39.2.5.1 for permit exemption individual.

"Small arms ammunition, primers, smokeless propellants and black powder stored in original containers and stored in a locked cabinet, closet or box when not in use as provided in Section 1.12.8.50." Per **527 C.M.R Chapter 1**, Section 1.12.8.39.1.1.4.

NOTE: A firearm (or magazine) certainly is NOT considered an "original container" to lock away with ammo inside it. But after careful scrutiny, there is nothing in the M.G.L. that says you cannot properly store a loaded firearm. Checking with a representative with the state fire Marshall, he said that the code on storage refers to the bulk storage of ammunition, if you have questions about that contact them. In a state police newsletter discussing firearms safety, they "recommend" that firearms are stored unloaded. A section on the Mass.gov website concerning firearms also notes that firearms "should" be stored unloaded. Further, no case law specifically covering a properly stored or kept firearm, that happens to be loaded can be found by us or even the clerk we reached out to from the Massachusetts Law Library. If you are able to find a statute, regulation or case law concerning this, please let me know. You make the distinction/call you feel comfortable with and perhaps seek legal counsel.

Consider though if a loaded and chambered firearm became hot enough during a fire the gun would go off just as if you pulled the trigger yourself. A fireman's job is dangerous enough without the added danger of inadvertently being shot.

It is better to be pro-active and do a little more than what is thought to be required, than to take chances on being charged over misconceptions in vague law.

NOTE: Storage by Permit increases the amounts of ammo, primers, smokeless propellants and black powder in private use that you may have. Be aware that when you apply for and are approved for a permit to store more than quantities listed above you consent to periodic inspections by the Fire Marshall or his designee.

Gun Sense #38 Traffic Stops in MA.

This question comes up quite frequently in my classes: "Do I have to tell the police that I have a gun or a gun license if I get pulled over?" I will start by saying that in many other states when a police officer pulls you over and if you do have a gun license, the first words out of your mouth will have to be "I have a gun license." If you do not say that as the first thing out of your mouth you will be arrested. If you say "hello" before you say "I have a gun license," you will be arrested. But this IS NOT a requirement/law here in MA...yet....

When you are pulled over on the highways or byways in MA you are not being pulled over because you happen to be a legal gun license holder. No, you most likely are being pulled over for a motor vehicle violation/infraction of some sort, typically speeding as the most common reason.

As a gun license holder of a MA LTC or FID you maybe, or you might not be carrying or have a long gun in the car at the time when you are pulled over. The following is an important tip for you to seriously consider for handguns. Even though most of us can easily reach our glove box from behind the steering wheel in the little shoe boxes that pass as cars these days and even though you would be considered under "direct control," because you can easily reach the glovebox, NEVER have a handgun where your car registration "lives." Do you see where I am going with this? The police officer asking for your driver's license, proof of insurance and registration does not know you from a hole in the wall. He does NOT need to see a handgun tumble from your glovebox, bad things could happen to you from there...use your own imagination on this one. He/she would have a legitimate reason to be very upset with you. If you feel like having a handgun in your glove box keep the registration SOMEWHERE ELSE, maybe on your visor...

When the officer runs your information in his cruiser computer he may see that you are a legal gun license holder, so what? As I said before, you are not being pulled over because you happen to be a legal gun license holder. If the officer asks if you are carrying, this is as far as that conversation needs to go: "Yes sir I am" or if not "No sir, not today." Don't lie about it, there is no legitimate reason for the conversation about a legal gun license to go any farther. If a police officer says he would like to search your car and you know there is no reason or "probable cause" for him to do so, don't be bullied, ask if he has a search warrant, this should end any fishing trip in its tracks.

There are police officers out there (hopefully very few) that may try to treat you badly because they personally do not like the idea of anyone having a gun license or maybe they are young (rookies) and possess far more authority than they possess maturity, not a very good combination for public relations/service. My advice is to politely listen to the unprofessional rant, at the end of the tirade ask for his/her badge number and name. Write the Chief a letter clearly detailing what happened including time of day and date, any witnesses etc, then "cc" (carbon copy) it at the end of the letter to the towns selectmen by name, to your lawyer by name and to your personal "file." Be sure to send it certified mail with return receipt to all listed, this way everyone will be on the same "sheet of music" about the unprofessional bully in this matter. You will be doing the Chief/town a favor in the long run. The Chief may already have complaints against this person and will or should know he needs to nip it in the bud before it costs the town an expensive lawsuit(s).

Gun Sense #39 MA Application/"Interview" Process & Steps/Tips.

After you receive your State Firearm Safety Certification the first thing you should know is that it will be a waste of your time if you go to the police station thinking that you can just walk in and fill out the gun permit application. 99% of police stations will send you away and tell you to make an appointment. So save your time by following these tips and good advice. It is not really an "Interview" in the sense you might think. What they want is for you to fill out an application and they take your picture, fingerprints, safety certification and your $100.

Save anything/everything you give to the police by making copies for your records, ANYTHING! Duplication is key!

If you want to check the status of your LTC application, call the Firearms Record Bureau:

The Department of Criminal Justice Information Services (Information in Appendix A)

1. Call the police station first, ask for the person in charge of licensing, get his/her name, extension # and email, if he/she has no email get the police department email. The email will be real handy when it is time to renew your license six years later because three months before your birthday you should contact the police by email to let them know your license will be expiring and that you would like to set up an appointment to fill out an application to renew it. SAVE the email as proof you contacted the police and started the process. If your birthday comes and you have not yet filled out the application because the police have not brought you in for an appointment, by law they will have to honor your "expired" license, it will be valid and in force until you get the new license. You will be issued a receipt, email them again with an attached copy of the original email.

OH NO! If you forget to start the process to renew and your birthday passes by before you think about it, then you realize it and run to the station very concerned that your license has expired, the police can tell you that since you allowed it to expire you will need to turn in your guns. They can also fine you for allowing it to expire, that fine is on the books though I have not heard of anyone being fined. If you now have no license you cannot legally take your guns to the station, you will need someone else to go with you that does have a license. A friend or relative can hold your guns for you but will need to write a note to the police that has this information on it: Name, gun license #, address, phone# and the note saying he will take responsibility for your guns while you renew your license, by law the police will/should accept this. Some police Chiefs may tell you to take the firearm safety course for another certificate first, as a hoop to put you through, this is not in law.

The moral to this story should be not to forget to start the process. Even though the state is supposed to send you a notice that your license is about to expire three months before it expires, don't hold your breath for that notice. I have been renewing my license since 1970 and have NEVER received a notice, some of my friends have and others have not, so it is a hit or miss proposition.

NOTE: If you decide that you no longer want a license, before it expires you would need to be rid of the gun(s) in your name by selling or giving them away and utilizing the E-FA-10 form(s) online at the MA State Police, read **Gun Sense #36 Inheritance and Other Firearm Transactions, Form (E-FA10).**

2. Take note of the date of your application appointment, go 40 days out and note that date on your calendar, this is the "window" they have to deny or approve your LTC permit. If you are denied you will receive a letter (by law) from the police stating why (this can be appealed, read **Gun Sense #13 Specific to MA Petition for Judicial Review** and **Gun Sense #20 MA Misdemeanor? Been Denied Your Gun Permit/License?**). After 40 days if you have not been denied, you`re not going to be. Every town has experienced longer than the normal turnaround time legally prescribed by the state (the state has/is breaking their own law) for these licenses. Now you need to just be patient. You will be given a receipt when you reapply on time, this will keep your expired license in force until the State issues you your new license, no matter how long that takes.

3. Next, as you look at the front of the application you will see license choices. If you are 21 years or older, check off "License to Carry." If you are under age 21, choose "Firearms Identification Card (FID)." As you read, you will find a question that asks for your reason for the license, put three words here: For LTC, "Any Lawful Purpose." If for some bizarre

reason (known only to them) the police in your town does not like giving a license for lawful reasons, use this as your second choice "For Personal Protection." It is only a silly matter of semantics as far as I can see. For FID, "Target and Hunting" (Read **Gun Sense #26 MA Hunter Safety Class Information.**). If you are required to bring letters of recommendation please read **Gun Sense # 33 MA "Letters of Recommendation" & Gun License Help.** If you are required to write a letter as to what your "reason" or "need" is for wanting a license please read **Gun Sense #19 "Reason" Letter for MA LTC.** If they try to insist that they are going to give you a license with restriction(s) that you do not want, politely refuse it and tell them you would like a letter from them stating why you are being denied the license you applied for. If you know you should not be denied as stated in 4 below, stand your ground and don't be needlessly bullied. Read **Gun Sense #13 Specific to MA Petition for Judicial Review.**

4. There are three set reasons to be denied: If you have been a Felon, if you have been convicted of Substance Abuse or if you have been incarcerated in a Mental Facility against your will (by court order). There is a fourth reason also, "dishonesty," by leaving out something that's on your legal record. If the police want to deny based on a non-statutory reason, they now need to petition the court to gain permission to do so (as of 8-13-2014). Read **Gun Sense #34 MA CORI Report Info** concerning your potential criminal history.

Gun Sense #34 MA CORI Report Info, Excerpt: There is a range of questions about being convicted for certain things. The application is not looking for parking tickets/moving violations. It is absolutely imperative that if you have been in front of a judge at some point in your life for some other reason, even if ultimately nothing came of it, you need to mention it, it is already part of your record and they want you to repeat what they already know about you. If something was dismissed make sure you emphasize that it was dismissed, "continued without a finding," or, "expired." If you leave something out it is deemed a "lie by omission" (dishonesty) and grounds for denial, take this advice seriously!

5. There is not much room on the application to write down what you may need to say about something that once happened to you. So at home write it on a sheet of paper to the best of your recollection and make a copy of it for your gun file because you will need this information every six years. When/if you come to a question that pertains to you

write "see attached paperwork." If you want a copy of your state CORI record (that you could also submit) read **Gun Sense #34 MA CORI Report Info** and follow the prompts.

Save anything you give to the police by making copies for your records, ANYTHING!

6. When you renew your license in six years you will need to submit a signed affidavit stating: "That no guns were lost or stolen within the last six years." If that were to happen, you would need to report it as soon as you became aware of it and then it cannot be used against you for a license renewal (by law as of 8-13-2014).

NOTE: Some towns will act as if, because you have never had a gun license before or because of your age, that they instead want to give you a restricted license like an FID instead of the LTC you are legally eligible for. Here is a note you can and should put onto your application if you live in a town such as this: "I have met the criteria as set down by the law, age or experience notwithstanding." The police enforce existing law, not invent new laws.

Synonyms: Notwithstanding, despite, in spite of imply that something is true even though there are obstacles or opposing conditions. The three expressions may be used practically interchangeably. Notwithstanding suggests, however, a hindrance of some kind: "Notwithstanding the long delay, I shall still go." Despite indicates that there is an active opposition: "Despite procrastination and disorganization, they finished the project." In spite of implies meeting strong opposing forces or circumstances that must be taken into account: "She succeeded in spite of many discouragements."

Gun Sense #40 The Right to Remain Silent has Changed, be Aware!

The below article was sent to me by Jeff Wernick of Second Call Defense. He has encouraged me to share it. I feel it is vital information that can protect you in the future, but I hope that you never need it. Education is power.

The article can be read here:

https://www.buckeyefirearms.org/5th-amendment-update-why-silence-no-longer-golden

For more information visit:

Second Call Defense

http://www.secondcalldefense.org/

In my opinion, I would just ask the police up front, is this a custodial or non-custodial interrogation? Handcuffs could be a clue if it is custodial.

Gun Sense #41 Gun Law Changes in MA 8-13-2014.

H.4376 Accomplished many positive things for MA gun owners including Juniors.

Critical Training language correction for juniors allows trainers to provide firearms to junior shooters and hunters with parental consent. This allows juniors to apply for their FID card a year early, age 14 and receive their card at 15, price $25.

NOTE: Age 15 up to 18, the fee for FID is $25, as stated in **Chapter 140 M.G.L. Section 129B (9C):**

"Except as provided in clause (9B), the fee for an application for a firearm identification card for any person under the age of 18 shall be $25, which shall be payable to the licensing authority and shall not be prorated or refunded in the case of revocation or denial. The licensing authority shall retain 50 per cent of the fee and the remaining portion shall be deposited into the General Fund. Notwithstanding any general or special law to the contrary, licensing authorities shall deposit quarterly that portion of the firearm identification card application fee which is to be deposited into the General Fund, not later than January 1, April 1, July 1 and October 1 of each year."

Pepper Spray: Persons over the age of 18 will no longer need an FID card to buy pepper spray. 15-17 year old persons can still possess pepper spray but must have an FID card or class D license.

FID: Chiefs must FIRST petition the court to deny someone his/her FID card. Because it is in the courts, it will give Gun Owners Action League (GOAL) and Com2A the ability to track what Chiefs are up to.

NOTE: In MA, courts will probably err with the Chief as the courts here are not very gun friendly, as we all know. So this still could allow abuse from certain Chiefs that frown on mere civilians having firearms. The courts should override Chiefs in frivolous cases if there were actual justice in play, time will tell.

Both licenses: The term "prohibited person" will now be used for both licenses, FID and LTC, instead of "unsuitable." This change in language provides a much needed change in the framework around who may be denied.

The former 90 day Grace Period is now GONE. Gun owners will now receive a receipt upon renewal which makes their old license valid until the state gets off its thumbs and sends to you your new license. With that receipt and your expired license you may still buy guns and ammo.

NOTE: Don't lose that receipt, ALWAYS make copies of ANYTHING gun related and file it!

Mental Health: Added language so that people who voluntarily seek mental health care WILL NOT be listed as a prohibited person through the NICS. This information is/has been private and confidential between you and your doctor anyway if the courts were never involved, it's not in your record.

Olympic style handguns: There will now be exemptions for the sale of Olympic style handguns in MA. They were previously not legal to transfer by licensed dealers in MA.

NOTE: It finally dawned over Marble Head that criminals have never committed any crimes with Olympic handguns.

Curios and Relic Collectors: Collectors can now purchase handguns and other firearms that once did not comply with the so-called approved firearms roster.

NOTE: Antique bolt action "assault" rifles, break open revolvers and such.

Online Portal: Newly created online portal for face to face E-FA-10 transfers, preserving private sales. Go to the MA State Police website, see **Gun Sense #36 Inheritance and Other Firearm Transactions, Form (E-FA10).**

NOTE: Remember, you can only sell up to four firearms in a linear year on your LTC.

LTC: The class A+B Licenses were eliminated. Going forward there will be only one License to Carry (LTC) in MA. If you already have a class B license it will remain in effect until it expires.

NOTE: Please read **Gun Sense #39 MA Application/"Interview" Process & Steps/Tips.**

Chiefs now have to put denials in writing for the LTC within 40 days of you applying (the police have been known to violate this 40 day law, if this happens please read **Gun Sense #13 Specific to MA Petition for Judicial Review.**). For the first time, gun owners can appeal their LTC restrictions in District Court. Now the burden of proof is on the police Chief to defend the denial or restriction in the District Court.

NOTE: We should have never been guilty until proven innocent in the first place! This may burden some Chiefs from arbitrarily denying people offhand, as some of them were infamous for doing in the past.

Confiscation: If your firearms get confiscated, the licensing authority (the police) shall at that time inform the person(s) in writing of their ability to transfer their firearms to an independently licensed individual.

NOTE: This one is curious. You always could do this, they just did not tell you outright, so I made it a point to tell people in my class of their right to do this. Please read **Gun Sense # 46 Firearms Confiscated in MA?**

Lost or Stolen Firearm(s): A person, who in good faith, reports their firearm lost or stolen, in a timely manner (when you discover it is missing), shall NOT make the police consider him/her a "prohibited person."

NOTE: There is a new requirement when renewing your license that you write an affidavit stating that: "No guns were lost or stolen from me within the last six years." Obviously if there had been you would have reported it anyway…..gee.

Military Personnel: The time for an active duty military member to renew their license has gone from 90 days to 180 days. Active duty military members are now exempted from having to take the mandatory gun safety training classes.

NOTE: In my opinion this sets them up for failure, not knowing the state gun laws is a recipe for felony charges. I suggest strongly that you read these following chapters so you are not blindsided by the laws (I'm sure that you have better things to do with your money and time than to be in court): Gun Sense **#39**, **#37**, **#22**, **#41**, **#3**, **#13**, **#14**, **#35**, **#36**, **#33**, **#19**, **#20**, **#34 & #38**

These will not take long to read, thank you for your service to our country!

Recap:

Police Chiefs gain discretion over the issuance of FID cards, however they must petition the District Court in order to deny an FID card for any non-statutory reason.

Court ordered commitments (and relief) relative to mental illness, alcohol and substance abuse will now be reported to the Federal National Instant Check System (NICS).

Suitability is better defined.

Improved opportunities to appeal suspended, revoked, denied or restricted licenses to carry.

Expired licenses remain valid indefinitely if the renewal process has been started prior to your license expiring.

NOTE: Contact the police by email at least three months before your license expires, save that email as proof you started the renewal process, don't lose that email!

Reduced penalties for failing to renew a license.

NOTE: If you decide that you no longer want a gun license, legally get rid of your guns (E-FA-10/ or gun dealer) prior to your license expiring. Now you're off the radar because you never go back to renew anyway. OK? See **Gun Sense #36 Inheritance and Other Firearm Transactions, Form (E-FA10).**

License renewals now require an affidavit stating that: "The licensee (you), has not had any firearms lost or stolen since their last license was issued."

Increased penalties for carrying on school grounds, improper storage and failure to report a lost or stolen firearm.

Elimination of the Class B license to carry-GONE!

Elimination of the licensing requirement to possess or buy pepper spray for anyone 18 or older, but age 15-17 still need an FID or class D license to buy pepper spray.

Requirement to report face to face firearm(s) transfers in "real time" E-FA-10 form, See **Gun Sense #36 Inheritance and Other Firearm Transactions, Form (E-FA10).**

Is this new legislation great? No, but it is better than it was with more room for improvement. If you stop putting the same people in office over and over maybe things will improve more.

Gun Sense #42 Legal Resident Aliens (Federal Law).

Question: Can a LEGAL Resident Alien apply now for a License to Carry (LTC) in Massachusetts?

Answer: Yes, a Legal Resident Alien (Green Card Holder) can apply for an LTC on the SAME BASIS as a citizen. It is the result of the federal court, Fletcher v. Haas decision, found here:

Civil Action No. 11-10644-DPW.

http://volokh.com/wp-content/uploads/2012/03/fletcher.pdf

If you run into a Police Department that refuses to process your application even though you are a Legal Resident Alien, please contact Comm2A:

Commonwealth Second Amendment Inc.

http://www.comm2a.org/

Contact Information (Information in Appendix A)

Permanent legal resident aliens (Green Card Holders) are treated the same as citizens with a license duration of six years and the $100 fee. The case was all about fairness for legal resident aliens – and we scored a decisive win.

NOTE: A yearly license fee for Non-residents is $100 per year, which I believe is designed to discourage people from out-of-state.

"GREEN CARD" Information: I verified this information through the Framingham State Police, who also verified it through the Firearms Record Bureau in Chelsea MA.

If you have a so-called green card and are a nonresident, you must still take the state approved firearm safety class before applying for either an FID or LTC.

1. Call the Firearm Records Bureau at (617) 660-4600, ask for a permit application to apply for a non-resident alien license.

The Department of Criminal Justice Information Services (Information in Appendix A)

2. You can take the MA Firearm Safety class any time and hang on to the certificate as proof you took the required course.

Gun Sense #43 MA Gun Registration Misconception.

The MA E-FA10 form is a transfer of ownership form. It is not gun registration. When you buy a firearm at the gun store or from an individual, you need to fill out the E-FA10 form online now (by law), to transfer ownership of that firearm. If you did not do that in MA you would be committing a felony. See NOTE below as to why this is not registration. Read **Gun Sense #36 Inheritance and Other Firearm Transactions, Form (E-FA10)** and **Gun Sense #45 Gun Registration UNCONSTITUTIONAL.**

If you want to register your firearm(s) on a voluntary basis only, in MA you can, but why would you? Hold off on that.

When registration is the goal of any government body it is always proceeded with unconstitutional, very dire threats to the entire population of the impending penalties/prison time, if you don't comply by such-n-such a date you will become an overnight felon, we will come after you, we will kick in your doors…! Those types of threats. Such as oath breakers in Connecticut and New York have just tried to impose on the citizens of those two states as of the deadline 1-1-2014, using the lie of "gun control" to stop mental cases or Islamic terrorists from killing people as a reason. Only a very small fraction have complied (best kept media secret), the rest have publicly said to the oath breakers in office to "Go to hell, come take them!" The police have said they will not enforce the dictate because it would needlessly put them in harm's way. Now, there are very nervous politicians in those two states, as they should be….

If you move into MA from out of state with your firearms, you have 180 days to get a LTC to legally keep them. In the meantime they would need to be properly stored under MA law (Read **Gun Sense #22 MA "Stored & Kept"' and "Direct Control."**). You could not use them until you received your MA license. Once you obtain your LTC you are under NO obligation to turn in a list of your firearms. If you want to sell any of them in the future, at that point you would be required to file the E-FA10 Transfer of Ownership form.

NOTE: MA Firearms records are EXEMPTED from the public records statute. Chapter 4 M.G.L. Section 7 (26)(j). The Firearm Record Bureau may not disseminate firearms records "…to any person, firm, corporation, entity or agency except criminal justice agencies as defined in chapter six and except to the extent such information relates solely to the person making the request and is necessary to the official interests of the entity making the request." Chapter 66 M.G.L. Section 10(d). Such as Law Enforcement in tracking ownership of a gun that was used in a crime.

Gun Sense #44 KSG 12ga Shotgun Demonstration.

In 2015 I bought my first KSG pump action shotgun, I was intrigued by the fact it could hold 15 2/34" 12 gauge shot shells. I was raised around shotguns of all action types and the KSG was unique to say the least. I loaded it with dummy rounds from Brownell' to test its function and immediately discovered that the factory feed tube selector switch was inadequate to proper functionality of the shotgun.

The selector switch was recessed too much and made switching feed tubes impossible to do without removing one of your hands from controlling the gun, leading to fumbling around trying to find the switch. To me that was a major flaw.

I started finding youtube videos about the gun and in all cases I watched the same problematic situation where the operator of the KSG, when it came time to switch to the second feed tube, would have to stop. In many videos the gun is pointed at his feet looking for the switch, remove his hand from the trigger or from the forend, switch tubes then reconfigure the gun to begin shooting again. There is nothing remotely "tactical" about doing that, for a gun that is touted as a "tactical" shotgun. Looking for the switch in a stressful situation could get you killed!

In all the KSG videos I found and there were many, the quickest someone could empty the shotgun ranged from 24 seconds to over one minute, because of the switch. I felt there should be a better way. As you used the gun you could keep your hands where they belong and your eyes on the task/target/situation, not looking for a selector switch.

I started experimenting and after awhile came up with the prototype to what is now the FTSS, (feed tube selector switch), pat. pending. I then made a couple videos, first showing it's smooth functionality and second showing in contrast to all the other videos out there, the speed it could be used. Fifteen rounds in 9 seconds was the demonstration and I actually held back a little.

My Speed demonstration was only meant to show an obvious contrast to any other available switch out. There were claims made but lacking any demonstration to back them up by the manufacturers.

I will be making another video with our new Flipper attachment and expect to fire fifteen rounds in 7 seconds or less.

Here is the link for the Selector Switch and video:

(FTSS) Feed Tube Selector Switch

http://www.shotgunswitch.com/

Pat. Pending 62/159,719
Solution De Innovation LLC

Gun Sense #45 Gun Registration UNCONSTITUTIONAL.

It falls under Section 103(i) in the Brady Law:

(i) PROHIBITION RELATING TO ESTABLISHMENT OF REGISTRATION SYSTEMS WITH RESPECT TO FIREARMS- No department, agency, officer, or employee of the United States may–

(1) require that any record or portion thereof generated by the system established under this section be recorded at or transferred to a facility owned, managed, or controlled by the United States or any State or political subdivision thereof; or

(2) use the system established under this section to establish any system for the registration of firearms, firearm owners, or firearm transactions or dispositions, except with respect to persons prohibited, (convicted criminals) by section 922 (g) or (n) of title 18, United States Code or State law, from receiving a firearm.

NOTE: "...the right to keep and bear arms shall not be infringed." Infringe means to encroach. You cannot even encroach on that right. Anything which restricts in any manner the right to keep and bear arms for the law abiding is Unconstitutional.

The answer to that question decides what type of country we live in: a constitutional republic, where individuals have unalienable rights, or an unlimited democracy where individuals have only privileges the fickle majority grants them.

"Shall not be infringed" is powerful language. Up there with "Congress shall make no law…"

Requiring paperwork and disclosure of private information are all infringements.

It's real easy, "SHALL NOT BE INFRINGED."

If the feds are data basing gun owners, they are infringing their right to keep and bear arms by requiring an unreasonable action on the part of the gun owner. A database has the potential to be abused, therefore it is in itself an infringement of the right to own a firearm.

"Guard with jealous attention the public liberty. Suspect everyone who approaches that jewel. Unfortunately, nothing will preserve it but downright force. Whenever you give up that force, you are inevitably ruined." - Patrick Henry

Take heed from this very astute warning fellow Americans...

NOTE: In MA, The E-FA-10 form is not a gun registration form, it is a transfer of ownership form, from the gun store to you or from you to another person. By law it can NOT be used to determine what you own unless a firearm is part of a criminal investigation.

NOTE: MA Firearms records are EXEMPTED from the public records statute. Chapter 4 M.G.L. Section 7 (26)(j). The Firearm Record Bureau (FRB) may not disseminate firearms records "...to any person, firm, corporation, entity or agency except criminal justice agencies as defined in chapter six and except to the extent such information relates solely to the person making the request and is necessary to the official interests of the entity making the request." Chapter 66 M.G.L. Section 10(d). Such as Law Enforcement in tracking ownership of a gun that was used in a crime.

Gun Sense #46 Firearms Confiscated in MA?

Things happen sometimes that are not under our control, we are all susceptible to being blindsided from time to time. If someone pulls a 209A restraining order against you for instance, while they are having an alcohol induced fit etc. and suddenly the police are there taking your firearms/ammo away, here is something for you to consider.

At the time of confiscation, by law, the police are supposed to do two things.

1. As of 8-13-2014 under bill H.4376, If your firearms are confiscated, the licensing authority (the police) shall at that time inform the person(s) in writing of their ability to transfer their firearms to an independently licensed individual OR dealer. After the 209-A has been terminated by the court the plaintiff may reacquire their firearm(s).

2. The officer shall, at the time of confiscation, provide to the person whose firearm(s)/ammo has been confiscated, a written inventory and receipt for any/all of the firearms/ammo confiscated and the officer and his employer shall exercise due care in the handling, holding and storage of these items. Nothing listed on the inventory should mysteriously be missing later on when/if the court terminates the disqualifying conditions....

So now that you know this. If there is someone that you can trust who will help you, this is a template letter he/she can use to present to the police in order to legally take custody of your firearm(s) if they are confiscated.

John Q. Doe II
John's Address Line 1
John's Address Line 2
John's City, State Zip
John's Phone Number

Date

Chief of Police (His/Her Name if you know it)
Police Department Name

Police Department Address Line 1
Police Department City, State Zip

Dear Chief of Police *(His/Her name if you know it)*:

I John Q. Doe II, LTC # 12345678A, of 123 Main St. (name of town) zip code, phone #. With the permission of (person's name), who was recently under a 209A restraining order, will take transfer of said person's firearm(s) and ammunition as listed on the enclosed/attached copy of official inventory list, as is a legal procedure under H.4376 passed on 8-13-2014. I will keep them stored as to maintain compliance with applicable state firearm storage.

Sincerely,

Signature

John Q. Doe II

Signature of person whose weapons were confiscated

Name of person whose weapons were confiscated.

I would add this whole section along with the letter:

Directly from the 188th session 2013-2014, H.4376, Sec. 42, **Chapter 140 M.G.L. Section 129D**; An Act Relative to Reduction of Gun Violence.

"Section 129D of said chapter 140, as so appearing, is hereby amended by striking out the first paragraph and inserting in place thereof the following paragraph:

Upon revocation, suspension or denial of an application for a firearm identification card pursuant to section 129B or for any firearms license if the firearm identification card is not then in force or for any machine gun license, the person whose application was so revoked, suspended or denied shall without delay deliver or surrender to the licensing authority where the person resides all firearms, rifles, shotguns and machine guns and ammunition which the person then possesses unless an appeal of the revocation or suspension is pending.

The person or the person's legal representative shall have the right, at any time up to 1 year after the delivery or surrender, to transfer the firearms, rifles, shotguns and machine guns and ammunition to any licensed dealer or any other person legally permitted to purchase or take possession of the firearms, rifles, shotguns and machine guns and ammunition and, upon notification in writing by the purchaser or transferee and the former owner, the licensing authority shall within 10 days deliver the firearms, rifles, shotguns and machine guns and ammunition to the transferee or purchaser and the licensing authority shall observe due care in the receipt and holding of any such firearm, rifle, shotgun or machine gun and ammunition; provided, however, that the purchaser or transferee shall affirm in writing that the purchaser or transferee shall not in violation of section 129C transfer the firearms, rifles, shotguns or machine guns or ammunition to the former owner.

The licensing authority shall at the time of delivery or surrender inform the person in writing of the authority's ability, within 1 year after delivery or surrender, to transfer the firearms, rifles, shotguns and machine guns and ammunition to any licensed dealer OR OTHER PERSON LEGALLY PERMITTED, (as in licensed) TO PURCHASE OR TAKE POSSESSION."
#

In my opinion, reasoning to the contrary does not reflect what H.4376, passed on 8-13-2014, clearly states in the above section. As this outline does not describe a transfer of ownership or use of an FA-10 form, it is merely a written transfer to another licensed individual taking custody, not ownership of the firearms until any disqualifying conditions have been dropped. It is true that a licensed individual can sell up to four firearms in a year and more through an FFL but it is also true that this cannot be done legally by someone with a suspended license, so it does not pertain for this transfer.

NOTE: If the police don't know or pretend not to know this about this law and refuse to research it or turn over the firearms/ammo, your second step should be to send the police Chief the request by certified mail return receipt. If then he will not be reasonable, your next step would be to go to court and petition a judge, who is supposed to know the laws. He should inform the police to release the firearms to you per law. I hope no one has to go to this extreme, but guns can be a big tug of war....see **Gun Sense #13 Specific to MA Petition for Judicial Review**.

NOTE: Section 44 said **Chapter 140 M.G.L Section 129D**, as so appearing, is hereby further amended by inserting after the third paragraph the following paragraph:

"If the licensing authority cannot reasonably ascertain a lawful owner within 180 days of acquisition by the authority, the authority may, in its discretion, trade or dispose of surplus, donated, abandoned or junk firearms, rifles, shotguns or machineguns or ammunition to properly licensed distributors or firearms dealers. The proceeds of the sale or transfer shall be remitted or credited to the municipality in which the authority presides to purchase weapons, equipment or supplies or for violence reduction or suicide prevention; provided, however, that no firearm, rifle, shotgun or machinegun or ammunition classified as having been used to carry out a criminal act pursuant to section 131Q shall be considered surplus, donated, abandoned or junk for the purpose of this section."

NOTE: Section 44 is a great incentive for the police to cling to the firearms and to block transfer under any pretense to someone you would want to hold them for you pending any court decision. Legal/illegal theft of valuable property is what this section could be used for. So stalling for 180 days would be in their best interest. Contact the Commonwealth Second Amendment Lawyers if this happens. You can visit them on the web at:

Commonwealth Second Amendment Inc.

http://www.comm2a.org/

Contact Information (Information in Appendix A)

Also, there are no stipulations in H.4376 as to a 209A, versus any other reason why the police would not turn the guns over to a licensed individual.

I hope this is helpful, of course it may not be applicable to cover all reasons for confiscation.

Gun Sense #47 26 States That Honor Your MA LTC.

This is a list of 26 States that honor your MA LTC. Be advised that this list can change without notice from year to year so before you travel to any of these states, give their State House a call and ask for the firearm licensing division to confirm that they still honor the MA license.

Alabama
Alaska
Arizona
Arkansas
Idaho
Indiana
Iowa
Kansas
Kentucky
Maine
Michigan
Mississippi
Missouri
Montana
Nevada
New Hampshire
North Carolina
Ohio
Oklahoma
South Dakota
Tennessee
Texas
Utah
Vermont
Virginia
Wisconsin

The following states have permitless carry which allows anyone that can legally possess a firearm carry concealed: Alaska, Arizona, Kansas, Maine, Mississippi, Missouri, New Hampshire, Vermont, West Virginia. Some restrictions may apply. Check each state for its own restrictions.

And if you want to see what states honor the multi-state licenses scroll down the information at my states tab at **www.mafirearmsafety.com**.

Gun Sense #48 Nomenclature of Various Firearms- ATF.

The information from these two links is important. You should understand the firearm you own and its parts:

ATF Guidebook - Importation & Verification of Firearms, Ammunition, and Implements of War Terminology & Nomenclature

https://www.atf.gov/file/61811/download

Terminology & Nomenclature

https://www.atf.gov/firearms/firearms-guides-importation-verification-firearms-ammunition-and-implements-war-terminology

Specifically covering:

Handgun — Pistol
Handgun — Revolver
Bolt Action
Lever Action
Self-Loading Action (Semiautomatic)
Slide/Pump Action
Top Break Action

Gun Sense #49 BATF Pays a Visit to MA Officials 4-20-18.

THE PAST:

The Firearms Reform bill s.2367, was passed by the MA House and Senate making it law on 6-29-2004. It created the Firearms Licensing Review Board (FLRB). Firearm license applicants disqualified by a prior misdemeanor conviction could now file a petition for review (Read **Gun Sense #20 MA Misdemeanor? Been Denied Your Gun Permit/License?**) in front of a seven member board. The petition could be filed five years after the conviction, adjudication, commitment, probation or parole (this is now under legal challenge).

The Firearms Reform bill s.2367 merely took the existing state references to Federal law and fixed the language to a point in time in 1994. Lawmakers followed that Federal language supposedly in 2004 as well, and believed the net effect on MA gun owners should be zero.

Since 2004, under **Chapter 140 M.G.L. Section 130B**, people who were previously denied a firearm license were able to sometimes successfully petition the FLRB to regain or gain a firearm license. Police Chiefs would ultimately have the final say but normally were comfortable with the findings of the FLRB.

PRESENT DAY:

On 4-20-18, the Federal Bureau of Alcohol, Tobacco and Firearms (BATF) had a meeting with the MA Criminal Justice Information Services (DCJIS) and the Executive Office of Public Safety and Security. In the meeting the BATF outlines how the state has been violating Federal law 18 U.S.C. / 922 (g) and 18 U.S.C./ 921 (a) (20) since 2004 (concerning disqualifiers to ownership of firearms). The BATF "advises" that the licenses that were approved through the FLRB appeals process should now all be revoked. This now would render the FLRB impotent in the future. "Advice" politicians are happy to follow...

People who lawfully went through the FLRB appeals process, approximately 340 of them, many in law Enforcement, all good people, are now, suddenly and severely impacted by this turn of events. These people did everything right, unknowingly under what was obviously fraudulent law.

The state should have to reimburse the people the money they had to spend to go through that process, plus any renewals they had to pay over the years.

When the topic is firearms the politicians now pretend to be concerned about running afoul of Federal laws, but exhibit no such concern about running afoul of Federal Immigration or Federal marijuana laws....

Article VI of the Constitution states that Federal law takes priority when it clashes with state law. Where is that concern?

Two examples of hypocrisy by politicians and police in MA concerning an aversion of running afoul of Federal laws:

7-24-17, The Highest Court in MA Declares the Commonwealth a Sanctuary State.

https://takecareblog.com/blog/the-highest-court-in-massachusetts-declares-the-commonwealth-a-sanctuary-state

2-27-18, State Police Chiefs Back New Version of Sanctuary State bill.

https://www.bostonglobe.com/metro/2018/02/27/state-police-chiefs-back-new-version-sanctuary-state-bill/YHNnxoppUuaHX9LgF30Z2O/story.html

Both of these are gross and clear violations of Federal Immigration laws.

Let's not even talk about Federal Marijuana laws the state willingly violates....

The DCJIS FLRB has no authority to revoke or suspend licenses currently in force. Police Chiefs can simply allow licenses to expire in due course, there should be no manufactured panic by politicians or police.

The Governor should stop feigning panic to strip guns away from these people "immediately," people who lawfully held firearms for years with no abuses.

The guns were also bought legally by these people and are private property. Is the state going to reimburse the cost of the firearms that are seized? Or are they going to willfully violate the Fourth, Fifth and possibly the Ninth Amendment, as well?

The people affected need to lawyer-up and take the state to court. And Federal law concerning appeals should be made so people are not banned for life for some minor youthful indiscretions that amounted to nothing.

IMPORTANT NOTE: The courts have started hearing cases, overturning decisions and have reinstated licenses to people in this circumstance. Any denials must go before a court in order to be overturned.

Gun Sense #50 Active Duty Service People in MA.

2014 the legislature passed laws concerning firearms etc. and one was about active duty military people. They will no longer be required to take a safety course in order to apply for their gun license. I think it is a nice "gesture" (or is it?), in recognition of our service men and women. But I also look at it another way, just because you no longer need the course, does that mean magically, "somehow," you will know what your legal responsibilities are and what the gun law "do's and don'ts" are?

An infraction of any gun law(s) usually means a felony count against you! In my opinion this is likely setting up our service people up for failure. Are politicians looking at this as a "we give you the LTC with one hand and take it away with the other" ploy?

I am a pessimist when it comes to politicians and their motives for doing anything (usually self-serving motives) in this anti-gun state. So, if anyone you know is active duty and would like a gun license in MA please refer them to these chapters before applying for their license: Gun Sense **#39, #37, #22, #41, #3, #13, #14, #35, #36, #33, #19, #20, #34 & #38**. This way they will be informed about what they MUST know if they do not want a felony count against them in the future and loss of gun rights for life, fair enough? Please pass this on. If they have issues after follow the advice in those chapters, have them contact me:

Contact Information in "About the Author" Section

Children, Their Future Rights, are we Overlooking Them?

I initially got involved with giving the state required basic firearm safety course when my son became old enough (15) to apply for his firearm identification card (FID). I started looking for an instructor that would give the course. At that time it was a separate course than the one given for the license to carry (LTC). I found instructors, but each one told me they only gave the LTC course, good only for 21 and older. "There was more money in it" an instructor told me. I retorted by saying to him (because by then I was starting to get fed up) "When you dinosaurs go extinct the shooting sports will go extinct with you because you ignored the kids!"

I could not believe how short sighted these people were. So I became a state instructor, my son was my first classroom "victim" for his FID card, then I began giving the course to the 15-20 year old group exclusively. Now the course will cover either age group with no distinctions.

I know how important it is to include our youth in the shooting sports, that is how I started, it is the only way these traditions have any hope of surviving into the future. I think that we as adults kind of overlook how important it really is to talk to our children about their rights under the Constitution. If we don't talk to them how will they ever know? Share your passion of firearm freedom with them. Don't depend on the public school system to educate them about their Second Amendment right to keep and bear arms. Schools/teachers and their unions, are anti Second Amendment, their ultimate agenda is to rewrite history by leaving out or "re-interpreting" whole sections of our Constitution and passing it off as factual to our children, by making the framers of the Constitution nary a footnote in history. So please talk to your children about their rights if you don't want them to lose these rights.

We fight hard to keep a certain class of politicians in line concerning our rights, we do not overlook their assaults on the Constitution, we can get very energized at the polls to "kick the bums out" as we should at the ballet box. But stop and think, do you take the time to explain the way you feel about your freedoms to your children? Do you take the time t' make sure they understand that these freedoms can only survive if t' too fight someday against the agendas of a few bad people willi· abuse their powers while holding political office? It has to com you, as the adult, as it did from your parents or grandparents, when the terror that was WWII was very real in their lives. They held their freedoms very dear indeed.

The importance of this seems to become more and more diluted, as the years pass, than when I was young. Try a test to see what, if anything, has been taught to your children about the Constitution, the framers or the Bill of Rights in school. Simply ask them if they have ever heard of the history behind the forming of American Independence, you may be shocked at their answers or lack thereof. It will be a clear message and duty for you to teach them yourself in this area.

The Constitution is only as strong as the current generation who protect it. If our young have no idea it exists, their rights will cease to exist along with their freedoms in the not so distant future. Firearm rights are the keystone of those freedoms.

This is a quote from an original Patriot who understood this all too well:

"The voice of tradition, I trust, will inform posterity of our struggles for freedom. If our descendants be worthy the name of Americans they will preserve and hand down to their latest posterity the transactions of the present times." - Patrick Henry

Zero Gun Sense = Uzi Submachine Gun Tragedy in Westfield MA.

When I first heard the story of the tragedy of an eight year old boy dying at the Westfield MA gun club, my initial reaction was anger at the gun club and sympathy for the young boy's family. I had to wonder what was going on in the minds of these so-called firearm instructors? There had to have been more than one instructor at an event that allowed the public in to shoot. There also should have been a "Range Master" overseeing the event and the other instructors. If all of these instructors were certified and dedicated to safety, it is hard for me to understand how this fatality would or could have happened (But I do have a good idea)?

I have read that the eight year old was being watched by a 15 year old "instructor," OK, maybe this 15 year old could have been certified, how, I'm not sure, but for sub machine guns, not very probable. In any case I would want proof of any certification and in what discipline. The certifications should have all been on display. I have heard people say that the blame lies with the dead boy's father, a doctor, I strongly disagree with that and I will tell you why...

When we go to a doctor we entrust our care to him, we know that his field is medicine and that we should be in good hands even though we do not understand all he is doing. He has had years of education in his background. The same can be held as true for many other trades or professions. Examples can go on and on. In this case with the boy's father, he brought his son to what looked to him to be an unusual and interesting event. This event was being run by people that were supposed to know what they were doing in the field of firearms, so the father placed his faith in that, as did many others that day.

There is a lot more that goes into having the label of "Firearm Instructor" on your shirt, you should have accumulated knowledge and understanding about many types of firearms and the characteristic's. This can take years. An individual that becomes a firearm instructor should understand how to reload many types of ammunition and understand the ballistics, trajectories and pressures involved, and understand basic kinetics. He should know how to strip down many kinds of firearms and understand the inner workings. At the very least, he should know how to instruct people in the proper mechanics or elements of shooting from very basic to advanced. To do this he needs to be able to study people in order to correct what they are doing wrong while they shoot. He should be no less than an expert shot himself in all manner of firearms in order to impart more effectively what he knows to others about the fundamentals.

All this takes dedication to the sport. I feel very strongly that the eight year old boy that died was not served by people with this dedication to the firearms sport or he would be alive today. Did the 15 year old have all this accumulated knowledge? I would say the answer is no, he has not lived long enough or become mature enough. The people that were running the event actually allowed safety to be trumped by perceived "fun," which lead directly to the boy's death. Firearms are far too unforgiving of foolish mistakes. When it comes to firearms a true instructor knows that safety can never be trumped by "fun," it would never be allowed. This death can be summed up in one unfortunate word, negligence.

A Micro Uzi is a fully automatic weapon and should have never, under any circumstances been placed in an eight year old's hands. A child that age is years away from having developed the muscular strength, coordination or understanding to handle such a weapon, for this not to be understood by these so-called instructors is in and of itself criminal negligence in my opinion. Whatever justice is meted out in court will have been fully deserved. I do not hold the 15 year old "instructor" to blame, only the imbeciles that put him in charge. Sadly the court can never return the little boy to his family, but hopefully it will send a loud and clear message to gun clubs to have instructors that will never allow fun to trump safety.

UZI Tragedy in Westfield, Part 2.

This is a follow up to ***Zero Gun Sense = Uzi Submachine Gun Tragedy in Westfield MA.*** Fast forward, in the Boston Herald on 8-21-2010, I read that the former police Chief of Pelham, Edward Fleury, the organizer of that fateful event where an eight year old boy died, has filed a motion that the charges be dropped because he says that he could not have "foreseen" the accident. I find it fascinating that any judge would even consider the motion.

It is true that when we rise in the morning we really do not know what will happen to us, we have certain expectations of how our day will unfold or hope it will unfold. We cannot control or foresee everything...of course not. A drunk, or some nitwit texting, crosses over the center line and there is absolutely no time on your part to react...you could not foresee this, this may kill you, this is one example, the list can go on and on....

I do not believe for a second (unless he is a complete imbecile) that Edward Fleury, who professes himself to be a "firearm instructor" would not have foreseen that something bad would/could happen by putting a fully automatic Micro Uzi into the hands of an eight year old boy. If Fleury is actually telling the truth about not being able to "foresee" this accident, why then was a complete imbecile allowed to run a firearms event of this nature? As the Range Master/organizer, Fleury had final say in the events of that day.

To highlight the point in another way...why not have Fleury give a child a hand grenade. Could Fleury claim he could not "foresee" an accident? The child may or may not pull the pin, you can't really "foresee" what he will do, but you can prevent something bad from happening by not giving the child a grenade in the first place! You can control certain circumstances like this by applying a smidgen of sense. The boy would have enjoyed being introduced to the proper use of a .22 cal. bolt action rifle also.

If Fleury really did not understand the characteristics of a Micro Uzi submachine gun and that an eight year old would not have the understanding, strength or physical coordination to control such a weapon, that would, at the very least, boil down to gross incompetence on his part and for that he and others involved should pay. He allowed perceived "fun" to trump safety and good sense. I hope the judge dismisses the motion and goes on with the trial.

UPDATE: On January 1, 2011, Fleury was acquitted of involuntary manslaughter and the three counts of furnishing a machine-gun to minors. He had organized the event and allowed a 15 year old with no instructor credentials to oversee the victim use a Micro Uzi. While I find it incredible that he was cleared of all charges, the MA jury has spoken. Two others, Domenico Spano and Carl Giuffre are accused of supplying the Micro Uzi, they have pleaded "not guilty" and await trial.

UPDATE: Nine year old girl accidentally kills instructor in Arizona with the exact same type of weapon as in above story, a Micro Uzi. This is another case of "Fun" before safety gone very bad:

Girl, 9, kills Arizona Shooting Instructor With Uzi in Accident

http://news.yahoo.com/girl-nine-kills-arizona-shooting-instructor-uzi-accident-202638510.html

Common Sense, The Meaning Has Flip Flopped.

Common sense used to mean to me, in an overall general way, the prevailing notion of what was the right, proper or safe thing to do throughout many varied real life situations. These days I view the term "common sense" as a misnomer. I don't want to be associated with the "common," as in generally accepted "sensible" notions of today.

What is common sense today? I don't believe that common sense, intended in any good way, exists much anymore. It now defines a whole new concept in the overall social mentality. Using good sense now is actually very uncommon behavior. For instance, someone who pulls off to the side of the road to call or text is using uncommon sense, as in "good," ask yourself, do you see that happening very often? "Common ignorance" more aptly describes and has completely eclipsed the "common sense" of old, especially with the advent of cell phones, used on our public roadways.

Driving distractedly/ignorantly is now the norm, not the exception where cell phones are concerned. Vast numbers of people, everywhere you care to look, appear oblivious to the necessity of paying undivided attention to their surroundings as that one ton (or more) missile they are behind the wheel of, hurtles blindly along. Blindly? Sure, ask yourself…, while you're texting, who is driving? Texting behind the wheel must be more important to people than life itself…, theirs' or anyone else's. FACT, people are dying on the roadways all across the country due to driving and texting or are victims of it. Depending on your speed, when you take your eyes off the road to text, your vehicle can travel anywhere from 50 to 300 feet in one second before you look back at the road! On some unconscious level I guess many people are in a hurry to go to the "bone yard," sadly, they can bring innocent people with them in many cases! "Common sense," now translated, is really "common ignorance" and it is prevailing. For it to be said that you have "uncommon sense" would be a compliment, you're not being part of the "herd."

When I notice a vehicle moving along erratically (which is often), invariably the driver will be texting or yapping on a cell phone. How in the world did we ever make it from point A to point B before cell phones were invented? I guess maybe we just had to pay attention to the road. When/if we make it to our destinations today, it is much less safely now than it was in the shaky past, you're surrounded by what is now the prevailing "common sense," that's spooky. The drunks are still out there, as they were in the past, but they now are also yapping/texting on cell phones as they weave happily along, double jeopardy for you and I! Pedestrians, cyclists, children, motorcyclists…their lives are in your hands. Are your hands on the wheel and your mind on the road?

On the political front, when I hear a politician exclaim that "this" or "that" bill is the common sense thing to do. I cringe and wonder if any of the clowns will actually read it first before taking a vote. Their collective ideas on what is "common sense" are now leading the nation down the road to financial ruin at this very moment. What we need now are politicians with "uncommon" sense, certainly not the status quo. You can't keep voting for the same buffoons and expect different results! That only means we are not paying attention or using good sense!

On the topic of "common sense" in the shooting sports, I will tell people in my class that before they ever fire a gun to be certain of their target and of what is beyond it. Not only at the shooting range but also while hunting…not to get so caught up in the excitement of shooting at a deer that you have tunnel vision of what or who may be beyond. That is just common sense someone will usually say. I counter that with, if it is such "common sense" why are we always reading, on a fairly regular basis, about accidental shootings in the woods? Please, don't use the prevailing "common sense," today, as individuals we need to start exercising more "uncommon sense."

Evil Guns? (by Ed Sinnott).

NOTE: This was sent to me by Ed Sinnott, an old friend I have known since the 8th grade. I had sent him a simple notice that I had put a "For Sale" tab on my website. As part of the description, I had mentioned that it was better than craigslist in that you could also put "evil" guns for sale. That is what spurred Ed to send me this history lesson about, not evil guns, but instead evil men. I thought it would be nice to share for your consideration. So when you hear talk of "Gun Control" take a closer look at the people doing the talking, a very very close look.

Evil Guns?

A funny thought, without them how much evil was in the world before the availability of guns to the common man? We take for granted that the industrial revolution made guns available to the average "common" man.

Before that, in our human history, the powerful rulers had control of the weapons, they only armed loyal men under their control. The men fought and died for the commands of a ruling class. It was said the Bill of Rights declared men to be equal and Samuel Colt and his guns made them truly equal. Disarmed men were easy to control when faced with armed men under the commands of a ruling class.

When the Founding Fathers wrote the Bill of Rights, they fully understood what it was like to be under the rule of the rich...those that were armed and therefore powerful. They fully knew if there were armed citizens then, and only then, could they ever hope to protect themselves from these "EVIL" men with their greedy ambitions. They knew of how "EVIL" men planed, schemed and wanted to exploit, control and rule the now independent freemen of the newly formed United States.

By giving the common man the gun, they hoped that men would have and use when necessary, the equalizing tool called the gun, to protect the principals of this new freedom. They also knew having every able man armed would help discourage any attacks from another nation. Having a fully armed citizenry would make for a sizable army. If there were to be a battle, the men would also know the fight would be to keep them free and not just to please a king. It was a good plan.

Now we face the even more insidious weapon of greed. It is through the use of money to manipulate and control us, to become subjects to a ruling class who has much of everything already under their control. It is this "EVIL" that is by far more deadly to any of us than any gun will ever be. This weapon of economic control threatens our country, our citizens and our future.

Sad, the gun will not do much to stop the evil greed of men who rule from a distance and other countries as they lay our freedoms, economies and futures to waste without ever firing a shot...All they need do to kill us is to adjust some numbers on a computer screen to change our money...All that we were and ever could be....is gone forever....The United States, the greatest hope for all mankind, will be lost because the gun could not find the target....of this evil.

Now a word from a Great American:

"I believe that banking institutions are more dangerous to our liberties than standing armies. If the American people ever allow private banks to control the issue of their currency, first by inflation, then by deflation, the banks and corporations that will grow up around the banks will deprive the people of all property- until their children wake up homeless on the continent their fathers conquered." - Thomas Jefferson

NRA and Relevance.

Gun control sounds reasonable when politicians speak on it and the media lets the phrase slide on by without any follow-up questions. Gun control has nothing, what-so-ever to do with crime or guns. They are the scapegoat, it is one hundred percent about attempting political control over our lives. You see, there are plenty of laws already on the books dealing with crime, yet crime happens, laws cannot stop evil intent and when a particularly brutal crime grabs the headlines, most politicians see an opportunity to get their mugs in the paper or on television to push their anti-gun, anti-Second Amendment agenda/crap. The billionaire socialist Bloomberg, once mayor of New York City is one such example, all high profile New York/MA/CA/NJ/Chicago politicians are prime examples.

The politicians and police, in their frustration to stop crime focus their attention on an easy target, you. This is why the NRA is the hated organization of many socialist leaning politicians, because the NRA comes to your defense. The NRA has over four million members and fights extremely hard to preserve our Second Amendment freedoms. Is the NRA relevant? You bet your firearm freedom it is. There are an estimated 100 million law abiding gun owners in the United States, if they were to all suddenly join the NRA, politicians would pale and never dare speak of gun control again, it would become political suicide to do so. Is the NRA relevant, again, you bet your overall freedom it is. And because so many politicians hate the NRA that is all the endorsement I need to be a member.

For more information on the NRA:

Contact Information (Information in Appendix A)

NOTE: There is also available in Massachusetts a group called The Gun Owners Action League (GOAL). This is the state club, representing the NRA. Like the NRA, GOAL fights for the rights of the law abiding gun owner, in Massachusetts, offers training and disseminates information. For more information find:

Contact Information (Information in Appendix A)

Constitutional Amendment for the Gun Control Crowd.

GUN CONTROL...You know, actually there is a constitutional procedure to remove or change any part of the Constitution, all it takes is 2/3rds of all 50 state legislature's to ratify the change and it becomes law.

Instead of trying to usurp the Constitution why don't the progressive liberals simply remove the Second Amendment constitutionally? Do you know the answer to that? I know the answer to that..., the progressives/liberals/communists/democrats/socialists, whatever name it is that they want to hide behind this month, know that real American patriots will never allow it and the lie that gun control will stop crime is just that, a lie.

It is about CONTROL period. Every dictator throughout history worth his weight in lies knows the best way to control the masses is to first disarm them. Any American that does not want to own a firearm has that freedom of choice, but as an American he or she should support and defend his fellow Americans' God given right to self-defense and Constitutional right to do it by way of firearms, if they so choose. It is an American birthright.

Now stop splitting hairs scheming about abolishing America's gun rights, taking my firearms will not stop ONE criminal from committing a criminal act and if so-called Democrats decide to be in an honest debate they would concede that, only that does not mesh with their little agenda. We are on to your statism game.

"Guard with jealous attention the public liberty, suspect everyone who approaches that jewel. Unfortunately, nothing will preserve it but downright force. Whenever you give up that force you are ruined." - Patrick Henry

Bloomberg's Gun Control....

There's no doubt America needs to curb gun use and possession, the question is whose guns? There are 34,500 members on the NYPD and in 2012 they fatally shot 16 people. That gives Bloomberg's former army a rate of 46 shooting deaths per 100,000, killing people at a clip that dwarfs any civilian level in the country....

To put it into perspective, Chicago, an American city known for gun violence, hit its peak murder rate of 34 per 100,000 in 1992. American law enforcement is increasingly militarized, why? Radley Balko reports in his book *Rise of the Warrior Cop*: "Driven by martial rhetoric and the availability of military style equipment, from bayonets and M-16 rifles, to armored personnel carriers, American police forces have often adopted a mindset previously reserved for the battlefield." So while gun violence has markedly declined, why do the police have such a military buildup? What do they think they are preparing to do?

While Bloomberg is squaring up to spread irrational fears about armed Mormon cattle ranchers and NRA members gone wild, we should be more worried about guns in the hands of the police. One unidentified (to protect the guilty) Connecticut police officer recently stated that he can hardly wait until he gets the order to kick in doors to confiscate firearms...I guess he just needs the "go ahead" from oath breaking politicians to gleefully become a state sanctioned thief.

For Bloomberg to further his agenda he is counting/playing on the majority of the public's ignorance about guns to push his disarmament agenda/scheme for CONTROL, a time honored tactic of any tyrant worth his weight in lies....

The biggest most irresponsible gun owner in the country isn't some redneck or a deranged teen plotting a massacre from his basement, it is the STATE, in my opinion. There is a lot of history to back that opinion up. Governments have been responsible for wholesale genocide throughout history....but first the People had to be disarmed!

Laws of any sort cannot prevent bad human behaviors. The term "Crime Prevention" means nothing to any educated person in the gun control debate.

Can violence be prevented by any law? If laws did prevent bad things from happening there would be no violent crimes or crime at all. Is that the case, anywhere in the world? NO. Example, prisons are the most controlled places on Earth and there is plenty of crime/violence/murder going on inside those locked little societies. How then can laws/wishful thinking prevent violence in an open free society? It can't.

We need laws of course, I am not saying that we don't. They are in place to prosecute the people that are caught after they commit the crimes, which are against these laws. That's all. If they even get caught. The police are the cleanup crew, after the gruesome crime/fact. Mainly, they are revenue collectors, with quotas to fill the state coffers, taking from people they know are working for a living (speeding tickets and such). Tougher to get money from criminals….they can't.

Can any law keep guns out of the hands of criminals? Of course not. The gun ban crowd knows this, they claim their cause is to stop crimes with guns, they hope the majority of the public cannot see through that lie. Their aim is disarmament of law abiding citizens, plain and simple. Why? CONTROL, hard to CONTROL the masses if they are allowed to have firearms….

So remember this…any candidate(s) that are spouting gun control are liars bent on control of YOU. Any gun owner who would vote for any candidate(s) that are spouting gun control would be the equivalent of a turkey voting in favor of Thanksgiving!

Warnings of Yesteryear for Today.

"A nation can survive its fools, and even the ambitious. But it cannot survive treason from within. An enemy at the gates is less formidable, for he is known and carries his banner openly. But the traitor moves amongst those within the gate freely, his sly whispers rustling through...all the alleys, heard in the very halls of government itself. For the traitor appears not a traitor; he speaks in accents familiar to his victims, and he wears their face and their arguments, he appeals to the baseness that lies deep in the hearts of all men. He rots the soul of a nation, he works secretly and unknown in the night to undermine the pillars of the city, he infects the body politic so that it can no longer resist. A murderer is less to fear. The traitor is the plague." - Marcus Tullius Cicero

Rome then, Washington D.C. today....

1. "An unconstitutional act is not law; it confers no rights; it imposes no duties; it affords no protection; it creates no office; it is in legal contemplation, as inoperative as though it had never been passed." Norton v. Shelby County, US Supreme Court Decision 118 US 425, 442 (in 1886)

This was at a time when no one in political office pretended that they did not understand our Constitution....

2. "Patriots are not revolutionaries trying to overthrow government. Patriots are counter-revolutionaries trying to prevent government from overthrowing the U.S. Constitution." - Author unknown

3. Executive Orders are now circumventing Congress while they sit on their hands doing nothing!

4. "The strength of the Constitution lies entirely in the determination of each citizen to defend it. Only if every single citizen feels duty bound to do his share in this defense are constitutional rights secure." - Albert Einstein

So defend it or it will not be there for your descendants, as it was for you...starting first in the voting booth!

Liberal vs. Conservative.

If a Conservative doesn't like guns, he doesn't buy any. If a Liberal doesn't like guns, he wants all guns outlawed and will try to undermine the Constitution to do it.

If a Conservative sees a foreign threat, he thinks about ways to defeat his enemy. A Liberal wonders how he can surrender gracefully and still look good. Can you say "set time frame exit strategy?"

If a Conservative is down-and-out, he thinks about how he may better his situation. A Liberal wonders who is going to take care of him. Can you say "welfare?"

If a Conservative decides he needs a health care plan, he goes about shopping for it or he may choose a job that provides it. A Liberal demands that the rest of us provide his health care, can you say "Obamacare" or "Romneycare?"

If a Conservative doesn't like a radio or TV show host, he switches the channel. Liberals demand that those they don't like be shut down.

NOTE: Shut down through the proposed implementation of their so-called Fairness Doctrine. The only problem is that there is nothing fair about it for conservative points of view, it would silence those views. Let's make sure that does not happen, be aware, pay attention.

A Conservative does not believe that murderous enemy terrorist combatants, who intentionally target civilians, should be given Constitutional rights, he believes those rights are to be reserved for American citizens. Liberals (progressives) want to extend our rights and protections to foreign terrorists (and illegals in general) with no thought of the exorbitant cost to the tax payer of course, or the deficit.

Some ideas from other sources, heavily edited, with "factoids" added by me. I thought these things ring so true that I should share them.

I'm not Politically Correct...you Offended?

To The Editor:

This letter is not politically correct, mainly because it deals in truth and "common sense," the latter being a quaint old term rapidly fading into history. For a long while now I have been witnessing anti Second Amendment "spin" spew forth from the major media outlets. It seems no one wants to address crime control, only gun control, regardless of the spin, they are not one and the same.

When our public servants swear their oaths of office, to uphold the Constitution, some of them turn around and try to diminish your Rights by passing gun control measures. That my friends is an affront to you and the Constitution they swore to uphold! The Second Amendment truly is our first Right, the only Right that ensures the rest will endure. I am using emphasis on the word "Right" so it can be clearly understood that it is not a privilege. There is no Bill of Privileges! In this country if you are convicted of a felony, you forfeit your Right to firearm ownership along with your Right to be free.

The media would and does, imply, strongly, that by definition legal gun owners are criminals. WRONG! We do not always agree with another person or groups' point of view, but agree or not, we should all defend the Right under the First Amendment for everyone to express their view. You or I do not have to own a firearm, that is our free decision, but as an American, you should defend your fellow Americans Right under the Second Amendment to own firearms if they so choose. It is an American birthright. To erode any of our Constitution in an unconstitutional manner is to invite the collapse of the entire document and all of our freedoms. I do not understand our public servants, the media and certain lawyers who feign ignorance?

The communists would use any means to justify the end result. This was not lost on the media, they embrace the strategy. When anything goes to get what you want, the truth is the first victim. In this country a push for total gun confiscation is underway, driven by the media elite and bad (i.e. treasonous) politicians. For every story where a crime is committed with a gun it is heralded by the media, there are other instances (reported by the NRA), where a crime is prevented and the intended victim, who saves himself or others, goes unreported. This kind of discrimination on the part of the media is very thoughtfully designed to build negative public opinion against gun ownership, the media works extremely hard trying to manipulate how people think about the subject of gun control.

There are greed driven trial lawyers that have their sights set on legitimate gun makers who are engaged in lawful commerce. These greed driven trial lawyers claim that if a gun maker's firearm is used in a crime then the gun maker should be liable for any consequences the criminal may have caused! Ridiculous, but true. These suits should be laughed out of every courtroom at every turn, otherwise what other type of ludicrous law suits will spring up next, on what other legitimate business manufacturer? These suits violate constitutional and civil Rights, including the First, Second and Ninth Amendments. This is just another way to circumvent the Second Amendment unconstitutionally. By trying to bankrupt gun makers that make the only constitutionally protected consumer product, these lawyers try to do away with a source of protection for all Americans.

As can easily be shown in England, Australia and Canada to name a few, crime has skyrocketed in all areas after gun confiscation took place. You may guess correctly that criminals fail to turn in their guns! This goes unreported by the media, it is a lie by its very omission. The trouble is, it will be your Right to self-defense that certain trial lawyers, the media and some of your public servants are trying to take from you. There were bad people before guns were invented and there will be bad people (with guns), even after the guns of every law abiding citizen are confiscated, you cannot legislate evil intent away.

On the whole, sadly enough, the police only serve as the "clean-up crew" after the crime is committed. It really is your first duty and your Right to be able to defend yourself and your family. You should NEVER allow anyone to take away your Right to self-defense! Call your public servant, let him or her know how you feel, remind them of their oath, the gun control legislation that they block today may save your life tomorrow.

NOTE: Submitted on 2-29-2000 – to three papers, but not printed, no surprise there!

Humble Observation of a Beleaguered Tax Payer.

To The Editor:

Draconian taxation legislation has amounted to a chronic case of deprivation of necessities that in turn will and is, turning the people against the arrogance of their elected officials. The time of "turning" seems to be drawing nearer. As in the days of George Washington, before the American Revolution and the taxations that became a major factor in the overthrow of an arrogant British occupation, unrest prevailed. Unrest is yet again slowly coming to a seemingly inescapable head. Taxation is now at a much higher percentage than it ever was under British rule before the Colonists put an end to it by going to war. I guess politicians never read history? My mistake, they don't read anything before they vote.

Apparently greed and power are the only driving factors for politicians in Washington DC...the only reason they run for office it seems. Americans certainly recognize this in a deepening recession and are becoming much less tolerant then they would otherwise be. Enough of this enormous drain on the American people! Even now politicians are dreaming and scheming up more creative ways to add extra layers of taxation on all of us, just take a minute of your day from other distractions and watch the news.

You have to call your public servants and tell them to vote NO to any new taxes, tell them to do away with all the so called temporary taxes of the last forty five years, the taxes that have burdened Americans for so long. Tell them to stop pouring billions upon billions, even trillions of OUR money into lost causes brought on by inept, greedy CEOs. We are all now unwilling shareholders of failed corporations, car companies, banks, mortgage institutions, etc.

The way again to prosperity, allow people their hard earned money, to spend the way they see fit to spend it, then sit back and watch the economy take off! It is a no brainer, if they had brains. As it has so clearly demonstrated, BIG government only translates into BIG money MISMANAGEMENT and inevitably, attempted constitutional infringements!

"My reading of history convinces me that most bad government results from too much government." - Thomas Jefferson

We the Problem – A Preamble to our Ignorance.

"We the People," in the good old days (way, way back), that used to mean something. When people had better control of government, when people paid more attention and less taxes, when politicians meant their oath of office, before all kinds of electronic distractions...Now it begins, WE the PROBLEM, for sure.

Can we really blame the embedded hogs (Representatives) feeding at the government trough? Not really. They have no idea that they may be doing anything wrong, why should they, they are never punished by WE the PROBLEM! They do as they please, not as we want. Our Representatives are caught acting inappropriately all the time, just open any newspaper or turn on any talk radio program, watch any television set. They will say anything just to get elected and once they are in office they set about trying to change our Constitution to suit their own personal little agendas and they never come through with any of those promises they made to get elected! Hell, they are in! The chase is on! Watch out! Incumbents never lose! No matter what happens, no matter how much of our tax money is wasted on pork projects and complete corruption, no matter how many immoral or unethical or criminal scandals politicians are caught in they are rarely ever punished by WE the PROBLEM at the voting booth!

Both parties stink, they could care less about you. Sure at voting time they love you, they surely take certain factions within each party for granted. They do not have to promise anything to get the hardliner (brainless) votes. The so-called independent voters are the ones politicians will get real creative in their lies to snare the coveted swing voters. No matter how many decades we see their mugs again and again running for another four to six year term, we just keep rewarding them, over and over and over! Why in the world would they or could they, ever know they have done anything wrong? Because WE the PROBLEM keep re-electing them.

They draw up the laws they will not lower themselves to follow, these laws are meant for the little people, not for scofflaw politicians. Don't forget that this problem is also at the state level, not just DC! I would love to see a third party mount a viable challenge and win! Let's call it the American or Constitutional or Tea Party. If that were to happen it would scare the bejesus out of the Republicans and the Democrats, really shake up their little house of ill repute so-to-speak.

We have a chance at the polls to really shake up the status quo, the incentive for change in DC is compelling. The health care debacle is one economic killer, the porkulus plan was another economic killer, bailing out huge firms with our tax dollars was extremely ill conceived and we are now heading for higher inflation just over the horizon. The morons in office don't read the laws they pass! Do you really think that by voting the same faces back in every term you will somehow get a different result? Obviously WE the PROBLEM do and have foolishly believed that! But will WE continue too?

Congress is a luxury liner with no apparent rudder, their only answer is to tax everything and everyone, in a recession no less! WE the PROBLEM allow them. We have a choice, we can remain WE the PROBLEM or we can once more become WE the PEOPLE, what's it going to be? Are you fed up with the BS yet? Our Founding Fathers never intended for Representatives to make careers, dynasties or millions out of the job. Term limits not only for a President but for ALL of them!

November tell them all with a hearty, YOU'RE FIRED!

My Definition of a Politician.

I will give you my definition of how a Representative becomes a politician...

When we vote for a new candidate we want someone who will represent us and honor their oath of office by defending our Constitution, ALL of it, not cherry pick what they like. We call these people Representatives and they are public servants, in the public domain, in short, public property, in either party.

Now somewhere along the line they start losing sight that they are supposed to represent The People. They instead start to represent special lobbyist groups that are made up of big money and people who do not even live in the district the representative comes from. This means he/she no longer cares about his/her constituents...that is the moment he/she becomes a Politician. It now becomes all about shortsighted agenda(s), self-interests and no longer the will of The People who put him/her there.

I hope that was helpful? When they get to this point, it is time to BOOT THEM OUT on their ear, for freedom's sake!

"A free people ought not only be armed and disciplined but they should have sufficient arms and ammunition to maintain a status of independence from any who might attempt to abuse them, which would include their own government." - George Washington

Another Type of Solution.

Back in 2010, yet again Mother Nature devastated another area in the world (Haiti), with a powerful earthquake. When all is said and done the human toll may be high, the cost astronomical in this small impoverished nation. President Obama, like other presidents before him when natural disaster strikes, has promised help. Of course, this is the humanitarian and right thing to do.

Even in the face of certain economic ruin at home, Americans will once again show that it has the most empathetic and generous people in the history of the world. How long can this generosity last? I believe the socialization of America will put an end to it eventually. I also believe that there is a better way to help the world where poverty/hunger are the rule and not the exception, I think it would create work and give pride to the citizens of poor nations. Simply throwing money at a problem, as history shows, will not solve the problem. You can give food to the hungry today, but teach them to grow food and they will feed themselves forever, becoming independent of further outside help. When disasters strike around the world I never see other nations come to the financial rescue of these devastated areas in any significant way, do you? That burden is put squarely on the American tax payer, even as the rest of the world continues to hate us regardless of our humanitarian efforts.

If America does not go bankrupt directly due to inept socialist politicians, it will most certainly go bankrupt by default due to disasters caused by Mother Nature around the world. America cannot keep pace monetarily with these disasters indefinitely. I would like to see any president start a program that would teach the rest of the world to feed itself and convince other nations to become partners in that effort.

The key to do that is through irrigation. Agriculture and irrigation go successfully hand in hand and can be taught. The ancient Roman Empire started building aqueducts around 312 BC, they built 11 of them totaling 359 miles coming into Rome, delivering about 50 million gallons of water each day! Rome also built aqueducts in Spain, North Africa and France. One aqueduct built by Rome, in Segovia Spain, is still in use today. There is another type of aqueduct known as a qanat, in use through the deserts of Iran today. Aqueducts can enable irrigation and enable cities to survive as they grow too large to be supported by local water sources and most importantly help feed regions that are now starving. If the Roman Empire could put such ancient un-mechanized technology to such good use, surely in this age of computers and space travel we should certainly be up to the task? Building these irrigation systems would put people to work, the end result would feed the hungry within their own boarders and help raise them from poverty and starvation in the process.

The population of the world is ever growing and resources are becoming more depleted. If a concentrated effort to teach agriculture is not seriously considered, the world will be in serious trouble within mere decades. In the long term it would save the American tax payer the burden of supporting the world. It would be preemptive and in everyone's best interest.

Holiday Cheer?

I was listening to the news the other day when they reported what I thought was an astonishing statistic, that there were 33 million people in the US still in debt from what they had bought last Christmas! This being twelve months later, do you find that as shocking as I do? I was never brought up under the good example made by my parents to think that Christmas was the one day of the year set aside which obligated everyone to go broke. That whole notion, I am sure, was the brainchild of retail stores and banks pushing "easy credit."

Christmas to me means a family get-together, a very nice meal, going to the midnight mass thanking God for our blessings. It was never about how much money you could spend trying to "one-up" everyone else. I know that commercialism is not the intended meaning of Christmas, never was. People have been brainwashed to think it is about the "things" you get.

My mother has always said that you get what you need when you need it, at any time of year and only if you can stay within the budget. I agree. She is from an era that was devoid of the temptations of credit cards, the "buy now pay later" traps. She is from the era of pay cash or do without until you could pay cash. We need urgently to get back to that way of thinking.

I guess the 33 million people that are still in debt from last year have put upon themselves the added (needless) stress of how to pay for this Christmas also. The best things in life are free….It is hard to wean yourself from the "easy credit" trap while trying to impress people with "things…."

Start by getting back to the basics, just being glad that your family is together and well, by enjoying each other's company. People do not love one another based on what they can buy each other, that is not love. Simple thoughtful and caring actions are the real measure of love, not "things." The whole world would be better off without the traps of "easy credit." May the true Spirit of Christmas find you and yours well.

APPENDIX A – RESOURCES

The U.S. Bill of Rights

https://billofrightsinstitute.org/wp-content/uploads/2018/12/Bill-of-Rights-for-Website.pdf

The Department of Criminal Justice Information Services

https://www.mass.gov/orgs/department-of-criminal-justice-information-services

The DCJIS is the main "go to" concerning everything firearms and pertaining to criminal records. Other resources through them are outlined below.

200 Arlington St.
Suite 2200
Chelsea, MA 02150
Phone: (617) 660-4600
Fax: (617) 660-4613

* **Criminal Records Check Services**
https://www.mass.gov/criminal-record-check-services

* **Firearm Services (Firearms Records Bureau)**
https://www.mass.gov/firearms-services

* **Information for Victims (of crime)**
https://www.mass.gov/information-for-victims

* Information for Researchers
https://www.mass.gov/information-for-researchers

* Resources for CJIS Vendors
https://www.mass.gov/resources-for-cjis-vendors

* Public Records for DCJIS
https://www.mass.gov/public-records-for-dcjis

Mass.gov Link to Gun Laws

https://www.mass.gov/lists/massachusetts-firearms-laws

Mass.gov Link to Approved Firearms Roster

https://www.mass.gov/lists/approved-firearms-rosters

Mass.gov Link to 527 CMR (BOARD OF FIRE PREVENTION REGULATIONS)

https://www.mass.gov/files/documents/2018/02/02/FEA_527%20CMR._2015_%20unofficial%20Effective%20January%201%2C%202018%20_1.pdf

Massachusetts Gun Transaction Portal

https://mircs.chs.state.ma.us/fa10/action/home?app_context=home&app_action=presentTrans

The National Sport Shooting Foundation (NSSF)

https://www.nssf.org/safety/

This is the firearms industry trade organization. Here you can get information on the Project Childsafe Program, "Own it? Respect it. Secure it" initiative, Safety Literature, Safety Videos, Suicide Prevention information and Wildfire Prevention information.

National Shooting Sports Foundation
Flintlock Ridge Office Center
11 Mile Hill Road
Newtown, CT 06470
Phone: (203) 426-1320
Fax: (203) 426-1087

The National Rifle Association (NRA)

https://home.nra.org/

The NRA is the premier firearms safety & rights organization. Founded in 1871 to educate young men in marksmanship in the post Civil War era. The NRA has several bodies and services available.

National Rifle Association of America
11250 Waples Mill Road
Fairfax, VA 22030
Phone: (800) 672-3888

* **NRA Eddie Eagle Program**
https://eddieeagle.nra.org/

Phone: (800) 231-0752
Email: **eddie@nrahq.org**

* NRA Training
https://firearmtraining.nra.org/

Email: **nrainstructors@nrahq.org**

* NRA Institute for Legislative Action
https://www.nraila.org/

* NRA Foundation
https://www.nrafoundation.org/

Contributions Phone: (877) 672-4483
Grants Phone: (800) 554-9498
Friends of NRA Phone: (703) 267-1351
Email: **nraf@nrahq.org**

Gun Owners Action League (GOAL)

https://goal.org/

This is the state club, representing the NRA. Like the NRA, GOAL fights for the rights of the law abiding gun owner, in Massachusetts, offers training and disseminates information.

GOAL
361 West Main Street
Northborough, MA 01532
Phone: (508) 393-5333

The General Court of the Commonwealth of Massachusetts

https://malegislature.gov/

The General Court of the Commonwealth of Massachusetts concerns everything legislative in the state. This resource will connect you with your legislators, allow you to view bills, access the Massachusetts General Laws, etc.

Massachusetts Statehouse
24 Beacon St.
Boston, MA 02133
Main Phone: (617) 722-2000
Tour Desk Phone: (617) 727-3676

* **Contact your Legislators**
https://malegislature.gov/StateHouse/Contact

Phone: (617) 722-2000

* **Massachusetts General Laws**
https://malegislature.gov/Laws/GeneralLaws

* **Massachusetts Constitution**
https://malegislature.gov/Laws/GeneralLaws

* **Hearings and Events**
https://malegislature.gov/Events

Commonwealth Second Amendment Inc.

https://www.comm2a.org/

The Commonwealth Second Amendment Inc. or Comm2A, is a grassroots civil rights organization dedicated to the protection of the Second Amendment in Massachusetts.

Commonwealth Second Amendment Inc.
PO Box 301398
Jamaica Plain, MA 02130
Phone: (617) 942-0660
Email: **info@comm2a.org**

Massachusetts Hunter Education Program

https://www.mass.gov/massachusetts-hunter-education-program

MassWildlife Field Headquarters
1 Rabbit Hill Road
Westborough, MA 01581
Program Office Phone: (508) 389-7820
Course Enrollment Phone: (508) 389-7830
Email: **hunter.education@mass.gov**

Division of Fisheries and Wildlife MASSWILDLIFE

https://www.mass.gov/orgs/division-of-fisheries-and-wildlife

MassWildlife Field Headquarters
1 Rabbit Hill Road
Westborough, MA 01581
Phone: (508) 389-6300
Fax: (508) 389-7890
Email: **Mass.Wildlife@state.ma.us**

* MassFishHunt – Online portal for hunting/fishing licenses and reporting
https://www.ma.wildlifelicense.com/IS/Customer/InternetCustomerSearch

* MassFishHunt License Agent Map – Where to get a License in Person
https://www.mass.gov/service-details/massfishhunt-license-agent-map

USA Carry

https://www.usacarry.com/

This is a great resource for anything concealed carry. They have excellent reciprocity maps and stay up to date on agreements. Overall a good place to look at for firearms information across the country, especially if you carry.

APPENDIX B – IMPORTANT FORMS

* **Massachusetts Resident FID/LTC Application**
https://www.mass.gov/files/documents/2017/12/13/Updated%20LTC_FID%20card%20app%20-%20REVISED%2005.19.15.pdf

* **Massachusetts Non-Resident FID/LTC Application**
https://www.mass.gov/files/documents/2018/12/06/Non-resident%20Application%20-%20REVISED%2001.01.18_2.pdf

* **Mail in Criminal Offender Record Information (CORI) Personal Request Form**
https://www.mass.gov/files/2017-06/adult-personal-criminal-record-request-form.pdf

* **Change of Address Form for FID and LTC**
https://www.mass.gov/files/documents/2016/09/tf/change-of-address-notification-rev-08-20-13.pdf

* **Petition for Review by the Firearm Licensing Review Board**
https://www.mass.gov/files/documents/2016/09/sd/petition-and-instruction-letter.pdf

APPENDIX C – LETTER EXAMPLES

Reason Letter

Your Name
Your Address Line 1
Your Address Line 2
Your City, State Zip
Your Phone Number

Date

Chief of Police (His/Her Name if you know it)
Police Department Name
Police Department Address Line 1
Police Department City, State Zip

Dear Chief of Police (His/Her name if you know it):

I am currently applying for my LTC and would like it for "All Lawful Purposes," as this would cover any contingency/reason that I would ever need for its use. I am a devoted family man/woman to my wife/husband and children and as such, must think of their protection. I pray that I would never be forced into a situation by a criminal(s) that would put the lives of my family and or myself in jeopardy. So, while I hope for the best, I would like to be prepared for the worst, wherever I may lawfully do so.

I realize that there are bad people in the world that do not follow the laws of man nor God. As important as I know the jobs of policemen are, I am not naïve. I realize they cannot be everywhere at once, especially in our homes at night guarding us. Is anyone anywhere truly safe from a violent criminal act? Not if the news is correct. This is why I feel strongly that as the head of my household, the defense of my family is MY immediate duty and responsibility and it falls to me first and foremost.

Thank you sir for your understanding in this matter.

Cordially,

Your Signature

Your Name
CC: Your Attorney's Name

Letter of Recommendation

John Doe
John's Address Line 1
John's Address Line 2
John's City, State Zip
John's Phone Number

Date

Chief of Police (His/Her Name if you know it)
Police Department Name
Police Department Address Line 1
Police Department City, State Zip

Dear Chief of Police (*His/Her name if you know it*):

I have known *Your Name* for *X* number of years and have no reason to believe he/she should not attain a gun license. He/she has always been level headed in my view. Any questions please feel free to call me.

Thank you,

John Doe Signature

John Doe

Firearm Custody Letter in the Event of Confiscation

John Q. Doe II
John's Address Line 1
John's Address Line 2
John's City, State Zip
John's Phone Number

Date

Chief of Police (His/Her Name if you know it)
Police Department Name
Police Department Address Line 1
Police Department City, State Zip

Dear Chief of Police (*His/Her* name if you know it):

I John Q. Doe II, LTC # 12345678A, of 123 Main St. (name of town) zip code, phone #. With the permission of (person's name), who was recently under a 209A restraining order, will take transfer of said person's firearm(s) and ammunition as listed on the enclosed/attached copy of official inventory list, as is a legal procedure under H.4376 passed on 8-13-2014. I will keep them stored as to maintain compliance with applicable state firearm storage.

Sincerely,

signature

John Q. Doe II

Signature of person whose weapons were confiscated

Name of person whose weapons were confiscated.

APPENDIX D - Massachusetts General Law (M.G.L.) Chapter 140 Firearm Sections

Section 121: Firearms sales; definitions; antique firearms; application of law; exceptions

Section 121. As used in sections 122 to 131Q, inclusive, the following words shall, unless the context clearly requires otherwise, have the following meanings:?

"Ammunition", cartridges or cartridge cases, primers (igniter), bullets or propellant powder designed for use in any firearm, rifle or shotgun. The term "ammunition" shall also mean tear gas cartridges.

"Assault weapon", shall have the same meaning as a semiautomatic assault weapon as defined in the federal Public Safety and Recreational Firearms Use Protection Act, 18 U.S.C. section 921(a)(30) as appearing in such section on September 13, 1994, and shall include, but not be limited to, any of the weapons, or copies or duplicates of the weapons, of any caliber, known as: (i) Avtomat Kalashnikov (AK) (all models); (ii) Action Arms Israeli Military Industries UZI and Galil; (iii) Beretta Ar70 (SC?70); (iv) Colt AR?15; (v) Fabrique National FN/FAL, FN/LAR and FNC; (vi) SWD M?10, M?11, M?11/9 and M?12; (vi) Steyr AUG; (vii) INTRATEC TEC?9, TEC?DC9 and TEC?22; and (viii) revolving cylinder shotguns, such as, or similar to, the Street Sweeper and Striker 12; provided, however, that the term assault weapon shall not include: (i) any of the weapons, or replicas or duplicates of such weapons, specified in appendix A to 18 U.S.C. section 922 as appearing in such appendix on September 13, 1994, as such weapons were manufactured on October 1, 1993; (ii) any weapon that is operated by manual bolt, pump, lever or slide action; (iii) any weapon that has been rendered permanently inoperable or otherwise rendered permanently unable to be designated a semiautomatic assault weapon; (iv) any weapon that was manufactured prior to the year 1899; (v) any weapon that is an antique or relic, theatrical prop or other weapon that is not capable of firing a projectile and which is not intended for use as a functional weapon and cannot be readily modified through a combination of available parts into an operable assault weapon; (vi) any semiautomatic rifle that cannot accept a detachable magazine that holds more than five rounds of ammunition; or (vii) any semiautomatic shotgun that cannot hold more than five rounds of ammunition in a fixed or detachable magazine.

"Conviction", a finding or verdict of guilt or a plea of guilty, whether or not final sentence is imposed.

"Deceptive weapon device", any device that is intended to convey the presence of a rifle, shotgun or firearm that is used in the commission of a violent crime, as defined in this section, and which presents an objective threat of immediate death or serious bodily harm to a person of reasonable and average sensibility.

"Firearm", a pistol, revolver or other weapon of any description, loaded or unloaded, from which a shot or bullet can be discharged and of which the length of the barrel or barrels is less than 16 inches or 18 inches in the case of a shotgun as originally manufactured; provided, however, that the term firearm shall not include any weapon that is: (i) constructed in a shape that does not resemble a handgun, short-barreled rifle or short-barreled shotgun including, but not limited to, covert weapons that resemble key-chains, pens, cigarette-lighters or cigarette-packages; or (ii) not detectable as a weapon or potential weapon by x-ray machines commonly used at airports or walk- through metal detectors.

"Gunsmith", any person who engages in the business of repairing, altering, cleaning, polishing, engraving, blueing or performing any mechanical operation on any firearm, rifle, shotgun or machine gun.

"Imitation firearm", any weapon which is designed, manufactured or altered in such a way as to render it incapable of discharging a shot or bullet.

"Large capacity feeding device", (i) a fixed or detachable magazine, box, drum, feed strip or similar device capable of accepting, or that can be readily converted to accept, more than ten rounds of ammunition or more than five shotgun shells; or (ii) a large capacity ammunition feeding device as defined in the federal Public Safety and Recreational Firearms Use Protection Act, 18 U.S.C. section 921(a)(31) as appearing in such section on September 13, 1994. The term "large capacity feeding device" shall not include an attached tubular device designed to accept, and capable of operating only with,.22 caliber ammunition.

"Large capacity weapon", any firearm, rifle or shotgun: (i) that is semiautomatic with a fixed large capacity feeding device; (ii) that is semiautomatic and capable of accepting, or readily modifiable to accept, any detachable large capacity feeding device; (iii) that employs a rotating cylinder capable of accepting more than ten rounds of ammunition in a rifle or firearm and more than five shotgun shells in the case of a shotgun or firearm; or (iv) that is an assault weapon. The term "large capacity weapon" shall be a secondary designation and shall apply to a weapon in addition to its primary designation as a firearm, rifle or shotgun and shall not include: (i) any weapon that was manufactured in or prior to the year 1899; (ii) any weapon that operates by manual bolt, pump, lever or slide action; (iii) any weapon that is a single-shot weapon; (iv) any weapon that has been modified so as to render it permanently inoperable or otherwise rendered permanently unable to be designated a large capacity weapon; or (v) any weapon that is an antique or relic, theatrical prop or other weapon that is not capable of firing a projectile and which is not intended for use as a functional weapon and cannot be readily modified through a combination of available parts into an operable large capacity weapon.

"Length of barrel" or "barrel length", that portion of a firearm, rifle, shotgun or machine gun through which a shot or bullet is driven, guided or stabilized and shall include the chamber.

"Licensing authority", the Chief of police or the board or officer having control of the police in a city or town, or persons authorized by them.

"Machine gun", a weapon of any description, by whatever name known, loaded or unloaded, from which a number of shots or bullets may be rapidly or automatically discharged by one continuous activation of the trigger, including a submachine gun.

"Purchase" and "sale" shall include exchange; the word "purchaser" shall include exchanger; and the verbs "sell" and "purchase", in their different forms and tenses, shall include the verb exchange in its appropriate form and tense.

"Rifle", a weapon having a rifled bore with a barrel length equal to or greater than 16 inches and capable of discharging a shot or bullet for each pull of the trigger.

"Sawed-off shotgun", any weapon made from a shotgun, whether by alteration, modification or otherwise, if such weapon as modified has one or more barrels less than 18 inches in length or as modified has an overall length of less than 26 inches.

"Semiautomatic", capable of utilizing a portion of the energy of a firing cartridge to extract the fired cartridge case and chamber the next round, and requiring a separate pull of the trigger to fire each cartridge.

"Shotgun", a weapon having a smooth bore with a barrel length equal to or greater than 18 inches with an overall length equal to or greater than 26 inches, and capable of discharging a shot or bullet for each pull of the trigger.

"Violent crime", shall mean any crime punishable by imprisonment for a term exceeding one year, or any act of juvenile delinquency involving the use or possession of a deadly weapon that would be punishable by imprisonment for such term if committed by an adult, that: (i) has as an element the use, attempted use or threatened use of physical force or a deadly weapon against the person of another; (ii) is burglary, extortion, arson or kidnapping; (iii) involves the use of explosives; or (iv) otherwise involves conduct that presents a serious risk of physical injury to another.

"Weapon", any rifle, shotgun or firearm.

Where the local licensing authority has the power to issue licenses or cards under this chapter, but no such licensing authority exists, any resident or applicant may apply for such license or firearm identification card directly to the colonel of state police and said colonel shall for this purpose be the licensing authority.

The provisions of sections 122 to 129D, inclusive, and sections 131, 131A, 131B and 131E shall not apply to:

(A) any firearm, rifle or shotgun manufactured in or prior to the year 1899;

(B) any replica of any firearm, rifle or shotgun described in clause (A) if such replica: (i) is not designed or redesigned for using rimfire or conventional centerfire fixed ammunition; or (ii) uses rimfire or conventional centerfire fixed ammunition which is no longer manufactured in the United States and which is not readily available in the ordinary channels of commercial trade; and

(C) manufacturers or wholesalers of firearms, rifles, shotguns or machine guns.

Section 121A: Identification of firearms; certificate by ballistics expert as prima facie evidence

Section 121A. A certificate by a ballistics expert of the department of the state police or of the city of Boston of the result of an examination made by him of an item furnished him by any police officer, signed and sworn to by such expert, shall be prima facie evidence of his findings as to whether or not the item furnished is a firearm, rifle, shotgun, machine gun, sawed off shotgun or ammunition, as defined by section one hundred and twenty-one, provided that in order to qualify as an expert under this section he shall have previously qualified as an expert in a court proceeding.

Section 122: Licenses; contents; fingerprints of applicants; procedure on refusal of license; fees; punishment for improper issuance

Section 122. The Chief of police or the board or officer having control of the police in a city or town, or persons authorized by them, may, after an investigation into the criminal history of the applicant to determine eligibility for a license under this section, grant a license to any person except an alien, a minor, a person who has been adjudicated a youthful offender, as defined in section fifty-two of chapter one hundred and nineteen, including those who have not received an adult sentence or a person who has been convicted of a felony or of the unlawful use, possession or sale of narcotic or harmful drugs, to sell, rent or lease firearms, rifles, shotguns or machine guns, or to be in business as a gunsmith. Every license shall specify the street and number of the building where the business is to be carried on, and the license shall not protect a licensee who carries on his business in any other place. The licensing authority to whom such application is made shall cause one copy of said applicant's fingerprints to be forwarded to the department of the state police, who shall within a reasonable time thereafter advise such authority in writing of any criminal record of the applicant. The taking of fingerprints shall not be required in issuing a renewal of a license, if the fingerprints of said applicant are on file with the department of the state police. The licensing authority to whom such application is made shall cause one copy of such application to be forwarded to the commissioner of the department of criminal justice information services. Any person refused a license under this section may within ten days thereafter apply to the colonel of state police for such license, who may direct that said licensing authorities grant said license, if, after a hearing, he is satisfied there were no reasonable grounds for the refusal to grant such license and that the applicant was not barred by the provisions of law from holding such a license. The fee for an application for a license issued under this section shall be $100, which shall be payable to the licensing authority and shall not be prorated or refunded in case of revocation or denial. The licensing authority shall retain $25 of the fee; $50 of the fee shall be deposited into the general fund of the commonwealth; and $25 of the fee shall be deposited in the Firearms Fingerprint Identity Verification Trust Fund. A person licensed to sell, rent or lease firearms, rifles, shotguns or machine guns shall not be assessed any additional fee for a gunsmith's license. Whoever knowingly issues a license in violation of this section shall be punished by imprisonment for not less than six months nor more than two years in a jail or house of correction.

Section 122A: Record of licenses; notice to department of criminal justice information services; sales record books

Section 122A. The licensing authority, under section one hundred and twenty-two, shall record all issued licenses in books, forms or electronic files kept for that purpose, and upon the granting of any such license or renewal thereof or renewal of an expired license shall send notice thereof to the department of criminal justice information services in a manner prescribed by the commissioner of the department of criminal justice information services; provided, however, that said executive director shall promulgate rules and regulations to ensure the prompt collection, exchange, dissemination, and distribution of such license information. The commissioner of the department of criminal justice information services, upon the application of the licensee, at a price not in excess of the cost thereof, shall furnish said licensee with the necessary sales record books to be kept by him as provided in section one hundred and twenty-three.

Section 122B: Sale of ammunition; license; fees; rules and regulations; refusal, suspension or revocation of license; judicial review; penalties

Section 122B. No person shall sell ammunition in the commonwealth unless duly licensed. The Chief of police or the board or officer having control of the police in a city or town, or persons authorized by them, may, after an investigation into the criminal history of the applicant to determine eligibility to be licensed under this section, grant a license to any person, except an alien, a minor, a person who has been adjudicated a youthful offender, as defined in section fifty-two of chapter one hundred and nineteen, including those who have not received an adult sentence or a person who has been convicted of a felony in any state or federal jurisdiction, or of the unlawful use, possession or sale of narcotic or harmful drugs, to sell ammunition. Every license shall specify the street and number, if any, of the building where the business is to be carried on. The licensing authority to whom such application is made shall cause one copy of the application to be forwarded to the commissioner of the department of criminal justice information services, who shall within a reasonable time thereafter advise such authority in writing of any criminal record disqualifying the applicant. The fee for an application for a license to sell ammunition shall be $100, which shall be payable to the licensing authority and shall not be prorated or refunded in case of revocation or denial. The licensing authority shall retain $25 of the fee; $50 of the fee shall be deposited into the general fund of the commonwealth; and $25 of the fee shall be deposited in the Firearms Fingerprint Identity Verification Trust Fund. The licensing authority to whom such application is made shall cause one copy of any approved application to be forwarded to the commissioner of the department of criminal justice information services.

Any lawfully incorporated sporting or shooting club shall, upon application, be licensed to sell or supply ammunition for regulated shooting on their premises, as for skeet, target or trap shooting; provided, however, that such club license shall, in behalf of said club, be issued to and exercised by an officer or duly authorized member of the club who himself possesses a firearm identification card or a license to carry a firearm and who would not be disqualified to receive a license to sell ammunition in his own right. The licensing authority may revoke or suspend a license to sell ammunition for violation of any provision of this chapter.

The secretary of the executive office of public safety may establish such rules and regulations as he may deem necessary to carry out the provisions of this section.

Any person refused a license under this section or once issued a license under this section has had said license suspended or revoked may obtain a judicial review of such refusal, suspension or revocation by filing within thirty days of such refusal, suspension or revocation a petition for review thereof in the district court having jurisdiction in the city or town in which the applicant filed for such license, and a justice of said court, after a hearing, may direct that a license be issued the applicant if satisfied there was no reasonable ground for refusing such license and that the applicant was not prohibited by law from holding the same.

Whoever not being licensed, as hereinbefore provided, sells ammunition within the commonwealth shall be punished by a fine of not less than five hundred nor more than one thousand dollars or by imprisonment for not less than six months nor more than two years.

Section 122C: Illegal sale or possession of self-defense spray; penalty for violation

Section 122C. (a) As used in this section and section 122D, "self-defense spray" shall mean chemical mace, pepper spray or any device or instrument which contains, propels or emits a liquid, gas, powder or other substance designed to incapacitate.

(b) Whoever, not being licensed as provided in section 122B, sells self-defense spray shall be punished by a fine of not more than $1,000 or by imprisonment in a house of correction for not more than 2 years.

(c) Whoever sells self-defense spray to a person younger than 18 years of age, if the person younger than 18 years of age does not have a firearms identification card, shall be punished by a fine of not more than $300.

(d) A person under 18 years of age who possesses self-defense spray and who does not have a firearms identification card shall be punished by a fine of not more than $300.

Section 122D: Persons prohibited from purchase or possession of self-defense spray; penalty for violation

Section 122D. No person shall purchase or possess self-defense spray who:

(i) in a court of the commonwealth, has been convicted or adjudicated a youthful offender or delinquent child as defined in section 52 of chapter 119 for the commission of: (A) a felony; (B) a misdemeanor punishable by imprisonment for more than 2 years; (C) a violent crime as defined in section 121; (D) a violation of a law regulating the use, possession, ownership, transfer, purchase, sale, lease, rental, receipt or transportation of weapons or ammunition for which a term of imprisonment may be imposed; or (E) a violation of a law regulating the use, possession or sale of a controlled substance as defined in section 1 of chapter 94C including, but not limited to, a violation under said chapter 94C; provided, however, that except for the commission of a violent crime or a crime involving the trafficking of controlled substances, if the person has been so convicted or adjudicated or released from confinement, probation or parole supervision for such conviction or adjudication, whichever occurs last, for 5 or more years immediately preceding the purchase or possession, that person may purchase or possess self-defense spray;

(ii) in another state or federal jurisdiction, has been convicted or adjudicated a youthful offender or delinquent child for the commission of: (A) a felony; (B) a misdemeanor punishable by imprisonment for more than 2 years; (C) a violent crime as defined in section 121; (D) a violation of a law regulating the use, possession, ownership, transfer, purchase, sale, lease, rental, receipt or transportation of weapons or ammunition for which a term of imprisonment may be imposed; or (E) a violation of a law regulating the use, possession or sale of a controlled substance as defined in section 1 of chapter 94C; provided, however, that, except for the commission of a violent crime or a crime involving the trafficking of weapons or controlled substances, if the person has been so convicted or adjudicated or released from confinement, probation or parole supervision for such conviction or adjudication, whichever occurs last, for 5 or more years immediately preceding the purchase or possession and that applicant's right or ability to possess a rifle or shotgun has been fully restored in the jurisdiction wherein the subject conviction or adjudication was entered, then that person may purchase or possess self-defense spray;

(iii) has been committed to any hospital or institution for mental illness unless the person obtains, prior to purchase or possession, an affidavit of a licensed physician or clinical psychologist attesting that such physician or psychologist is familiar with the applicant's mental illness and that in the physician's or psychologist's opinion the applicant is not disabled by such an illness in a manner that shall prevent the applicant from possessing self-defense spray;

(iv) is or has been in recovery from or committed based upon a finding that the person is a person with an alcohol use disorder or a substance use disorder or both unless a licensed physician or clinical psychologist deems such person to be in recovery from such condition, in which case, such person may purchase or possess self-defense spray after 5 years from the date of such confinement or recovery; provided, however, that prior to such purchase or possession of self-defense spray, the applicant shall submit an affidavit issued by a licensed physician or clinical psychologist attesting that such physician or psychologist knows the person's history of treatment and that in that physician's or psychologist's opinion the applicant is in recovery;

(v) at the time of the application, is younger than 15 years of age;

(vi) at the time of the application, is at least 15 years of age but less than 18 years of age unless the applicant submits with the application a certificate from the applicant's parent or guardian granting the applicant permission to apply for a card;

(vii) is an alien who does not maintain lawful permanent residency or is an alien not residing under a visa pursuant to 8 U.S.C ? 1101(a)(15)(U), or is an alien not residing under a visa pursuant to 8 U.S.C. ? 1154(a)(1)(B)(ii)(I) or is an alien not residing under a visa pursuant to 8 U.S.C. ? 1101(a)(15)(T)(i)(I)?(IV);

(viii) is currently subject to: (1) an order for suspension or surrender issued pursuant to section 3B or 3C of chapter 209A or section 7 of chapter 258E; or (2) a permanent or temporary protection order issued pursuant to chapter 209A or section 7 of chapter 258E; or

(ix) is currently the subject of an outstanding arrest warrant in any state or federal jurisdiction.

Whoever purchases or possesses self-defense spray in violation of this section shall be punished by a fine of not more than $1,000 or by imprisonment in a house of correction for not more than 2 years or both such fine and imprisonment.

Section 123: Conditions of licenses

[First paragraph effective until January 1, 2021. For text effective January 1, 2021, see below.]

Section 123. A license granted under section one hundred and twenty-two shall be expressed to be and shall be subject to the following conditions:? First, That the provisions in regard to the nature of the license and the building in which the business may be carried on under it shall be strictly adhered to. Second, That every licensee shall, before delivery of a firearm, rifle or shotgun, make or cause to be made a true, legible entry in a sales record book to be furnished by the commissioner of the department of criminal justice information services and to be kept for that purpose, specifying the complete description of the firearm, rifle or shotgun, including the make, serial number, if any, type of firearm, rifle or shotgun, and designation as a large capacity weapon, if applicable, whether sold, rented or leased, the date of each sale, rental or lease, the license to carry firearms number or permit to purchase number and the identification card number in the case of a firearm or the identification card number or the license to carry firearms number in the case of a rifle or shotgun, the sex, residence and occupation of the purchaser, renter or lessee, and shall before delivery, as aforesaid, require the purchaser, renter or lessee personally to write in said sales record book his full name. Said book shall be open at all times to the inspection of the police. Third, That the license or a copy thereof, certified by the official issuing the same, shall be displayed on the premises in a position where it can easily be read. Fourth, That no firearm, rifle or shotgun, or machine gun shall be displayed in any outer window of said premises or in any other place where it can readily be seen from the outside. Fifth, That the licensee shall submit a record of all sales, rentals and leases forthwith at the time of such sale, rental or lease via electronic communication link to the commissioner of the department of criminal justice information services. Sixth, That every firearm, rifle or shotgun shall be unloaded when delivered. Seventh, That no delivery of a firearm shall be made to any person not having a license to carry firearms issued under the provisions of section one hundred and thirty-one nor shall any delivery of a rifle or shotgun or ammunition be made to any minor nor to any person not having a license to carry firearms issued under the provisions of section one hundred and thirty-one or a firearm identification card issued under the provisions of section one hundred and twenty-nine B nor shall any large capacity firearm or large capacity feeding device therefor be delivered to any person not having a Class A license to carry firearms issued under section 131 nor shall any large capacity rifle or shotgun or large capacity feeding device therefor be delivered to any person not having a Class A or Class B license to carry firearms issued under said section 131; provided, however, that delivery of a firearm by a licensee to a person possessing a valid permit to purchase said firearm issued under the provisions of section one hundred and thirty-one A and a valid firearm identification card issued under section one hundred and twenty-nine B may be made by the licensee to the purchaser's residence or place of business, subject to the restrictions imposed upon such permits as provided under section 131A. Eighth, That no firearm shall be sold, rented or leased to a minor or a person who has not a permit then in force to purchase, rent or lease the same issued under section one hundred and thirty-one A, and a firearm identification card issued under the provisions of section one hundred and twenty-nine B, or unless such person has a license to carry firearms issued under the provisions of section one hundred and thirty-one; nor shall any rifle or shotgun be sold, rented or leased to a person who has not a valid firearm identification card as provided for in section one hundred and twenty-nine B, or has a license to carry firearms as provided in section one hundred and thirty-one; that no large capacity firearm nor large capacity feeding device therefor shall be sold, rented, leased or transferred to any person not having (i) a Class A license to carry firearms issued under section 131 or (ii) a proper permit issued under section 131A and a firearm identification card issued under section 129B; that no large capacity rifle or shotgun nor large capacity feeding device therefor shall be sold to any person not having a Class A or Class B license to carry firearms issued under said section 131; and that no machine gun shall be sold, rented or leased to any person who has not a license to possess the same issued under section one hundred and thirty-one. Ninth, That upon the sale, rental or lease of a firearm, subject to a permit to purchase issued under the provisions of section one hundred and thirty-one A, the licensee under section one hundred and twenty-two shall take up such permit to purchase and shall endorse upon it the date and place of said sale, rental or lease, and shall transmit the same to the executive director of the criminal history systems board; and that upon the sale, rental or lease of a machine gun shall endorse upon the license to possess the same the date and place of said sale, rental or lease, and shall within seven days transmit a notice thereof to said executive director. In case of a sale under the provisions of section one hundred and thirty-one E the licensee under section one hundred and twenty-two shall write in the sales record book the number of the license to carry firearms issued the purchaser under the provisions of section one hundred and thirty-one, or the number of the firearm identification card issued the purchaser under the provisions of section one hundred and twenty-nine B, whichever is applicable under the provisions of condition Eighth of this section. Tenth, That this license shall be subject to forfeiture as provided in section one hundred and twenty-five for breach of any of its conditions, and that, if the licensee hereunder is convicted of a violation of any such conditions, this license shall thereupon become void. Eleventh, That the second, fifth, eighth and ninth conditions shall not apply to a gunsmith with regard to repair or remodeling or servicing of firearms, rifles or shotguns unless said gunsmith has manufactured a firearm, rifle or shotgun for the purchaser, but said gunsmith shall keep records of the work done by him together with the names and addresses of his customers. Such records shall be kept open for inspection by the police at all times. Twelfth, That any licensee shall keep records of each sale, rental or lease of a rifle or shotgun, specifying the description of said rifle or shotgun, together with the name and address of the purchaser, renter or lessee, and the date of such transaction. Thirteenth, That the current validity of any firearm identification card, license to carry firearms or permit to purchase, rent or lease firearms presented, and that the person presenting said card, license or permit is the lawful holder thereof, shall be verified by the licensee prior to any sale, rental or lease of a rifle, shotgun, firearm or large capacity feeding device; and, upon being presented with such card or license that is expired, suspended or revoked, the licensee shall notify the licensing authority of the presentment of such expired, suspended or revoked card, license or permit; and further, the licensee may take possession of such card or license provided that, in such case, such licensee shall: (i) issue a receipt, in a form provided by the commissioner of the department of criminal justice information services, to the holder thereof which shall state that the holder's card or license is expired, suspended or revoked, was taken by such licensee and forwarded to the licensing authority by whom it was issued and such receipt shall be valid for the date of issuance for the purpose of providing immunity from prosecution under section 10 of chapter 269 for unlawfully possessing a firearm, rifle or shotgun or large capacity weapon; (ii) notify the cardholder or licensee of his requirement to renew said card or license; and (iii) forward such expired card or license to the licensing authority forthwith; provided, however, that such licensee shall be immune from civil and criminal liability for good faith compliance with the provisions herein. Fourteenth, That the licensee shall conspicuously post at each purchase counter the following warning in bold type not less than one inch in height: "IT IS UNLAWFUL TO STORE OR KEEP A FIREARM, RIFLE, SHOTGUN OR MACHINE GUN IN ANY PLACE UNLESS THAT WEAPON IS EQUIPPED WITH A TAMPER-RESISTANT SAFETY DEVICE OR IS STORED OR KEPT IN A SECURELY LOCKED CONTAINER.", and that such licensee shall provide said warning, in writing, to the purchaser or transferee of any firearm, rifle, shotgun or machine gun in bold type not less than one-quarter inch in height, and further that the licensee shall conspicuously post and distribute at each purchase counter a notice providing information on suicide prevention developed and provided by the division on violence and injury prevention within the department of public health. The department of public health shall develop and make available on its website for download a sign providing the information on suicide prevention. Fifteenth, That all licensees shall maintain a permanent place of business that is not a residence or dwelling wherein all transactions described in this section shall be conducted and wherein all records required to be kept under this section shall be so kept. Sixteenth, That no licensee shall sell, lease, rent, transfer or deliver or offer for sale, lease, rent, transfer or delivery to any person any assault weapon or large capacity feeding device that was not otherwise lawfully possessed on September 13, 1994. Seventeenth, That any licensee from whom a rifle, shotgun, firearm or machine gun is lost or stolen shall report such loss or theft to the licensing authority and the executive director of the criminal history systems board forthwith. Such report shall include a complete description of the weapon, including the make, model, serial number and caliber and whether such weapon is a large capacity weapon. Eighteenth, That no licensee shall sell, rent, lease, transfer or deliver or offer for sale, lease, transfer or delivery any firearm, to any purchaser in the commonwealth unless such sale is to a business entity that is primarily a firearm wholesaler and the sale, by its terms, prohibits the purchaser from reselling such firearm to a firearm retailer or consumer in the commonwealth if such firearm has a frame, barrel, cylinder, slide or breechblock that is composed of: (i) any metal having a melting point of less than 900 degrees Fahrenheit; (ii) any metal having an ultimate tensile strength of less than 55,000 pounds per square inch; or (iii) any powdered metal having a density of less than 7.5 grams per cubic centimeter. This clause shall not apply to any make and model of firearm for which a sample of three firearms in new condition all pass the following test: Each of the three samples shall fire 600 rounds, stopping every 100 rounds to tighten any loose screws and to clean the gun if required by the cleaning schedule in the user manual, and as needed to refill the empty magazine or cylinder to capacity before continuing. For any firearm that is loaded in a manner other than via a detachable magazine, the tester shall also pause every 50 rounds for ten minutes. The ammunition used shall be the type recommended by the firearm manufacturer in its user manual or, if none is recommended, any standard ammunition of the correct caliber in new condition. A firearm shall pass this test if it fires the first 20 rounds without a malfunction, fires the full 600 rounds with not more than six malfunctions and completes the test without any crack or breakage of an operating part of the firearm. The term "crack" or "breakage" shall not include a crack or breakage that does not increase the danger of injury to the user. For purposes of evaluating the results of this test, malfunction shall mean any failure to feed, chamber, fire, extract or eject a round or any failure to accept or eject a magazine or any other failure which prevents the firearm, without manual intervention beyond that needed for routine firing and periodic reloading, from firing the chambered round or moving a new round into position so that the firearm is capable of firing the new round properly. "Malfunction" shall not include a misfire caused by a faulty cartridge the primer of which fails to detonate when properly struck by the firearm's firing mechanism. Nineteenth, That no licensee shall sell, rent, lease, transfer or deliver or offer for sale, lease, transfer or delivery any firearm to any purchaser in the commonwealth unless such sale is to a business entity that is primarily a firearms wholesaler, and the sale, by its terms, prohibits such purchaser from reselling such firearm to a firearm retailer or consumer in the commonwealth if such firearm is prone to accidental discharge which, for purposes of this clause, shall mean any make and model of firearm for which a sample of five firearms in new condition all undergo, and none discharge during, the following test: Each of the five sample firearms shall be: (a) test loaded; (b) set so that the firearm is in a condition such that pulling the trigger and taking any action that must simultaneously accompany the pulling of the trigger as part of the firing procedure would fire the handgun; and (c) dropped onto a solid slab of concrete from a height of one meter from each of the following positions: (i) normal firing position; (ii) upside down; (iii) on grip; (iv) on the muzzle; (v) on either side; and (vi) on the exposed hammer or striker or, if there is no exposed hammer or striker, the rearmost part of the firearm. If the firearm is designed so that its hammer or striker may be set in other positions, each sample firearm shall be tested as above with the hammer or striker in each such position but otherwise in such condition that pulling the trigger, and taking any action that must simultaneously accompany the pulling of the trigger as part of the firing procedure, would fire the firearm. Alternatively, the tester may use additional sample firearms of the same make and model, in a similar condition, for the test of each of these hammer striker settings. Twentieth, That no licensee shall sell, rent, lease, transfer or deliver or offer for sale, lease, transfer or delivery, any firearm to any purchaser in the commonwealth unless such sale is to a business entity that is primarily a firearm wholesaler, and the sale, by its terms, prohibits the purchaser from reselling such firearm to a firearm retailer or consumer in the commonwealth if such firearm is prone to: (i) firing more than once per pull of the trigger; or (ii) explosion during firing. Twenty-first, That no licensee shall sell, rent, lease, transfer or deliver or offer for sale, lease, transfer or delivery any firearm to any purchaser in the commonwealth unless such sale is to a business entity that is primarily a firearm wholesaler and the sale, by its terms, prohibits the purchaser from reselling such firearm to a firearm retailer or consumer in the commonwealth if such firearm has a barrel less than three inches in length, unless the licensee discloses in writing, prior to the transaction, to the prospective buyer, lessee, deliveree or transferee the limitations of the accuracy of the particular make and model of the subject firearm, by disclosing the make and model's average group diameter test result at seven yards, average group diameter test result at 14 yards and average group diameter test result at 21 yards. For purposes of this clause, "average group diameter test result" shall mean the arithmetic mean of three separate trials, each performed as follows on a different sample firearm in new condition of the make and model at issue. Each firearm shall fire five rounds at a target from a set distance and the largest spread in inches between the centers of any of the holes made in a test target shall be measured and recorded. This procedure shall be repeated two more times on the firearm. The arithmetic mean of each of the three recorded results shall be deemed the result of the trial for that particular sample firearm. The ammunition used shall be the type recommended by the firearm manufacturer in its user manual or, if none is recommended, any standard ammunition of the correct caliber in new condition. No licensee shall sell any rifle or shotgun, contrary to the provisions of section one hundred and thirty or section 131E.

[First paragraph as amended by 2014, 284, Secs. 23 and 24 effective January 1, 2021. See 2014, 284, Sec. 112. For text effective until January 1, 2021, see above.]

A license granted under section one hundred and twenty-two shall be expressed to be and shall be subject to the following conditions:? First, That the provisions in regard to the nature of the license and the building in which the business may be carried on under it shall be strictly adhered to. Second, That every licensee shall, before delivery of a firearm, rifle or shotgun, make or cause to be made a true, legible entry in a sales record book to be furnished by the commissioner of the department of criminal justice information services and to be kept for that purpose, specifying the complete description of the firearm, rifle or shotgun, including the make, serial number, if any, type of firearm, rifle or shotgun, and designation as a large capacity weapon, if applicable, whether sold, rented or leased, the date of each sale, rental or lease, the license to carry firearms number or permit to purchase number and the identification card number in the case of a firearm or the identification card number or the license to carry firearms number in the case of a rifle or shotgun, the sex, residence and occupation of the purchaser, renter or lessee, and shall before delivery, as aforesaid, require the purchaser, renter or lessee personally to write in said sales record book his full name. Said book shall be open at all times to the inspection of the police. Third, That the license or a copy thereof, certified by the official issuing the same, shall be displayed on the premises in a position where it can easily be read. Fourth, That no firearm, rifle or shotgun, or machine gun shall be displayed in any outer window of said premises or in any other place where it can readily be seen from the outside. Fifth, That the licensee shall submit a record of all sales, rentals and leases forthwith at the time of such sale, rental or lease via electronic communication link to the commissioner of the department of criminal justice information services. Sixth, That every firearm, rifle or shotgun shall be unloaded when delivered. Seventh, That no delivery of a firearm shall be made to any person not having a license to carry firearms issued under the provisions of section one hundred and thirty-one nor shall any delivery of a rifle or shotgun or ammunition be made to any minor nor to any person not having a license to carry firearms issued under the provisions of section one hundred and thirty-one or a firearm identification card issued under the provisions of section one hundred and twenty-nine B nor shall any large capacity firearm or large capacity feeding device therefor be delivered to any person not having a license to carry firearms issued under section 131 nor shall any large capacity rifle or shotgun or large capacity feeding device therefor be delivered to any person not having a license to carry firearms issued under said section 131; provided, however, that delivery of a firearm by a licensee to a person possessing a valid permit to purchase said firearm issued under the provisions of section one hundred and thirty-one A and a valid firearm identification card issued under section one hundred and twenty-nine B may be made by the licensee to the purchaser's residence or place of business, subject to the restrictions imposed upon such permits as provided under section 131A. Eighth, That no firearm shall be sold, rented or leased to a minor or a person who has not a permit then in force to purchase, rent or lease the same issued under section one hundred and thirty-one A, and a firearm identification card issued under the provisions of section one hundred and twenty-nine B, or unless such person has a license to carry firearms issued under the provisions of section one hundred and thirty-one; nor shall any rifle or shotgun be sold, rented or leased to a person who has not a valid firearm identification card as provided for in section one hundred and twenty-nine B, or has a license to carry firearms as provided in section one hundred and thirty-one; that no large capacity firearm nor large capacity feeding device therefor shall be sold, rented, leased or transferred to any person not having (i) a license to carry firearms issued under section 131 or (ii) a proper permit issued under section 131A and a firearm identification card issued under section 129B; that no large capacity rifle or shotgun nor large capacity feeding device therefor shall be sold to any person not having a license to carry firearms issued under said section 131; and that no machine gun shall be sold, rented or leased to any person who has not a license to possess the same issued under section one hundred and thirty-one. Ninth, That upon the sale, rental or lease of a firearm, subject to a permit to purchase issued under the provisions of section one hundred and thirty-one A, the licensee under section one hundred and twenty-two shall take up such permit to purchase and shall endorse upon it the date and place of said sale, rental or lease, and shall transmit the same to the executive director of the criminal history systems board; and that upon the sale, rental or lease of a machine gun shall endorse upon the license to possess the same the date and place of said sale, rental or lease, and shall within seven days transmit a notice thereof to said executive director. In case of a sale under the provisions of section one hundred and thirty-one E the licensee under section one hundred and twenty-two shall write in the sales record book the number of the license to carry firearms issued the purchaser under the provisions of section one hundred and thirty-one, or the number of the firearm identification card issued the purchaser under the provisions of section one hundred and twenty-nine B, whichever is applicable under the provisions of condition Eighth of this section. Tenth, That this license shall be subject to forfeiture as provided in section one hundred and twenty-five for breach of any of its conditions, and that, if the licensee hereunder is convicted of a violation of any such conditions, this license shall thereupon become void. Eleventh, That the second, fifth, eighth and ninth conditions shall not apply to a gunsmith with regard to repair or remodeling or servicing of firearms, rifles or shotguns unless said gunsmith has manufactured a firearm, rifle or shotgun for the purchaser, but said gunsmith shall keep records of the work done by him together with the names and addresses of his customers. Such records shall be kept open for inspection by the police at all times. Twelfth, That any licensee shall keep records of each sale, rental or lease of a rifle or shotgun, specifying the description of said rifle or shotgun, together with the name and address of the purchaser, renter or lessee, and the date of such transaction. Thirteenth, That the current validity of any firearm identification card, license to carry firearms or permit to purchase, rent or lease firearms presented, and that the person presenting said card, license or permit is the lawful holder thereof, shall be verified by the licensee prior to any sale, rental or lease of a rifle, shotgun, firearm or large capacity feeding device; and, upon being presented with such card or license that is expired, suspended or revoked, the licensee shall notify the licensing authority of the presentment of such expired, suspended or revoked card, license or permit; and further, the licensee may take possession of such card or license provided that, in such case, such licensee shall: (i) issue a receipt, in a form provided by the commissioner of the department of criminal justice information services, to the holder thereof which shall state that the holder's card or license is expired, suspended or revoked, was taken by such licensee and forwarded to the licensing authority by whom it was issued and such receipt shall be valid for the date of issuance for the purpose of providing immunity from prosecution under section 10 of chapter 269 for unlawfully possessing a firearm, rifle or shotgun or large capacity weapon; (ii) notify the cardholder or licensee of his requirement to renew said card or license; and (iii) forward such expired card or license to the licensing authority forthwith; provided, however, that such licensee shall be immune from civil and criminal liability for good faith compliance with the provisions herein. Fourteenth, That the licensee shall conspicuously post at each purchase counter the following warning in bold type not less than one inch in height: "IT IS UNLAWFUL TO STORE OR KEEP A FIREARM, RIFLE, SHOTGUN OR MACHINE GUN IN ANY PLACE UNLESS THAT WEAPON IS EQUIPPED WITH A TAMPER-RESISTANT SAFETY DEVICE OR IS STORED OR KEPT IN A SECURELY LOCKED CONTAINER.", and that such licensee shall provide said warning, in writing, to the purchaser or transferee of any firearm, rifle, shotgun or machine gun in bold type not less than one-quarter inch in height, and further that the licensee shall conspicuously post and distribute at each purchase counter a notice providing information on suicide prevention developed and provided by the division on violence and injury prevention within the department of public health. The department of public health shall develop and make available on its website for download a sign providing the information on suicide prevention. Fifteenth, That all licensees shall maintain a permanent place of business that is not a residence or dwelling wherein all transactions described in this section shall be conducted and wherein all records required to be kept under this section shall be so kept. Sixteenth, That no licensee shall sell, lease, rent, transfer or deliver or offer for sale, lease, rent, transfer or delivery to any person any assault weapon or large capacity feeding device that was not otherwise lawfully possessed on

September 13, 1994. Seventeenth, That any licensee from whom a rifle, shotgun, firearm or machine gun is lost or stolen shall report such loss or theft to the licensing authority and the executive director of the criminal history systems board forthwith. Such report shall include a complete description of the weapon, including the make, model, serial number and caliber and whether such weapon is a large capacity weapon. Eighteenth, That no licensee shall sell, rent, lease, transfer or deliver or offer for sale, lease, transfer or delivery any firearm, to any purchaser in the commonwealth unless such sale is to a business entity that is primarily a firearm wholesaler and the sale, by its terms, prohibits the purchaser from reselling such firearm to a firearm retailer or consumer in the commonwealth if such firearm has a frame, barrel, cylinder, slide or breechblock that is composed of: (i) any metal having a melting point of less than 900 degrees Fahrenheit; (ii) any metal having an ultimate tensile strength of less than 55,000 pounds per square inch; or (iii) any powdered metal having a density of less than 7.5 grams per cubic centimeter. This clause shall not apply to any make and model of firearm for which a sample of three firearms in new condition all pass the following test: Each of the three samples shall fire 600 rounds, stopping every 100 rounds to tighten any loose screws and to clean the gun if required by the cleaning schedule in the user manual, and as needed to refill the empty magazine or cylinder to capacity before continuing. For any firearm that is loaded in a manner other than via a detachable magazine, the tester shall also pause every 50 rounds for ten minutes. The ammunition used shall be the type recommended by the firearm manufacturer in its user manual or, if none is recommended, any standard ammunition of the correct caliber in new condition. A firearm shall pass this test if it fires the first 20 rounds without a malfunction, fires the full 600 rounds with not more than six malfunctions and completes the test without any crack or breakage of an operating part of the firearm. The term "crack" or "breakage" shall not include a crack or breakage that does not increase the danger of injury to the user. For purposes of evaluating the results of this test, malfunction shall mean any failure to feed, chamber, fire, extract or eject a round or any failure to accept or eject a magazine or any other failure which prevents the firearm, without manual intervention beyond that needed for routine firing and periodic reloading, from firing the chambered round or moving a new round into position so that the firearm is capable of firing the new round properly. "Malfunction" shall not include a misfire caused by a faulty cartridge the primer of which fails to detonate when properly struck by the firearm's firing mechanism. Nineteenth, That no licensee shall sell, rent, lease, transfer or deliver or offer for sale, lease, transfer or delivery any firearm to any purchaser in the commonwealth unless such sale is to a business entity that is primarily a firearms wholesaler, and the sale, by its terms, prohibits such purchaser from reselling such firearm to a firearm retailer or consumer in the commonwealth if such firearm is prone to accidental discharge which, for purposes of this clause, shall mean any make and model of firearm for which a sample of five firearms in new condition all undergo, and none discharge during, the following test: Each of the five sample firearms shall be: (a) test loaded; (b) set so that the firearm is in a condition such that pulling the trigger and taking any action that must simultaneously accompany the pulling of the trigger as part of the firing procedure would fire the handgun; and (c) dropped onto a solid slab of concrete from a height of one meter from each of the following positions: (i) normal firing position; (ii) upside down; (iii) on grip; (iv) on the muzzle; (v) on either side; and (vi) on the exposed hammer or striker or, if there is no exposed hammer or striker, the rearmost part of the firearm. If the firearm is designed so that its hammer or striker may be set in other positions, each sample firearm shall be tested as above with the hammer or striker in each such position but otherwise in such condition that pulling the trigger, and taking any action that must simultaneously accompany the pulling of the trigger as part of the firing procedure, would fire the firearm. Alternatively, the tester may use additional sample firearms of the same make and model, in a similar condition, for the test of each of these hammer striker settings. Twentieth, That no licensee shall sell, rent, lease, transfer or deliver or offer for sale, lease, transfer or delivery, any firearm to any purchaser in the commonwealth unless such sale is to a business entity that is primarily a firearm wholesaler, and the sale, by its terms, prohibits the purchaser from reselling such firearm to a firearm retailer or consumer in the commonwealth if such firearm is prone to: (i) firing more than once per pull of the trigger; or (ii) explosion during firing. Twenty-first, That no licensee shall sell, rent, lease, transfer or deliver or offer for sale, lease, transfer or delivery any firearm to any purchaser in the commonwealth unless such sale is to a business entity that is primarily a firearm wholesaler and the sale, by its terms, prohibits the purchaser from reselling such firearm to a firearm retailer or consumer in the commonwealth if such firearm has a barrel less than three inches in length, unless the licensee discloses in writing, prior to the transaction, to the prospective buyer, lessee, deliveree or transferee the limitations of the accuracy of the particular make and model of the subject firearm, by disclosing the make and model's average group diameter test result at seven yards, average group diameter test result at 14 yards and average group diameter test result at 21 yards. For purposes of this clause, "average group diameter test result" shall mean the arithmetic mean of three separate trials, each performed as follows on a different sample firearm in new condition of the make and model at issue. Each firearm shall fire five rounds at a target from a set distance and the largest spread in inches between the centers of any of the holes made in a test target shall be measured and recorded. This procedure shall be repeated two more times on the firearm. The arithmetic mean of each of the three recorded results shall be deemed the result of the trial for that particular sample firearm. The ammunition used shall be the type recommended by the firearm manufacturer in its user manual or, if none is recommended, any standard ammunition of the correct caliber in new condition. No licensee shall sell any rifle or shotgun, contrary to the provisions of section one hundred and thirty or section 131E.

Clauses Eighteenth to Twenty-first, inclusive, of the first paragraph shall not apply to: (i) a firearm lawfully owned or possessed under a license issued under this chapter on or before October 21, 1998; (ii) a firearm designated by the secretary of public safety, with the advice of the gun control advisory board, established pursuant to section 1311/2 of chapter 140, as a firearm solely designed and sold for formal target shooting competition; or (iii) a firearm designated by the secretary of public safety, with the advice of the gun control advisory board, established pursuant to section 131 1/2 of chapter 140, as a firearm or pistol solely designed and sold for Olympic shooting competition. The secretary of public safety shall compile lists, on a bi-annual basis, of firearms designated as "formal target shooting firearms" and "Olympic competition firearms" in accordance with this paragraph. Such lists shall be made available for distribution by the executive office of public safety and security.

No person licensed under the provisions of section 122 or section 122B shall sell, rent, lease, transfer or deliver any rifle, shotgun or firearm or ammunition or ammunition feeding device contrary to the provisions of section 130 or section 131E; and no such licensee shall sell, rent, lease, transfer or deliver any rifle, shotgun or firearm or ammunition or ammunition feeding device to any person who does not have in his possession the required firearm identification card or proof of exemption therefrom, license to carry firearms or permit to purchase, rent or lease firearms and who does not present such card, proof, license or permit to the licensee in person at the time of purchase, rental or lease. No person licensed under the provisions of section 122 or section 122B shall fill an order for such weapon, ammunition or ammunition feeding device that was received by mail, facsimile, telephone or other telecommunication unless such transaction or transfer includes the in-person presentation of the required card, proof, license or permit as required herein prior to any sale, delivery or any form of transfer of possession of the subject weapon, ammunition or ammunition feeding device. Transactions between persons licensed under section 122 or between federally licensed dealers shall be exempt from the provisions of this paragraph.

The licensing authority shall enter, one time per calendar year, during regular business hours, the commercial premises owned or leased by any licensee, wherein such records required to be maintained under this section are stored or maintained, and inspect, in a reasonable manner, such records and inventory for the purpose of enforcing the provisions of this section. If such records and inventory contain evidence of violations of this section, the inspecting officer shall produce and take possession of copies of such records and, in the event that the licensee subject to inspection does not possess copying equipment, the inspecting officer shall arrange to have copied, in a reasonable time and manner, such records that contain evidence of such violations and the costs for such copying shall be assessed against the owner of such records. Licensees found to be in violation of this section shall be subject to the suspension or permanent revocation of such license issued under section 122 and to the provisions of section 128. Nothing herein shall prohibit the licensing authority or the department of state police from conducting such inspections pursuant to a valid search warrant issued by a court of competent jurisdiction.

Notwithstanding the provisions of this section, a person licensed under the provisions of section one hundred and twenty-two, or section one hundred and twenty-two B, may sell or transfer firearms, rifles, shotguns, machine guns or ammunition at any regular meeting of an incorporated collectors club or at a gun show open to the general public; provided, however, that all other provisions of this section are complied with and that such sale or transfer is in conformity with federal law or regulations applicable to the transfer or sale of firearms, rifles, shotguns, machine guns or ammunition, including the restrictions imposed upon firearm identification cards issued under section 129B, licenses to carry firearms issued under section 131 and permits to purchase, lease or rent firearms issued under section 131A.

Section 124: Term of licenses

Section 124. Licenses issued under sections one hundred and twenty-two and one hundred and twenty-two B shall expire three years from the date of issuance.

Section 125: Forfeiture or suspension of licenses; notice

Section 125. The officials authorized to issue a license under section one hundred and twenty-two, after due notice to the licensee and reasonable opportunity for him to be heard, may declare his license forfeited, or may suspend his license for such period of time as they may deem proper, upon satisfactory proof that he has violated or permitted a violation of any condition thereof or has violated any provision of this chapter, or has been convicted of a felony. The pendency of proceedings before a court shall not suspend or interfere with the power to declare a forfeiture. If the license is declared forfeited, the licensee shall be disqualified to receive a license for one year after the expiration of the term of the license so forfeited. The commissioner of the department of criminal justice information services shall be notified in writing of any forfeiture under this section.

Section 126: Placards, signs or advertisements; prima facie evidence

Section 126. If there is exposed from, maintained in or permitted to remain on any vehicle or premises any placard, sign or advertisement purporting or designed to announce that firearms, rifles, shotguns or machine guns are kept in or upon such vehicle or premises or that an occupant of any vehicle or premises is a gunsmith, it shall be prima facie evidence that firearms, rifles, shotguns or machine guns are kept in or upon such vehicle or premises for sale or that the occupant is engaged in business as a gunsmith.

Section 127: Transfer of licenses

Section 127. The officials authorized to issue a license under section one hundred and twenty-two may transfer licenses from one location to another within the city or town in which the licenses are in force, but such transfer shall be granted only to the original licensee and upon the same terms and conditions upon which the license was originally granted. The commissioner of the department of criminal justice information services shall be notified in writing of any transfers made under this section.

Section 128: Penalty for violation of statute on selling, renting or leasing weapons; evidence on sale of machine gun

Section 128. Any licensee under a license described in section one hundred and twenty-three, and any employee or agent of such a licensee, who violates any provision of said section required to be expressed in the second, fourth, sixth, seventh, eighth, ninth, sixteenth, seventeenth, eighteenth, nineteenth, twentieth or twenty-first condition of said license, and except as provided in section one hundred and twenty-eight A, any person who, without being licensed as hereinbefore provided, sells, rents or leases a firearm, rifle, shotgun or machine gun, or is engaged in business as a gunsmith, shall be punished by a fine of not less than $1,000 nor more than $10,000, or by imprisonment for not less than one year nor more than ten years, or by both such fine and imprisonment.

Evidence that a person sold or attempted to sell a machine gun without being licensed under section one hundred and twenty-three shall, in a prosecution under this section, constitute prima facie evidence that such person is engaged in the business of selling machine guns.

Section 128A: Application of Sec. 128

Section 128A. The provisions of section one hundred and twenty-eight shall not apply to any person who, without being licensed as provided in section one hundred and twenty-two, sells or transfers a firearm, rifle or shotgun to a person licensed under said section one hundred and twenty-two, or to a federally licensed firearms dealer or to a federal, state or local historical society, museum or institutional collection open to the public. The provisions of section one hundred and twenty-eight shall not apply to any resident of the commonwealth who, without being licensed as provided in section one hundred and twenty-two, sells or transfers to other than a federally licensed firearms dealer or organization named above not more than four firearms, including rifles and shotguns in any one calendar year; provided, however, that the seller has a firearm identification card or a license to carry firearms, is an exempt person under the conditions of clauses (n), (o), (r) and (s) of the fourth paragraph of section one hundred and twenty-nine C, or is permitted to transfer ownership under the conditions of section one hundred and twenty-nine D and the purchaser has, in the case of sale or transfer of a firearm, a permit to purchase issued under the provisions of section one hundred and thirty-one A and a firearm identification card issued under section one hundred and twenty-nine B, or has such permit to purchase and is an exempt person under the provisions of section one hundred and twenty-nine C, or has been issued a license to carry firearms under the provisions of section one hundred and thirty, or in the case of sale or transfer of a rifle or shotgun, the purchaser has a firearm identification card or a license to carry firearms or is an exempt person as hereinbefore stated. Any sale or transfer conducted pursuant to this section shall comply with section 131E and shall, prior to or at the point of sale, be conducted over a real time web portal developed by the department of criminal justice information services. The department of criminal justice information services shall require each person selling or transferring a firearm, shotgun or rifle pursuant to this section to electronically provide, though the portal, such information as is determined to be necessary to verify the identification of the seller and purchaser and ensure that the sale or transfer complies with this section. Upon submission of the required information, the portal shall automatically review such information and display a message indicating whether the seller may proceed with the sale or transfer and shall provide any further instructions for the seller as determined to be necessary by the department of criminal justice information services. The department of criminal justice information services shall keep a record of any sale or transfer conducted pursuant to this section and shall provide the seller and purchaser with verification of such sale or transfer.

Section 128B: Unauthorized purchase of firearms; report to commissioner; penalties

Section 128B. Any resident of the commonwealth who purchases or obtains a firearm, rifle or shotgun or machine gun from any source within or without the commonwealth, other than from a licensee under section one hundred and twenty-two or a person authorized to sell firearms under section one hundred and twenty-eight A, and any nonresident of the commonwealth who purchases or obtains a firearm, rifle, shotgun or machine gun from any source within or without the commonwealth, other than such a licensee or person, and receives such firearm, rifle, shotgun or machine gun, within the commonwealth shall within seven days after receiving such firearm, rifle, shotgun or machine gun, report, in writing, to the commissioner of the department of criminal justice information services the name and address of the seller or donor and the buyer or donee, together with a complete description of the firearm, rifle, shotgun or machine gun, including the caliber, make and serial number. Whoever violates any provision of this section shall for the first offense be punished by a fine of not less than $500 nor more than $1,000 and for any subsequent offense by imprisonment in the state prison for not more than ten years.

Section 129: Fictitious name or address and other false information; penalties

Section 129. Whoever in purchasing, renting or hiring a firearm, rifle, shotgun or machine gun, or in making application for any form of license or permit issued in connection therewith, or in requesting that work be done by a gunsmith, gives a false or fictitious name or address or knowingly offers or gives false information concerning the date or place of birth, his citizenship status, occupation, or criminal record, shall for the first offense be punished by a fine of not less than five hundred nor more than one thousand dollars, or by imprisonment for not more than one year, or both; and for a second or subsequent offense, shall be punished by imprisonment for not less than two and one half years nor more than five years in the state prison.

Section 129A: Repealed, 1945, 254

Section 129B: Firearm identification cards; conditions and restrictions

Section 129B. A firearm identification card shall be issued and possessed subject to the following conditions and restrictions:

(1) Any person residing or having a place of business within the jurisdiction of the licensing authority or any person residing in an area of exclusive federal jurisdiction located within a city or town may submit to the licensing authority an application for a firearm identification card, or renewal of the same, which the licensing authority shall issue if it appears that the applicant is not a prohibited person. A prohibited person shall be a person who:

(i) has ever, in a court of the commonwealth, been convicted or adjudicated a youthful offender or delinquent child, or both as defined in section 52 of chapter 119, for the commission of: (A) a felony; (B) a misdemeanor punishable by imprisonment for more than 2 years ; (C) a violent crime as defined in section 121; (D) a violation of any law regulating the use, possession, ownership, transfer, purchase, sale, lease, rental, receipt or transportation of weapons or ammunition for which a term of imprisonment may be imposed; (E) a violation of any law regulating the use, possession or sale of controlled substances, as defined in section 1 of chapter 94C, including, but not limited to, a violation under said chapter 94C; or (F) a misdemeanor crime of domestic violence as defined in 18 U.S.C. 921(a)(33); provided, however, that, except for the commission of a felony, a misdemeanor crime of domestic violence, a violent crime or a crime involving the trafficking of controlled substances, if the applicant has been so convicted or adjudicated or released from confinement, probation or parole supervision for such conviction or adjudication, whichever occurs last, for 5 or more years immediately preceding such application, then the applicant's right or ability to possess a non-large capacity rifle or shotgun shall be deemed restored in the commonwealth with respect to such conviction or adjudication and that conviction or adjudication shall not disqualify the applicant for a firearm identification card;

(ii) has, in any other state or federal jurisdiction, been convicted or adjudicated a youthful offender or delinquent child for the commission of: (A) a felony; (B) a misdemeanor punishable by imprisonment for more than 2 years; (C) a violent crime as defined in section 121; (D) a violation of any law regulating the use, possession, ownership, transfer, purchase, sale, lease, rental, receipt or transportation of weapons or ammunition for which a term of imprisonment may be imposed; (E) a violation of any law regulating the use, possession or sale of controlled substances, as defined in section 1 of chapter 94C, including, but not limited to, a violation under said chapter 94C; or (F) a misdemeanor crime of domestic violence as defined in 18 U.S.C. 921(a)(33); provided, however, that, except for the commission of felony, a misdemeanor crime of domestic violence, a violent crime or a crime involving the trafficking of weapons or controlled substances, if the applicant has been so convicted or adjudicated or released from confinement, probation or parole supervision for such conviction or adjudication, whichever occurs last, for 5 or more years immediately preceding such application and the applicant's right or ability to possess a rifle or shotgun has been fully restored in the jurisdiction wherein the conviction or adjudication was entered, then the conviction or adjudication shall not disqualify such applicant for a firearm identification card;

(iii) is or has been: (A) except in the case of a commitment pursuant to sections 35 or 36C of chapter 123, committed to any hospital or institution for mental illness, alcohol or substance abuse, unless after 5 years from the date of the confinement, the applicant submits with the application an affidavit of a licensed physician or clinical psychologist attesting that such physician or psychologist is familiar with the applicant's mental illness, alcohol or substance abuse and that in the physician's or psychologist's opinion the applicant is not disabled by a mental illness, alcohol or substance abuse in a manner that should prevent the applicant from possessing a firearm, rifle or shotgun; (B) committed by an order of a court to any hospital or institution for mental illness, unless the applicant was granted a petition for relief of the court's order pursuant to said section 36C of said chapter 123 and submits a copy of the order for relief with the application; (C) subject to an order of the probate court appointing a guardian or conservator for a incapacitated person on the grounds that that applicant lacks the mental capacity to contract or manage affairs, unless the applicant was granted a petition for relief pursuant to section 56C of chapter 215 and submits a copy of the order for relief with the application; or (D) found to be a person with an alcohol use disorder or substance use disorder or both and committed pursuant to said section 35 of said chapter 123, unless the applicant was granted a petition for relief of the court's order pursuant to said section

35 of said chapter 123 and submits a copy of the order for relief with the application;

(iv) is at the time of the application younger than 14 years of age; provided however that the applicant shall not be issued the card until the applicant reaches the age of 15.

(v) is at the time of the application more than 14 but less than 18 years of age, unless the applicant submits with the application a certificate of a parent or guardian granting the applicant permission to apply for a card;

(vi) is an alien who does not maintain lawful permanent residency;

(vii) is currently subject to: (A) an order for suspension or surrender issued pursuant to section 3B or 3C of chapter 209A or a similar order issued by another jurisdiction; or (B) a permanent or temporary protection order issued pursuant to chapter 209A, a similar order issued by another jurisdiction, including an order described in 18 U.S.C. 922(g)(8);

(viii) is currently the subject of an outstanding arrest warrant in any state or federal jurisdiction;

(ix) has been discharged from the armed forces of the United States under dishonorable conditions;

(x) is a fugitive from justice; or

(xi) having been a citizen of the United States, has renounced that citizenship.

(11/2)(a) Notwithstanding paragraph (1) to the contrary, the licensing authority may file a petition to request that an applicant be denied the issuance or renewal of a firearm identification card, or to suspend or revoke such a card in the district court of jurisdiction. If the licensing authority files any such petition it shall be accompanied by written notice to the applicant describing the specific evidence in the petition. Such petition shall be founded upon a written statement of the reasons for supporting a finding of unsuitability pursuant to subsection (d).

(b) Upon the filing of a petition to deny the issuance or renewal of a firearm identification card, the court shall within 90 days hold a hearing to determine if the applicant is unsuitable under subsection (d) of this paragraph. Such a petition shall serve to stay the issuance or renewal of the firearm identification card pending a judicial determination on such petition.

(c) Upon the filing of a petition to suspend or revoke a firearm identification card, the court shall within 15 days determine whether there is sufficient evidence to support a finding that the applicant is unsuitable. Such petition shall serve to effect the suspension or revocation pending a judicial determination on the sufficiency of evidence. If a court determines that insufficient evidence exists to support a finding of unsuitability, the licensing authority shall not file a petition under this subsection for the same applicant within 75 days of the licensing authority's previous petition for that applicant. If a court determines that sufficient evidence exists to support a finding of unsuitability, the court shall within 75 days hold a hearing to determine if the applicant is unsuitable under subsection (d); provided, however, that such initial suspension or revocation shall remain in effect pending a judicial determination thereon.

(d) A determination of unsuitability shall be based on a preponderance of evidence that there exists: (i) reliable, articulable, and credible information that the applicant has exhibited or engaged in behavior to suggest the applicant could potentially create a risk to public safety; or (ii) existing factors that suggest that the applicant could potentially create a risk to public safety. If a court enters a judgment that an applicant is unsuitable the court shall notify the applicant in a writing setting forth the specific reasons for such determination. If a court has not entered a judgment that an applicant is unsuitable under this clause within 90 days for petitions under clause (ii) or within 75 days under clause (iii), the court shall enter a judgment that the applicant is suitable for the purposes of this paragraph.

(2) Within seven days of the receipt of a completed application for a card, the licensing authority shall forward one copy of the application and one copy of the applicant's fingerprints to the colonel of state police, who shall, within 30 days, advise the licensing authority, in writing, of any disqualifying criminal record of the applicant arising from within or

without the commonwealth and whether there is reason to believe that the applicant is disqualified for any of the foregoing reasons from possessing a card; provided, however, that the taking of fingerprints shall not be required in issuing the renewal of a card if the renewal applicant's fingerprints are on file with the department of state police. In searching for any disqualifying history of the applicant, the colonel shall utilize, or cause to be utilized, files maintained by the department of mental health, department of probation and statewide and nationwide criminal justice, warrant and protection order information systems and files including, but not limited to, the National Instant Criminal Background Check System. If the information available to the colonel does not indicate that the possession of a non-large capacity rifle or shotgun by the applicant would be in violation of state or federal law, he shall certify such fact, in writing, to the licensing authority within such 30 day period. The licensing authority shall provide to the applicant a receipt indicating that it received the applicant's application. The receipt shall be provided to the applicant within 7 days by mail if the application was received by mail or immediately if the application was made in person; provided, however, that the receipt shall include the applicants' name, address, current firearm identification card number, if any, the current card's expiration date, if any, the date when the application was received by the licensing authority, the name of the licensing authority and its agent that received the application, the licensing authority's address and telephone number, the type of application and whether it is an application for a new card or for renewal of an existing card; and provided further, that a copy of the receipt shall be kept by the licensing authority for not less than 1 year and a copy shall be furnished to the applicant if requested by the applicant.

(3) The licensing authority may not prescribe any other condition for the issuance of a firearm identification card and shall, within 40 days from the date of application, either approve the application and issue the license or deny the application and notify the applicant of the reason for such denial in writing; provided, however, that no such card shall be issued unless the colonel has certified, in writing, that the information available to him does not indicate that the possession of a rifle or shotgun by the applicant would be in violation of state or federal law.

(4) A firearm identification card shall be revoked or suspended by the licensing authority or his designee upon the occurrence of any event that would have disqualified the holder from being issued such card or from

having such card renewed or for a violation of a restriction provided under this section. Any revocation or suspension of a card shall be in writing and shall state the reasons therefor. Upon revocation or suspension, the licensing authority shall take possession of such card and receipt for fee paid for such card, and the person whose card is so revoked or suspended shall take all action required under the provisions of section 129D. No appeal or post-judgment motion shall operate to stay such revocation or suspension. Notices of revocation and suspension shall be forwarded to the commissioner of the department of criminal justice information services and the commissioner of probation and shall be included in the criminal justice information system. A revoked or suspended card may be reinstated only upon the termination of all disqualifying conditions.

(5) Any applicant or holder aggrieved by a denial, revocation or suspension of a firearm identification card, unless a hearing has previously been held pursuant to chapter 209A, may, within either 90 days after receipt of notice of such denial, revocation or suspension or within 90 days after the expiration of the time limit in which the licensing authority is required to respond to the applicant, file a petition to obtain judicial review in the district court having jurisdiction in the city or town wherein the applicant filed for or was issued such card. A justice of such court, after a hearing, may direct that a card be issued or reinstated to the petitioner if the justice finds that such petitioner is not prohibited by law from possessing such card.

[Paragraph (6) effective until January 1, 2021. For text effective January 1, 2021, see below.]

(6) A firearm identification card shall not entitle a holder thereof to possess: (i) a large capacity firearm or large capacity feeding device therefor, except under a Class A license issued to a shooting club as provided under section 131 or under the direct supervision of a holder of a Class A license issued to an individual under section 131 at an incorporated shooting club or licensed shooting range; or (ii) a non-large capacity firearm or large capacity rifle or shotgun or large capacity feeding device therefor, except under a Class A license issued to a shooting club as provided under section 131 or under the direct supervision of a holder of a Class A or Class B license issued to an individual under section 131 at an incorporated shooting club or licensed shooting range. A firearm

identification card shall not entitle a holder thereof to possess any rifle or shotgun that is, or in such manner that is, otherwise prohibited by law. A firearm identification card issued pursuant to subclause (vi) of clause (1) of section 122D shall be valid for the purpose of purchasing and possessing chemical mace, pepper spray or other similarly propelled liquid, gas or powder designed to temporarily incapacitate. Except as otherwise provided herein, a firearm identification card shall not be valid for the use, possession, ownership, transfer, purchase, sale, lease, rental or transportation of a rifle or shotgun if such rifle or shotgun is a large capacity weapon as defined in section 121.

[Paragraph (6) as amended by 2014, 284, Sec. 33 effective January 1, 2021. For text effective until January 1, 2021, see above.]

(6) A firearm identification card shall not entitle a holder thereof to possess: (i) a large capacity firearm or large capacity feeding device therefor, except under a license issued to a shooting club as provided under section 131 or under the direct supervision of a holder of a license issued to an individual under said section 131 at an incorporated shooting club or licensed shooting range; or (ii) a non-large capacity firearm or large capacity rifle or shotgun or large capacity feeding device therefor, except under a license issued to a shooting club as provided under said section 131 or under the direct supervision of a holder of a license issued to an individual under said section 131 at an incorporated shooting club or licensed shooting range. A firearm identification card shall not entitle a holder thereof to possess any rifle or shotgun that is, or in such manner that is, otherwise prohibited by law. A firearm identification card issued pursuant to subclause (vi) of clause (1) of section 122D, shall be valid to purchase and possess chemical mace, pepper spray or other similarly propelled liquid, gas or powder designed to temporarily incapacitate. Except as otherwise provided herein, a firearm identification card shall not be valid for the use, possession, ownership, transfer, purchase, sale, lease, rental or transportation of a rifle or shotgun if such rifle or shotgun is a large capacity weapon as defined in section 121.

[Paragraph (7) effective until January 1, 2021. For text effective January 1, 2021, see below.]

(7) A firearm identification card shall be in a standard form provided by the commissioner of the department of criminal justice information

services in a size and shape equivalent to that of a license to operate motor vehicles issued by the registry of motor vehicles pursuant to section 8 of chapter 90 and shall contain an identification number, name, address, photograph, fingerprint, place and date of birth, height, weight, hair color, eye color and signature of the cardholder and shall be marked "Firearm Identification Card" and shall provide in a legible font size and style the phone numbers for the National Suicide Prevention Lifeline and the Samaritans Statewide Helpline. If a firearm identification card is issued pursuant to clause (vi) of section 122D for the sole purpose of purchasing or possessing chemical mace, pepper spray or other similarly propelled liquid, gas or powder designed to temporarily incapacitate, such card shall clearly state that such card is valid for such limited purpose only. The application for such card shall be made in a standard form provided by the commissioner of the department of criminal justice information services which shall require the applicant to affirmatively state, under the pains and penalties of perjury, that he is not disqualified on any of the grounds enumerated in clauses (i) to (ix), inclusive, from being issued such card.

[Paragraph (7) as amended by 2014, 284, Sec. 35A effective January 1, 2021. See 2014, 284, Sec. 112. For text effective until January 1, 2021, see above.]

(7) A firearm identification card shall be in a standard form provided by the commissioner of the department of criminal justice information services in a size and shape equivalent to that of a license to operate motor vehicles issued by the registry of motor vehicles pursuant to section 8 of chapter 90 and shall contain an identification number, name, address, photograph, fingerprint, place and date of birth, height, weight, hair color, eye color and signature of the cardholder and shall be marked "Firearm Identification Card" and shall provide in a legible font size and style the phone numbers for the National Suicide Prevention Lifeline and the Samaritans Statewide Helpline. If a firearm identification card is issued for the sole purpose of purchasing or possessing chemical mace, pepper spray or other similarly propelled liquid, gas or powder designed to temporarily incapacitate, such card shall clearly state that such card is valid for such limited purpose only. The application for such card shall be made in a standard form provided by the commissioner of the department of criminal justice information services which shall require the applicant to affirmatively state, under the pains and penalties of

perjury, that he is not disqualified on any of the grounds enumerated in clauses (i) to (ix), inclusive, from being issued such card.

(8) Any person who knowingly files an application containing false information shall be punished by a fine of not less than $500 nor more than $1,000 or by imprisonment for not less than six months nor more than two years in a house of correction, or by both such fine and imprisonment.

(9) A firearm identification card shall be valid, unless revoked or suspended, for a period of not more than 6 years from the date of issuance, except that if the cardholder applied for renewal before the card expired, the card shall remain valid after the expiration date on the card for all lawful purposes, until the application for renewal is approved or denied; provided, however, if the cardholder is on active duty with the armed forces of the United States on the expiration date of the card, the card shall remain valid until the cardholder is released from active duty and for a period of not less than 180 days following such release, except that if the cardholder applied for renewal prior to the end of such period, the card shall remain valid after the expiration date on the card for all lawful purposes, until the application for renewal is approved or denied. A card issued on February 29 shall expire on March 1. The commissioner of criminal justice information services shall send electronically or by first class mail to the holder of a firearm identification card, a notice of the expiration of the card not less than 90 days before its expiration and shall enclose with the notice a form for the renewal of the card. The form for renewal shall include an affidavit whereby the applicant shall verify that the applicant has not lost a firearm or had a firearm stolen from the applicant's possession since the date of the applicant's last renewal or issuance. The commissioner of criminal justice information services shall include in the notice all pertinent information about the penalties that may be imposed if the firearm identification card is not renewed. The commissioner of criminal justice information services shall provide electronic notice of expiration only upon the request of a cardholder. A request for electronic notice of expiration shall be forwarded to the department on a form furnished by the commissioner. Any electronic address maintained by the department to provide electronic notice of expiration shall be considered a firearms record and shall not be disclosed except as provided in section 10 of chapter 66.

(9A) Except as provided in paragraph (9B), the fee for an application for a firearm identification card shall be $100, which shall be payable to the licensing authority and shall not be prorated or refunded in the case of revocation or denial. The licensing authority shall retain $25 of the fee; $50 of the fee shall be deposited in the General Fund; and $25 of the fee shall be deposited in the Firearms Fingerprint Identity Verification Trust Fund. Notwithstanding any general or special law to the contrary, licensing authorities shall deposit quarterly that portion of the firearm identification card application fee which is to be deposited into the General Fund, not later than January 1, April 1, July 1 and October 1 of each year.

[First paragraph of paragraph (9B) effective until January 1, 2021. For text effective January 1, 2021, see below.]

(9B) The application fee for a firearm identification card issued pursuant to clause (vi) of section 122D for the sole purpose of purchasing or possessing chemical mace, pepper spray or other similarly propelled liquid, gas or powder designed to temporarily incapacitate shall be $25, which shall be payable to the licensing authority and shall not be prorated or refunded in the case of revocation or denial. The licensing authority shall retain 50 per cent of the fee and the remaining portion shall be deposited in the General Fund. Notwithstanding any general or special law to the contrary, licensing authorities shall deposit quarterly that portion of the firearm identification card application fee which is to be deposited into the General Fund, not later than January 1, April 1, July 1 and October 1 of each year. There shall be no application fee for the renewal of a firearm identification card issued under this paragraph.

[First paragraph of paragraph (9B) as amended by 2014, 284, Sec. 35B effective January 1, 2021. See 2014, 284, Sec. 112. For text effective until January 1, 2021, see above.]

(9B) The application fee for a firearm identification card issued for the sole purpose of purchasing or possessing chemical mace, pepper spray or other similarly propelled liquid, gas or powder designed to temporarily incapacitate shall be $25, which shall be payable to the licensing authority and shall not be prorated or refunded in the case of revocation or denial. The licensing authority shall retain 50 per cent of the fee and the remaining portion shall be deposited in the General Fund.

Notwithstanding any general or special law to the contrary, licensing authorities shall deposit quarterly that portion of the firearm identification card application fee which is to be deposited into the General Fund, not later than January 1, April 1, July 1 and October 1 of each year. There shall be no application fee for the renewal of a firearm identification card issued under this paragraph.

A firearm identification card issued under this paragraph shall display, in clear and conspicuous language, that the card shall be valid only for the purpose of purchasing or possessing chemical mace, pepper spray or other similarly propelled liquid, gas or powder designed to temporarily incapacitate.

(9C) Except as provided in paragraph (9B), the fee for an application for a firearm identification card for any person under the age of 18 shall be $25, which shall be payable to the licensing authority and shall not be prorated or refunded in the case of revocation or denial. The licensing authority shall retain 50 per cent of the fee and the remaining portion shall be deposited into the General Fund. Notwithstanding any general or special law to the contrary, licensing authorities shall deposit quarterly that portion of the firearm identification card application fee which is to be deposited into the General Fund, not later than January 1, April 1, July 1 and October 1 of each year.

(10) Any person over the age of 70 shall be exempt from the requirement of paying a renewal fee for a firearm identification card.

(11) A cardholder shall notify, in writing, the licensing authority that issued such card, the Chief of police into whose jurisdiction such cardholder moves and the executive director of the criminal history systems board of any change of address. Such notification shall be made by certified mail within 30 days of its occurrence. Failure to so notify shall be cause for revocation or suspension of such card.

(12) Notwithstanding the provisions of section 10 of chapter 269, any person in possession of a non-large capacity rifle or shotgun whose firearm identification card issued under this section is invalid for the sole reason that it has expired, not including licenses that remain valid under paragraph (9) because the licensee applied for renewal before the license expired, but who shall not be disqualified from renewal upon application

therefor under this section, shall be subject to a civil fine of not less than $100 nor more than $5,000 and the provisions of said section 10 of said chapter 269 shall not apply; provided, however, that the exemption from the provisions of said section 10 of said chapter 269 provided herein shall not apply if: (i) such firearm identification card has been revoked or suspended, unless such revocation or suspension was caused by failure to give notice of a change of address as required under this section; (ii) revocation or suspension of such firearm identification card is pending, unless such revocation or suspension was caused by failure to give notice of a change of address as required under this section; or (iii) an application for renewal of such firearm identification card has been denied. Any law enforcement officer who discovers a person to be in possession of a rifle or shotgun after such person's firearm identification card has expired, meaning after 90 days beyond the stated expiration date on the card, or has been revoked or suspended solely for failure to give notice of a change of address shall confiscate any rifle or shotgun and such expired or suspended card then in possession, and such officer shall forward such card to the licensing authority by whom it was issued as soon as practicable. Any confiscated weapon shall be returned to the owner upon the renewal or reinstatement of such expired or suspended card within one year of such confiscation or such weapon may be otherwise disposed of in accordance with the provisions of section 129D. Pending the issuance of a renewed firearm identification card, a receipt for the fee paid, after five days following issuance, shall serve as a valid substitute and any rifle or shotgun so confiscated shall be returned, unless the applicant is disqualified. The provisions of this paragraph shall not apply if such person has a valid license to carry firearms issued under section 131 or 131F.

(13) Upon issuance of a firearm identification card under this section, the licensing authority shall forward a copy of such approved application and card to the executive director of the criminal history systems board, who shall inform the licensing authority forthwith of the existence of any disqualifying condition discovered or occurring subsequent to the issuance of a firearm identification card under this section.

(14) Nothing in this section shall authorize the purchase, possession or transfer of any weapon, ammunition or feeding device that is, or in such manner that is, prohibited by state or federal law.

(15) The secretary of the executive office of public safety, or his designee, may promulgate regulations to carry out the purposes of this section.

Section 129C: Application of Sec. 129B; ownership or possession of firearms or ammunition; transfers; report to commissioner; exemptions; exhibiting license to carry, etc. on demand

Section 129C. No person, other than a licensed dealer or one who has been issued a license to carry a pistol or revolver or an exempt person as hereinafter described, shall own or possess any firearm, rifle, shotgun or ammunition unless he has been issued a firearm identification card by the licensing authority pursuant to the provisions of section one hundred and twenty-nine B.

No person shall sell, give away, loan or otherwise transfer a rifle or shotgun or ammunition other than (a) by operation of law, or (b) to an exempt person as hereinafter described, or (c) to a licensed dealer, or (d) to a person who displays his firearm identification card, or license to carry a pistol or revolver.

A seller shall, within seven days, report all such transfers to the commissioner of the department of criminal justice information services according to the provisions set forth in section one hundred and twenty-eight A, and in the case of loss, theft or recovery of any firearm, rifle, shotgun or machine gun, a similar report shall be made forthwith to both the commissioner of the department of criminal justice information services and the licensing authority in the city or town where the owner resides. Whoever fails to report the loss or theft of a firearm, rifle, shotgun or machine gun or the recovery of a firearm, rifle, shotgun or machine gun previously reported lost or stolen to the commissioner of the department of criminal justice information services and the licensing authority in the city or town where the owner resides shall be punished by a fine of not less than $500 nor more than $1,000 for a first offense, by a fine of not less than $2,500 nor more than $7,500 for a second offense and by a fine of not less than $7,500 nor more than $10,000 or imprisonment for not less than 1 year nor more than 5 years, or by both such fine and imprisonment, for a third or subsequent offense. Failure to so report shall be a cause for suspension or permanent revocation of a person's firearm identification card or license to carry firearms, or both. Notwithstanding this paragraph or any general or special law to the contrary, no person, who in good faith, reports a loss or theft under this paragraph for the first time shall be subject to suspension, revocation or be considered unsuitable under section 131 for the renewal of a lawfully held firearm identification card or license to carry firearms; provided, however, that persons reporting loss or theft under this paragraph or under section 129B on a second or subsequent occasion may be subject to suspension, revocation or be considered unsuitable under said section 131 for the renewal of a lawfully held firearm identification card or license to carry firearms.

The provisions of this section shall not apply to the following exempted persons and uses:

(a) Any device used exclusively for signalling or distress use and required or recommended by the United States Coast Guard or the Interstate Commerce Commission, or for the firing of stud cartridges, explosive rivets or similar industrial ammunition;

(b) Federally licensed firearms manufacturers or wholesale dealers, or persons employed by them or by licensed dealers, or on their behalf, when possession of firearms, rifles or shotguns is necessary for manufacture, display, storage, transport, installation, inspection or testing;

(c) To a person voluntarily surrendering a firearm, rifle or shotgun and ammunition therefor to a licensing authority, the colonel of the state police or his designee if prior written notice has been given by said person to the licensing authority or the colonel of the state police, stating the place and approximate time of said surrender;

(d) The regular and ordinary transport of firearms, rifles or shotguns as merchandise by any common carrier;

(e) Possession by retail customers for the purpose of firing at duly licensed target concessions at amusement parks, piers and similar locations, provided that the firearms, rifles or shotguns to be so used are firmly chained or affixed to the counter and that the proprietor is in possession of a firearm identification card or license to carry firearms;

(f) Possession of rifles and shotguns and ammunition therefor by nonresident hunters with valid nonresident hunting licenses during hunting season;

(g) Possession of rifles and shotguns and ammunition therefor by nonresidents while on a firing or shooting range;

(h) Possession of rifles and shotguns and ammunition therefor by nonresidents traveling in or through the commonwealth, providing that any rifles or shotguns are unloaded and enclosed in a case;

(i) Possession of rifles and shotguns by nonresidents while at a firearm showing or display organized by a regularly existing gun collectors' club or association;

(j) Any resident of the commonwealth returning after having been absent from the commonwealth for not less than 180 consecutive days or any new resident moving into the commonwealth, with respect to any firearm, rifle or shotgun and any ammunition therefor then in his possession, for 60 days after such return or entry into the commonwealth;

(k) Any person under the age of fifteen with respect to the use of a rifle or shotgun by such person in hunting or target shooting, provided that such use is otherwise permitted by law and is under the immediate supervision of a person holding a firearm identification card or a license to carry firearms, or a duly commissioned officer, noncommissioned officer or enlisted member of the United States Army, Navy, Marine Corps, Air Force or Coast Guard, or the National Guard or military service of the commonwealth or reserve components thereof, while in the performance of his duty;

(l) The possession or utilization of any rifle or shotgun during the course of any television, movie, stage or other similar theatrical production, or by a professional photographer or writer for examination purposes in the pursuit of his profession, providing such possession or utilization is under the immediate supervision of a holder of a firearm identification card or a license to carry firearms;

(m) The temporary holding, handling or firing of a firearm for examination, trial or instruction in the presence of a holder of a license to carry firearms, or the temporary holding, handling or firing of a rifle or shotgun for examination, trial or instruction in the presence of a holder of a firearm identification card, or where such holding, handling or firing is for a lawful purpose;

(n) The transfer of a firearm, rifle or shotgun upon the death of an owner to his heir or legatee shall be subject to the provisions of this section, provided that said heir or legatee shall within one hundred and eighty days of such transfer, obtain a firearm identification card or a license to carry firearms if not otherwise an exempt person who is qualified to receive such or apply to the licensing authority for such further limited period as may be necessary for the disposition of such firearm, rifle or shotgun;

(o) Persons in the military or other service of any state or of the United States, and police officers and other peace officers of any jurisdiction, in the performance of their official duty or when duly authorized to possess them;

(p) Carrying or possession by residents or nonresidents of so-called black powder rifles, shotguns, and ammunition therefor as described in such paragraphs (A) and (B) of the third paragraph of section 121, and the carrying or possession of conventional rifles, shotguns, and ammunition therefor by nonresidents who meet the requirements for such carrying or possession in the state in which they reside.

[There is no clause (q).]

(r) Possession by a veteran's organization chartered by the Congress of the United States, chartered by the commonwealth or recognized as a nonprofit tax-exempt organization by the Internal Revenue Service and possession by the members of any such organization when on official parade duty or ceremonial occasions.

(s) Possession by federal, state and local historical societies, museums, and institutional collections open to the public, provided such firearms, rifles or shotguns are unloaded, properly housed and secured from unauthorized handling;

(t) the possession of firearms, rifles, shotguns, machine guns and ammunition, by banks or institutional lenders, or their agents, servants or employees, when the same are possessed as collateral for a secured commercial transaction or as a result of a default under a secured commercial transaction.

(u) Any nonresident who is eighteen years of age or older at the time of acquiring a rifle or shotgun from a licensed firearms dealer; provided, however, that such nonresident must hold a valid firearms license from his state of residence; provided, further, that the licensing requirements of such nonresident's state of residence are as stringent as the requirements of the commonwealth for a firearm identification card, as determined by the colonel of the state police who shall, annually, publish a list of those states whose requirements comply with the provisions of this clause.

Any person, exempted by clauses (o), (p) and (q), purchasing a rifle or shotgun or ammunition therefor shall submit to the seller such full and clear proof of identification, including shield number, serial number, military or governmental order or authorization, military or other official identification, other state firearms license, or proof of nonresidence, as may be applicable.

Nothing in this section shall permit the sale of rifles or shotguns or ammunition therefor to a minor under the age of eighteen in violation of section one hundred and thirty nor may any firearm be sold to a person under the age of 21 nor to any person who is not licensed to carry firearms under section one hundred and thirty-one unless he presents a valid firearm identification card and a permit to purchase issued under section one hundred and thirty-one A, or presents such permit to purchase and is a properly documented exempt person as hereinbefore described.

[Seventh paragraph effective until January 1, 2021. For text effective January 1, 2021, see below.]

Nothing in this section shall permit the sale or transfer of any large capacity rifle or shotgun or large capacity feeding device therefor to any person not in possession of a Class A or Class B license to carry firearms issued under section 131, or of any large capacity firearm or large capacity feeding device therefor to any person not in possession of a Class A license to carry firearms issued under section 131.

[Seventh paragraph as amended by 2014, 284, Sec. 41 effective January 1, 2021. See 2014, 284, Sec. 112. For text effective until January 1, 2021, see above.]

Nothing in this section shall permit the sale or transfer of a large capacity rifle, shotgun or firearm or large capacity feeding device therefor to a person not in possession of a license to carry firearms issued pursuant to section 131.

The possession of a firearm identification card issued under section one hundred and twenty-nine B shall not entitle any person to carry a firearm in violation of section ten of chapter two hundred and sixty-nine and, the possession of a firearm identification card issued under section 129B shall not entitle any person to possess any large capacity rifle or shotgun or large capacity feeding device therefor in violation of subsection (m) of said section 10 of said chapter 269.

Any person who, while not being within the limits of his own property or residence, or such person whose property or residence is under lawful search, and who is not exempt under this section, shall on demand of a police officer or other law enforcement officer, exhibit his license to carry firearms, or his firearm identification card or receipt for fee paid for such card, or, after January first, nineteen hundred and seventy, exhibit a valid hunting license issued to him which shall bear the number officially inscribed of such license to carry or card if any. Upon failure to do so such person may be required to surrender to such officer said firearm, rifle or shotgun which shall be taken into custody as under the provisions of section one hundred and twenty-nine D, except that such firearm, rifle or shotgun shall be returned forthwith upon presentation within thirty days of said license to carry firearms, firearm identification card or receipt for fee paid for such card or hunting license as hereinbefore described. Any person subject to the conditions of this paragraph may, even though no firearm, rifle or shotgun was surrendered, be required to produce within thirty days said license to carry firearms, firearm identification card or receipt for fee paid for such card, or said hunting license, failing which the conditions of section one hundred and twenty-nine D will apply. Nothing in this section shall prevent any person from being prosecuted for any violation of this chapter.

Section 129D: Surrender of firearms and ammunition to licensing authority upon denial of application for, or revocation of, identification card or license; right to transfer; sale by colonel of state police; rules and regulations

Section 129D. Upon revocation, suspension or denial of an application for a firearm identification card pursuant to section 129B or for any firearms license if the firearm identification card is not then in force or for any machine gun license, the person whose application was so revoked, suspended or denied shall without delay deliver or surrender to the licensing authority where the person resides all firearms, rifles, shotguns and machine guns and ammunition which the person then possesses unless an appeal of the revocation or suspension is pending. The person or the person's legal representative shall have the right, at any time up to 1 year after the delivery or surrender, to transfer the firearms, rifles, shotguns and machine guns and ammunition to any licensed dealer or any other person legally permitted to purchase or take possession of the firearms, rifles, shotguns and machine guns and ammunition and, upon notification in writing by the purchaser or transferee and the former owner, the licensing authority shall within 10 days deliver the firearms, rifles, shotguns and machine guns and ammunition to the transferee or purchaser and the licensing authority shall observe due care in the receipt and holding of any such firearm, rifle, shotgun or machine gun and ammunition; provided, however, that the purchaser or transferee shall affirm in writing that the purchaser or transferee shall not in violation of section 129C transfer the firearms, rifles, shotguns or machine guns or ammunition to the former owner. The licensing authority shall at the time of delivery or surrender inform the person in writing of the authority's ability, within 1 year after delivery or surrender, to transfer the firearms, rifles, shotguns and machine guns and ammunition to any licensed dealer or other person legally permitted to purchase or take possession.

The licensing authority, after taking possession of any firearm, rifle, shotgun, machine gun or ammunition by any means, may transfer possession of such weapon for storage purposes to a federally and state licensed dealer of such weapons and ammunition who operates a bonded warehouse on the licensed premises that is equipped with a safe for the secure storage of firearms and a weapon box or similar container for the secure storage of other weapons and ammunition; provided, however, that the licensing authority shall not transfer to such dealer possession of any weapon that is or may be evidence in any current or pending criminal case concerning a violation of any general or special law, rule or regulation governing the use, possession or ownership of such weapon. Any such dealer that takes possession of a weapon under the provisions of this section shall: (i) inspect such weapon; (ii) issue to the owner a receipt indicating the make, model, caliber, serial number and condition of each weapon so received; and (iii) store and maintain all weapons so received in accordance with such regulations, rules or guidelines as the secretary of the executive office of public safety may establish under this section. The owner shall be liable to such dealer for reasonable storage charges and may dispose of any such weapon as provided under this section by transfer to a person lawfully permitted to purchase or take possession of such weapon.

Firearms, rifles, shotguns or machine guns and ammunition not disposed of after delivery or surrender according to the provisions of this section shall be sold at public auction by the colonel of the state police to the highest bidding person legally permitted to purchase and possess said firearms, rifles, shotguns or machine guns and ammunition and the proceeds shall be remitted to the state treasurer. Any such weapon that is stored and maintained by a licensed dealer as provided under this section may be so auctioned at the direction of: (i) the licensing authority at the expiration of one year following initial surrender or delivery to such licensing authority; or (ii) the dealer then in possession, if the storage charges for such weapon have been in arrears for 90 days; provided, however, that in either case, title shall pass to the licensed dealer for the purpose of transferring ownership to the auctioneer; and provided further, that in either case, after deduction and payment for storage charges and all necessary costs associated with such surrender and transfer, all surplus proceeds, if any, shall be immediately returned to the owner of such weapon; provided, however, that no firearm, rifle, shotgun or machine gun or ammunition classified as having been used to carry out a criminal act pursuant to section 131Q shall be sold at public auction pursuant to this section.

If the licensing authority cannot reasonably ascertain a lawful owner within 180 days of acquisition by the authority, the authority may, in its discretion, trade or dispose of surplus, donated, abandoned or junk firearms, rifles, shotguns or machine guns or ammunition to properly licensed distributors or firearms dealers. The proceeds of the sale or transfer shall be remitted or credited to the municipality in which the authority presides to purchase weapons, equipment or supplies or for violence reduction or suicide prevention; provided, however, that no firearm, rifle, shotgun or machine gun or ammunition classified as having been used to carry out a criminal act pursuant to section 131Q shall be considered surplus, donated, abandoned or junk for the purposes of this section.

The secretary of the executive office of public safety may make and promulgate such rules and regulations as are necessary to carry out the provisions of this section.

Section 130: Sale or furnishing weapons or ammunition to aliens or minors; penalty

Section 130. Whoever sells or furnishes a rifle, shotgun or ammunition to any alien 18 years of age or older who does not hold a permit card issued to that alien pursuant to section 131H or, except as provided in this section or section 131E, whoever sells or furnishes any alien or any person under 18 years of age a rifle, shotgun, machine gun or ammunition, or whoever sells or furnishes to any person under 21 years of age a firearm or large capacity rifle or shotgun or ammunition therefor shall have the license to sell firearms, rifles, shotguns, machine guns or ammunition revoked and shall not be entitled to apply for such license for 10 years from the date of such revocation and shall be punished by a fine of not less than $1,000 nor more than $10,000, or by imprisonment in a state prison for not more than 10 years or by imprisonment in a house of correction for not more than 21/2 years or by both such fine and imprisonment.

Section 130 1/2: Lawfully furnishing weapons to minors for hunting, recreation, instruction and participation in shooting sports

Section 130 1/2. Notwithstanding section 130 or any general or special law to the contrary, it shall be lawful to furnish a weapon to a minor for hunting, recreation, instruction and participation in shooting sports while under the supervision of a holder of a valid firearm identification card or license to carry appropriate for the weapon in use; provided, however, that the parent or guardian of the minor granted consent for such activities.

Section 130A: Repealed, 1957, 688, Sec. 14

Section 130B: Firearm licensing review board; members; license applicants; hearings

Section 130B. (a) There shall be a firearm licensing review board, established within the department of criminal justice information services, in this section called the board, comprised of 7 members, 1 of whom shall be a member of the department of criminal justice information services appointed by the commissioner and who shall be the chair, 1 of whom shall be the secretary of public safety or his designee, 1 of whom shall be the colonel of state police or his designee, 1 of whom shall be appointed by the Massachusetts Chiefs of Police Association, 1 of whom shall be the attorney general or his designee, 1 whom shall be an attorney with litigation experience in firearm licensing cases and appointed by the governor from a list of qualified persons submitted to the governor by the Massachusetts Bar Association, and 1 of whom shall be a retired member of the judiciary and appointed by the governor.

(b) An applicant for a firearm identification card or license to carry who has been convicted of or adjudicated a delinquent child or youthful offender by reason of an offense or offenses punishable by 2 1/2 years imprisonment or less when committed under the laws of the commonwealth which was not: (a) an assault or battery on a family member or household member, as defined by section 1 of chapter 209A, except that the determination to be made under clause (e) of said section 1 of said chapter 209A shall be made by the review board, may, after the passage of 5 years from conviction, adjudication as a youthful offender or a delinquent child or release from confinement, commitment, probation or parole supervision for such conviction or adjudication, whichever is last occurring, file a petition for review of eligibility with the firearm licensing review board.

(c) The petitioner shall provide to the board a copy of a completed firearm identification card or license to carry application, which application shall have previously been submitted to the licensing authority or be submitted to the licensing authority contemporaneously with the petition filed with the board. The petitioner shall have the burden to prove his suitability to receive a firearm identification card or a license to carry by clear and convincing evidence. The board shall set a reasonable filing fee to file the petition.

(d) If the board determines, by 2/3rds vote, that: (i) the sole disqualifier for the petitioner is any conviction or adjudication as a youthful offender or a delinquent child for an offense or offenses punishable by 2 1/2 years imprisonment or less when committed under the laws of the commonwealth, arising out of a single incident and which does not otherwise disqualify the petitioner under subclauses (a), (d) or (e) of clause (i) or clauses (ii) to (ix), inclusive, of paragraph (1) of section 129B or subclauses (a), (d) or (e) of clause (i) or clauses (ii) to (vii), inclusive, of paragraph (d) of section 131, and which was not an assault or battery on a family member or household members, as defined by section 1 of chapter 209A, except that the determination to be made under clause (e) of said section 1 of said chapter 209A shall be made by the board; (ii) 5 years has passed since such conviction or adjudication or release from confinement, commitment, probation or parole supervision for such conviction or adjudication, whichever is last occurring; and (iii) by clear and convincing evidence, that the petitioner is a suitable person to be a firearm identification card or license to carry holder, the board shall determine that the petitioner's right or ability to possess a firearm is fully restored in the commonwealth with respect to such conviction or adjudication and that such conviction or adjudication shall not prohibit such petitioner from applying to a licensing authority for a firearm identification card or license to carry. The board shall make a determination on a petition within 60 days after receipt of the petition.

(e) The board shall hold hearings at such times and places as in its discretion it reasonably determines to be required, but not less than once every 90 days, and shall give reasonable notice of the time and place of the hearing to the petitioner. The board shall have the power to compel attendance of witnesses at hearings.

(f) All hearings shall be conducted in an informal manner, but otherwise according to the rules of evidence, and all witnesses shall be sworn by the chair. If requested by the petitioner and payment for stenographic services, as determined by the board, accompanies such request, the board shall cause a verbatim transcript of the hearing to be made. The board's decisions and findings of facts therefore shall be communicated in writing to the petitioner and to the licensing authority to whom the petitioner has applied or intends to apply within 20 days of rendering a decision.

(g) Members of the board shall serve without compensation, but shall be entitled to reasonable subsistence and travel allowances in the performance of their duties.

Section 131: Licenses to carry firearms; conditions and restrictions

[Introductory paragraph effective until January 1, 2021. For text effective January 1, 2021, see below.]

Section 131. All licenses to carry firearms shall be designated Class A or Class B, and the issuance and possession of any such license shall be subject to the following conditions and restrictions:

[Introductory paragraph as amended by 2014, 284, Sec. 46 effective January 1, 2021. See 2014, 284, Sec. 112. For text effective until January 1, 2021, see above.]

The issuance and possession of a license to carry firearms shall be subject to the following conditions and restrictions:

[Paragraphs (a) to (c) effective until January 1, 2021. For text effective January 1, 2021, see below.]

(a) A Class A license shall entitle a holder thereof to purchase, rent, lease, borrow, possess and carry: (i) firearms, including large capacity firearms, and feeding devices and ammunition therefor, for all lawful purposes, subject to such restrictions relative to the possession, use or carrying of firearms as the licensing authority deems proper; and (ii) rifles and shotguns, including large capacity weapons, and feeding devices and ammunition therefor, for all lawful purposes; provided, however, that the licensing authority may impose such restrictions relative to the possession, use or carrying of large capacity rifles and shotguns as it deems proper. A violation of a restriction imposed by the licensing authority under the provisions of this paragraph shall be cause for suspension or revocation and shall, unless otherwise provided, be punished by a fine of not less than $1,000 nor more than $10,000; provided, however, that the provisions of section 10 of chapter 269 shall not apply to such violation.

The colonel of state police may, after an investigation, grant a Class A license to a club or facility with an on-site shooting range or gallery, which club is incorporated under the laws of the commonwealth for the possession, storage and use of large capacity weapons, ammunition therefor and large capacity feeding devices for use with such weapons on the premises of such club; provided, however, that not less than one shareholder of such club shall be qualified and suitable to be issued such license; and provided further, that such large capacity weapons and ammunition feeding devices may be used under such Class A club license only by such members that possess a valid firearm identification card issued under section 129B or a valid Class A or Class B license to carry firearms, or by such other persons that the club permits while under the direct supervision of a certified firearms safety instructor or club member who, in the case of a large capacity firearm, possesses a valid Class A license to carry firearms or, in the case of a large capacity rifle or shotgun, possesses a valid Class A or Class B license to carry firearms. Such club shall not permit shooting at targets that depict human figures, human effigies, human silhouettes or any human images thereof, except by public safety personnel performing in line with their official duties.

No large capacity weapon or large capacity feeding device shall be removed from the premises except for the purposes of: (i) transferring such firearm or feeding device to a licensed dealer; (ii) transporting such firearm or feeding device to a licensed gunsmith for repair; (iii) target, trap or skeet shooting on the premises of another club incorporated under the laws of the commonwealth and for transporting thereto; (iv) attending an exhibition or educational project or event that is sponsored by, conducted under the supervision of or approved by a public law enforcement agency or a nationally or state recognized entity that promotes proficiency in or education about semiautomatic weapons and for transporting thereto and therefrom; (v) hunting in accordance with the provisions of chapter 131; or (vi) surrendering such firearm or feeding device under the provisions of section 129D. Any large capacity weapon or large capacity feeding device kept on the premises of a lawfully incorporated shooting club shall, when not in use, be secured in a locked container, and shall be unloaded during any lawful transport. The clerk or other corporate officer of such club shall annually file a report with the colonel of state police and the commissioner of the department of criminal justice information services listing all large capacity weapons and large capacity feeding devices owned or possessed under such license. The colonel of state police or his designee, shall have the right to inspect all firearms owned or possessed by such club upon request during regular business hours and said colonel may revoke or suspend a club license for a violation of any provision of this chapter or chapter 269 relative to the ownership, use or possession of large capacity weapons or large capacity feeding devices.

(b) A Class B license shall entitle a holder thereof to purchase, rent, lease, borrow, possess and carry: (i) non-large capacity firearms and feeding devices and ammunition therefor, for all lawful purposes, subject to such restrictions relative to the possession, use or carrying of such firearm as the licensing authority deems proper; provided, however, that a Class B license shall not entitle the holder thereof to carry or possess a loaded firearm in a concealed manner in any public way or place; and provided further, that a Class B license shall not entitle the holder thereof to possess a large capacity firearm, except under a Class A club license issued under this section or under the direct supervision of a holder of a valid Class A license at an incorporated shooting club or licensed shooting range; and (ii) rifles and shotguns, including large capacity rifles and shotguns, and feeding devices and ammunition therefor, for all lawful purposes; provided, however, that the licensing authority may impose such restrictions relative to the possession, use or carrying of large capacity rifles and shotguns as he deems proper. A violation of a restriction provided under this paragraph, or a restriction imposed by the licensing authority under the provisions of this paragraph, shall be cause for suspension or revocation and shall, unless otherwise provided, be punished by a fine of not less than $1,000 nor more than $10,000; provided, however, that the provisions of section 10 of chapter 269 shall not apply to such violation.

A Class B license shall not be a valid license for the purpose of complying with any provision under this chapter governing the purchase, sale, lease, rental or transfer of any weapon or ammunition feeding device if such weapon is a large capacity firearm or if such ammunition feeding device is a large capacity feeding device for use with a large capacity firearm, both as defined in section 121.

(c) Either a Class A or Class B license shall be valid for the purpose of owning, possessing, purchasing and transferring non-large capacity rifles and shotguns, and for purchasing and possessing chemical mace, pepper spray or other similarly propelled liquid, gas or powder designed to temporarily incapacitate, consistent with the entitlements conferred by a firearm identification card issued under section 129B.

[Paragraphs (a) to (c) as amended by 2014, 284, Sec. 47 effective January 1, 2021. See 2014, 284, Sec. 112. For text effective until January 1, 2021, see above.]

(a) A license shall entitle a holder thereof of a license to purchase, rent, lease, borrow, possess and carry: (i) firearms, including large capacity firearms, and feeding devices and ammunition therefor, for all lawful purposes, subject to such restrictions relative to the possession, use or carrying of firearms as the licensing authority considers proper; and (ii) rifles and shotguns, including large capacity weapons, and feeding devices and ammunition therefor, for all lawful purposes; provided, however, that the licensing authority may impose such restrictions relative to the possession, use or carrying of large capacity rifles and shotguns as it considers proper. A violation of a restriction imposed by the licensing authority under this paragraph shall be cause for suspension or revocation and shall, unless otherwise provided, be punished by a fine of not less than $1,000 nor more than $10,000; provided, however, that section 10 of chapter 269 shall not apply to a violation of this paragraph.

(b) The colonel of state police may, after an investigation, grant a license to a club or facility with an on-site shooting range or gallery, which club is incorporated under the laws of the commonwealth for the possession, storage and use of large capacity weapons, ammunition therefor and large capacity feeding devices for use with such weapons on the premises of the club; provided, however, that not less than 1 shareholder of the club shall be qualified and suitable to be issued a license; and provided further, that such large capacity weapons and ammunition feeding devices may be used under the club license only by a member that possesses a valid firearm identification card issued pursuant to section 129B or a valid license to carry firearms, or by such other person that the club permits while under the direct supervision of a certified firearms safety instructor or club member who, in the case of a large capacity firearm, possesses a valid license to carry firearms or, in the case of a large capacity rifle or shotgun, possesses a valid license to carry firearms. The club shall not permit shooting at targets that depict human figures, human effigies, human silhouettes or any human images thereof, except by public safety personnel performing in line with their official duties.

No large capacity weapon or large capacity feeding device shall be removed from the premises except to: (i) transfer the firearm or feeding device to a licensed dealer; (ii) transport the firearm or feeding device to a licensed gunsmith for repair; (iii) target, trap or skeet shoot on the premises of another club incorporated under the laws of the commonwealth and to transport thereto; (iv) attend an exhibition or educational project or event that is sponsored by, conducted under the supervision of or approved by a public law enforcement agency or a nationally or state recognized entity that promotes proficiency in or education about semiautomatic weapons and to transport thereto and therefrom; (v) hunt pursuant to chapter 131; or (vi) surrender the firearm or feeding device pursuant to section 129D. Any large capacity weapon or large capacity feeding device kept on the premises of a lawfully incorporated shooting club shall, when not in use, be secured in a locked container and shall be unloaded during any lawful transport. The clerk or other corporate officer of the club shall annually file a report with the colonel of state police and the commissioner of criminal justice information services listing all large capacity weapons and large capacity feeding devices owned or possessed under the license. The colonel or a designee may inspect all firearms owned or possessed by the club upon request during regular business hours and the colonel may revoke or suspend a club license for a violation of this chapter or chapter 269 relative to the ownership, use or possession of large capacity weapons or large capacity feeding devices.

(c) A license to carry firearms shall be valid to own, possess, purchase and transfer non-large capacity rifles and shotguns, consistent with the entitlements conferred by a firearm identification card issued under section 129B.

[First paragraph of paragraph (d) effective until January 1, 2021. For text effective January 1, 2021, see below.]

(d) Any person residing or having a place of business within the jurisdiction of the licensing authority or any law enforcement officer employed by the licensing authority or any person residing in an area of exclusive federal jurisdiction located within a city or town may submit to the licensing authority or the colonel of state police, an application for a Class A license to carry firearms, or renewal of the same, which the licensing authority or the colonel may issue if it appears that the applicant is not a prohibited person, as set forth in this section, to be issued a license and has good reason to fear injury to the applicant or the applicant's property or for any other reason, including the carrying of firearms for use in sport or target practice only, subject to the restrictions expressed or authorized under this section.

[First paragraph of paragraph (d) as amended by 2014, 284, Sec. 49 effective January 1, 2021. See 2014, 284, Sec. 112. For text effective until January 1, 2021, see above.]

(d) A person residing or having a place of business within the jurisdiction of the licensing authority or any law enforcement officer employed by the licensing authority or any person residing in an area of exclusive federal jurisdiction located within a city or town may submit to the licensing authority or the colonel of state police an application for a license to carry firearms, or renewal of the same, which the licensing authority or the colonel may issue if it appears that the applicant is not a prohibited person as set forth in this section to be issued a license and that the applicant has good reason to fear injury to the applicant or the applicant's property or for any other reason, including the carrying of firearms for use in sport or target practice only, subject to the restrictions expressed or authorized under this section.

A prohibited person shall be a person who:

(i) has, in a court of the commonwealth, been convicted or adjudicated a youthful offender or delinquent child, both as defined in section 52 of chapter 119, for the commission of (A) a felony; (B) a misdemeanor punishable by imprisonment for more than 2 years ; (C) a violent crime as defined in section 121; (D) a violation of any law regulating the use, possession, ownership, transfer, purchase, sale, lease, rental, receipt or transportation of weapons or ammunition for which a term of imprisonment may be imposed; (E) a violation of any law regulating the use, possession or sale of a controlled substance as defined in section 1 of chapter 94C including, but not limited to, a violation of said chapter 94C; or (F) a misdemeanor crime of domestic violence as defined in 18 U.S.C. 921(a)(33);

(ii) has, in any other state or federal jurisdiction, been convicted or adjudicated a youthful offender or delinquent child for the commission of (A) a felony; (B) a misdemeanor punishable by imprisonment for more than 2 years; (C) a violent crime as defined in section 121; (D) a violation of any law regulating the use, possession, ownership, transfer, purchase, sale, lease, rental, receipt or transportation of weapons or ammunition for which a term of imprisonment may be imposed; (E) a violation of any law regulating the use, possession or sale of a controlled substance as defined in said section 1 of said chapter 94C including, but not limited to, a violation of said chapter 94C; or (F) a misdemeanor crime of domestic violence as defined in 18 U.S.C. 921(a)(33);

(iii) is or has been (A) committed to a hospital or institution for mental illness, alcohol or substance abuse, except a commitment pursuant to sections 35 or 36C of chapter 123, unless after 5 years from the date of the confinement, the applicant submits with the application an affidavit of a licensed physician or clinical psychologist attesting that such physician or psychologist is familiar with the applicant's mental illness, alcohol or substance abuse and that in the physician's or psychologist's opinion, the applicant is not disabled by a mental illness, alcohol or substance abuse in a manner that shall prevent the applicant from possessing a firearm, rifle or shotgun; (B) committed by a court order to a hospital or institution for mental illness, unless the applicant was granted a petition for relief of the court order pursuant to said section 36C of said chapter 123 and submits a copy of the court order with the application; (C) subject to an order of the probate court appointing a guardian or conservator for a incapacitated person on the grounds that the applicant lacks the mental capacity to contract or manage the applicant's affairs, unless the applicant was granted a petition for relief of the order of the probate court pursuant to section 56C of chapter 215 and submits a copy of the order of the probate court with the application; or (D) found to be a person with an alcohol use disorder or substance use disorder or both and committed pursuant to said section 35 of said chapter 123, unless the applicant was granted a petition for relief of the court order pursuant to said section 35 and submits a copy of the court order with the application;

(iv) is younger than 21 years of age at the time of the application;

(v) is an alien who does not maintain lawful permanent residency;

(vi) is currently subject to: (A) an order for suspension or surrender issued pursuant to sections 3B or 3C of chapter 209A or a similar order issued by another jurisdiction; or (B) a permanent or temporary protection order issued pursuant to said chapter 209A or a similar order issued by another jurisdiction, including any order described in 18 U.S.C. 922(g)(8);

(vii) is currently the subject of an outstanding arrest warrant in any state or federal jurisdiction;

(viii) has been discharged from the armed forces of the United States under dishonorable conditions;

(ix) is a fugitive from justice; or

(x) having been a citizen of the United States, has renounced that citizenship.

The licensing authority may deny the application or renewal of a license to carry, or suspend or revoke a license issued under this section if, in a reasonable exercise of discretion, the licensing authority determines that the applicant or licensee is unsuitable to be issued or to continue to hold a license to carry. A determination of unsuitability shall be based on: (i) reliable and credible information that the applicant or licensee has exhibited or engaged in behavior that suggests that, if issued a license, the applicant or licensee may create a risk to public safety; or (ii) existing factors that suggest that, if issued a license, the applicant or licensee may create a risk to public safety. Upon denial of an application or renewal of a license based on a determination of unsuitability, the licensing authority shall notify the applicant in writing setting forth the specific reasons for the determination in accordance with paragraph (e). Upon revoking or suspending a license based on a determination of unsuitability, the licensing authority shall notify the holder of a license in writing setting forth the specific reasons for the determination in accordance with paragraph (f). The determination of unsuitability shall be subject to judicial review under said paragraph (f).

(e) Within seven days of the receipt of a completed application for a license to carry or possess firearms, or renewal of same, the licensing authority shall forward one copy of the application and one copy of the applicant's fingerprints to the colonel of state police, who shall within 30 days advise the licensing authority, in writing, of any disqualifying criminal record of the applicant arising from within or without the commonwealth and whether there is reason to believe that the applicant is disqualified for any of the foregoing reasons from possessing a license to carry or possess firearms. In searching for any disqualifying history of the applicant, the colonel shall utilize, or cause to be utilized, files maintained by the department of probation and statewide and nationwide criminal justice, warrant and protection order information systems and files including, but not limited to, the National Instant Criminal Background Check System. The colonel shall inquire of the commissioner of the department of mental health relative to whether the applicant is disqualified from being so licensed. If the information available to the colonel does not indicate that the possession of a firearm or large capacity firearm by the applicant would be in violation of state or federal law, he shall certify such fact, in writing, to the licensing authority within said 30 day period.

The licensing authority may also make inquiries concerning the applicant to: (i) the commissioner of the department of criminal justice information services relative to any disqualifying condition and records of purchases, sales, rentals, leases and transfers of weapons or ammunition concerning the applicant; (ii) the commissioner of probation relative to any record contained within the department of probation or the statewide domestic violence record keeping system concerning the applicant; and (iii) the commissioner of the department of mental health relative to whether the applicant is a suitable person to possess firearms or is not a suitable person to possess firearms. The director or commissioner to whom the licensing authority makes such inquiry shall provide prompt and full cooperation for that purpose in any investigation of the applicant.

The licensing authority shall, within 40 days from the date of application, either approve the application and issue the license or deny the application and notify the applicant of the reason for such denial in writing; provided, however, that no such license shall be issued unless the colonel has certified, in writing, that the information available to him does not indicate that the possession of a firearm or large capacity firearm by the applicant would be in violation of state or federal law.

The licensing authority shall provide to the applicant a receipt indicating that it received the application. The receipt shall be provided to the applicant within 7 days by mail if the application was received by mail or immediately if the application was made in person; provided, however, that the receipt shall include the applicant's name and address; current license number and license expiration date, if any; the date the licensing authority received the application; the name, address and telephone number of the licensing authority; the agent of the licensing authority that received the application; the type of application; and whether the application is for a new license or a renewal of an existing license. The licensing authority shall keep a copy of the receipt for not less than 1 year and shall furnish a copy to the applicant if requested by the applicant.

(f) A license issued under this section shall be revoked or suspended by the licensing authority, or his designee, upon the occurrence of any event that would have disqualified the holder from being issued such license or from having such license renewed. A license may be revoked or suspended by the licensing authority if it appears that the holder is no longer a suitable person to possess such license. Any revocation or suspension of a license shall be in writing and shall state the reasons therefor. Upon revocation or suspension, the licensing authority shall take possession of such license and the person whose license is so revoked or suspended shall take all actions required under the provisions of section 129D. No appeal or post-judgment motion shall operate to stay such revocation or suspension. Notices of revocation and suspension shall be forwarded to the commissioner of the department of criminal justice information services and the commissioner of probation and shall be included in the criminal justice information system. A revoked or suspended license may be reinstated only upon the termination of all disqualifying conditions, if any.

Any applicant or holder aggrieved by a denial, revocation, suspension or restriction placed on a license, unless a hearing has previously been held pursuant to chapter 209A, may, within either 90 days after receiving notice of the denial, revocation or suspension or within 90 days after the expiration of the time limit during which the licensing authority shall respond to the applicant or, in the case of a restriction, any time after a restriction is placed on the license pursuant to this section, file a petition to obtain judicial review in the district court having jurisdiction in the city or town in which the applicant filed the application or in which the license was issued. If after a hearing a justice of the court finds that there was no reasonable ground for denying, suspending, revoking or restricting the license and that the petitioner is not prohibited by law from possessing a license, the justice may order a license to be issued or reinstated to the petitioner or may order the licensing authority to remove certain restrictions placed on the license.

[Paragraph (g) effective until January 1, 2021. For text effective January 1, 2021, see below.]

(g) A license shall be in a standard form provided by the executive director of the criminal history systems board in a size and shape equivalent to that of a license to operate motor vehicles issued by the registry of motor vehicles pursuant to section 8 of chapter 90 and shall contain a license number which shall clearly indicate whether such number identifies a Class A or Class B license, the name, address, photograph, fingerprint, place and date of birth, height, weight, hair color, eye color and signature of the licensee. Such license shall be marked "License to Carry Firearms" and shall clearly indicate whether the license is Class A or Class B. The application for such license shall be made in a standard form provided by the executive director of the criminal history systems board, which form shall require the applicant to affirmatively state under the pains and penalties of perjury that such applicant is not disqualified on any of the grounds enumerated above from being issued such license.

[Paragraph (g) as amended by 2014, 284, Sec. 52 effective January 1, 2021. See 2014, 284, Sec. 112. For text effective until January 1, 2021, see above.]

(g) A license shall be in a standard form provided by the commissioner of criminal justice information services in a size and shape equivalent to that of a license to operate motor vehicles issued by the registry of motor vehicles pursuant to section 8 of chapter 90 and shall contain a license number which shall clearly indicate the name, address, photograph, fingerprint, place and date of birth, height, weight, hair color, eye color and signature of the licensee. The license shall be clearly marked "License to Carry Firearms". The license shall provide in a legible font size and style the phone numbers for the National Suicide Prevention Lifeline and the Samaritans Statewide Helpline. The application for such license shall be made in a standard form provided by the executive director of the criminal history systems board, which form shall require the applicant to affirmatively state under the pains and penalties of perjury that such applicant is not disqualified on any of the grounds enumerated above from being issued such license.

(h) Any person who knowingly files an application containing false information shall be punished by a fine of not less than $500 nor more than $1,000 or by imprisonment for not less than six months nor more than two years in a house of correction, or by both such fine and imprisonment.

[First paragraph of paragraph (i) effective until January 1, 2021. For text effective January 1, 2021, see below.]

(i) A license to carry or possess firearms shall be valid, unless revoked or suspended, for a period of not more than 6 years from the date of issue and shall expire on the anniversary of the licensee's date of birth occurring not less than 5 years nor more than 6 years from the date of issue; provided, however, that, if the licensee applied for renewal before the license expired, the license shall remain valid after its expiration date for all lawful purposes until the application for renewal is approved or denied. If a licensee is on active duty with the armed forces of the United States on the expiration date of the license, the license shall remain valid until the licensee is released from active duty and for a period not less than 180 days following the release; provided, however, that, if the licensee applied for renewal prior to the end of that period, the license shall remain valid after its expiration date for all lawful purposes until the application for renewal is approved or denied. An application for renewal of a Class B license filed before the license has expired shall not extend the license beyond the stated expiration date; provided, that the Class B license shall expire on the anniversary of the licensee's date of birth occurring not less than 5 years nor more than 6 years from the date of issue. Any renewal thereof shall expire on the anniversary of the licensee's date of birth occurring not less than 5 years but not more than 6 years from the effective date of such license. Any license issued to an applicant born on February 29 shall expire on March 1. The fee for the application shall be $100, which shall be payable to the licensing authority and shall not be prorated or refunded in case of revocation or denial. The licensing authority shall retain $25 of the fee; $50 of the fee shall be deposited into the general fund of the commonwealth and not less than $50,000 of the funds deposited into the General Fund shall be allocated to the Firearm Licensing Review Board, established in section 130B, for its operations and that any funds not expended by said board for its operations shall revert back to the General Fund; and $25 of the fee shall be deposited in the Firearms Fingerprint Identity Verification Trust Fund. For active and retired law enforcement officials, or local, state, or federal government entities acting on their behalf, the fee for the application shall be set at $25, which shall be payable to the licensing authority and shall not be prorated or refunded in case of revocation or denial. The licensing authority shall retain $12.50 of the fee, and $12.50 of the fee shall be deposited into the general fund of the commonwealth. Notwithstanding any general or special law to the contrary, licensing authorities shall deposit such portion of the license application fee into the Firearms Record Keeping Fund quarterly, not later than January 1, April 1, July 1 and October 1 of each year. Notwithstanding any general or special law to the contrary, licensing authorities shall deposit quarterly such portion of the license application fee as is to be deposited into the General Fund, not later than January 1, April 1, July 1 and October 1 of each year. For the purposes of section 10 of chapter 269, an expired license to carry firearms shall be deemed to be valid for a period not to exceed 90 days beyond the stated date of expiration, unless such license to carry firearms has been revoked.

[First paragraph of paragraph (i) as amended by 2014, 284, Sec. 54 effective January 1, 2021. See 2014, 284, Sec. 112. For text effective until January 1, 2021, see above.]

(i) A license to carry or possess firearms shall be valid, unless revoked or suspended, for a period of not more than 6 years from the date of issue and shall expire on the anniversary of the licensee's date of birth occurring not less than 5 years nor more than 6 years from the date of issue; provided, however, that, if the licensee applied for renewal before the license expired, the license shall remain valid after its expiration date for all lawful purposes until the application for renewal is approved or denied. If a licensee is on active duty with the armed forces of the United States on the expiration date of the license, the license shall remain valid until the licensee is released from active duty and for a period not less than 180 days following the release; provided, however, that, if the licensee applied for renewal prior to the end of that period, the license shall remain valid after its expiration date for all lawful purposes until the application for renewal is approved or denied. Any renewal thereof shall expire on the anniversary of the licensee's date of birth occurring not less than 5 years but not more than 6 years from the effective date of such license. Any license issued to an applicant born on February 29 shall expire on March 1. The fee for the application shall be $100, which shall be payable to the licensing authority and shall not be prorated or refunded in case of revocation or denial. The licensing authority shall retain $25 of the fee; $50 of the fee shall be deposited into the general fund of the commonwealth and not less than $50,000 of the funds deposited into the General Fund shall be allocated to the Firearm Licensing Review Board, established in section 130B, for its operations and that any funds not expended by said board for its operations shall revert back to the General Fund; and $25 of the fee shall be deposited in the Firearms Fingerprint Identity Verification Trust Fund. For active and retired law enforcement officials, or local, state, or federal government entities acting on their behalf, the fee for the application shall be set at $25, which shall be payable to the licensing authority and shall not be prorated or refunded in case of revocation or denial. The licensing authority shall retain $12.50 of the fee, and $12.50 of the fee shall be deposited into the general fund of the commonwealth. Notwithstanding any general or special law to the contrary, licensing authorities shall deposit such portion of the license application fee into the Firearms Record Keeping Fund quarterly, not later than January 1, April 1, July 1 and October 1 of each year. Notwithstanding any general or special law to the contrary, licensing authorities shall deposit quarterly such portion of the license application fee as is to be deposited into the General Fund, not later than January 1, April 1, July 1 and October 1 of each year. For the purposes of section 10 of chapter 269, an expired license to carry firearms shall be deemed to be valid for a period not to exceed 90 days beyond the stated date of expiration, unless such license to carry firearms has been revoked.

Any person over the age of 70 and any law enforcement officer applying for a license to carry firearms through his employing agency shall be exempt from the requirement of paying a renewal fee for a Class A or Class B license to carry.

(j)(1) No license shall be required for the carrying or possession of a firearm known as a detonator and commonly used on vehicles as a signaling and marking device, when carried or possessed for such signaling or marking purposes.

(2) No license to carry shall be required for the possession of an unloaded large capacity rifle or shotgun or an unloaded feeding device therefor by a veteran's organization chartered by the Congress of the United States, chartered by the commonwealth or recognized as a nonprofit tax-exempt organization by the Internal Revenue Service, or by the members of any such organization when on official parade duty or during ceremonial occasions. For purposes of this subparagraph, an "unloaded large capacity rifle or shotgun" and an "unloaded feeding device therefor" shall include any large capacity rifle, shotgun or feeding device therefor loaded with a blank cartridge or blank cartridges, so-called, which contain no projectile within such blank or blanks or within the bore or chamber of such large capacity rifle or shotgun.

(k) Whoever knowingly issues a license in violation of this section shall be punished by a fine of not less than $500 nor more than $1,000 or by imprisonment for not less than six months nor more than two years in a jail or house of correction, or by both such fine and imprisonment.

(l) The executive director of the criminal history systems board shall send electronically or by first class mail to the holder of each such license to carry firearms, a notice of the expiration of such license not less than 90 days prior to such expiration and shall enclose therein a form for the renewal of such license. The form for renewal shall include an affidavit in which the applicant shall verify that the applicant has not lost any firearms or had any firearms stolen from the applicant since the date of the applicant's last renewal or issuance. The taking of fingerprints shall not be required in issuing the renewal of a license if the renewal applicant's fingerprints are on file with the department of the state police. Any licensee shall notify, in writing, the licensing authority who issued said license, the Chief of police into whose jurisdiction the licensee moves and the executive director of the criminal history systems board of any change of address. Such notification shall be made by certified mail within 30 days of its occurrence. Failure to so notify shall be cause for revocation or suspension of said license. The commissioner of criminal justice information services shall provide electronic notice of expiration only upon the request of a cardholder. A request for electronic notice of expiration shall be forwarded to the department on a form furnished by the commissioner. Any electronic address maintained by the department for the purpose of providing electronic notice of expiration shall be considered a firearms record and shall not be disclosed except as provided in section 10 of chapter 66.

(m) Notwithstanding the provisions of section 10 of chapter 269, any person in possession of a firearm, rifle or shotgun whose license issued under this section is invalid for the sole reason that it has expired, not including licenses that remain valid under paragraph (i) because the licensee applied for renewal before the license expired, but who shall not be disqualified from renewal upon application therefor pursuant to this section, shall be subject to a civil fine of not less than $100 nor more than $5,000 and the provisions of section 10 of chapter 269 shall not apply; provided, however, that the exemption from the provisions of said section 10 of said chapter 269 provided herein shall not apply if: (i) such license has been revoked or suspended, unless such revocation or suspension was caused by failure to give notice of a change of address as required under this section; (ii) revocation or suspension of such license is pending, unless such revocation or suspension was caused by failure to give notice of a change of address as required under this section; or (iii) an application for renewal of such license has been denied. Any law enforcement officer who discovers a person to be in possession of a firearm, rifle or shotgun after such person's license has expired, meaning after 90 days beyond the stated expiration date on the license, has been revoked or suspended, solely for failure to give notice of a change of address, shall confiscate such firearm, rifle or shotgun and the expired or suspended license then in possession and such officer, shall forward such license to the licensing authority by whom it was issued as soon as practicable. The officer shall, at the time of confiscation, provide to the person whose firearm, rifle or shotgun has been confiscated, a written inventory and receipt for all firearms, rifles or shotguns confiscated and the officer and his employer shall exercise due care in the handling, holding and storage of these items. Any confiscated weapon shall be returned to the owner upon the renewal or reinstatement of such expired or suspended license within one year of such confiscation or may be otherwise disposed of in accordance with the provisions of section 129D. The provisions of this paragraph shall not apply if such person has a valid license to carry firearms issued under section 131F.

(n) Upon issuance of a license to carry or possess firearms under this section, the licensing authority shall forward a copy of such approved application and license to the executive director of the criminal history systems board, who shall inform the licensing authority forthwith of the existence of any disqualifying condition discovered or occurring subsequent to the issuance of a license under this section.

(o) No person shall be issued a license to carry or possess a machine gun in the commonwealth, except that a licensing authority or the colonel of state police may issue a machine gun license to:

(i) a firearm instructor certified by the municipal police training committee for the sole purpose of firearm instruction to police personnel;

(ii) a bona fide collector of firearms upon application or upon application for renewal of such license.

(p) The executive director of the criminal history systems board shall promulgate regulations in accordance with chapter 30A to establish criteria for persons who shall be classified as bona fide collectors of firearms.

(q) Nothing in this section shall authorize the purchase, possession or transfer of any weapon, ammunition or feeding device that is, or in such manner that is, prohibited by state or federal law.

(r) The secretary of the executive office of public safety or his designee may promulgate regulations to carry out the purposes of this section.

Section 1311/2: Gun control advisory board

Section 1311/2. The governor shall appoint a gun control advisory board, hereinafter referred to as the board. The board shall consist of seven individuals, one of whom shall be a member of the gun owners action league, one of whom shall be a police Chief selected from a list of four selected by the police chiefs association and one of whom shall be the director of the firearms record bureau within the department of criminal justice information services. It shall be the responsibility of the board to advise the executive office of public safety on matters relating to the implementation of sections 121 to 131P, inclusive, and section 2SS of chapter 29. The board shall serve without compensation and shall adopt operating rules and procedures for its organization and activities.

Section 1313/4: Roster of large capacity rifles, shotguns, firearms, and feeding devices

Section 1313/4. The secretary of public safety shall, with the advice of the gun control advisory board established pursuant to the provisions of section 1311/2, compile and publish a roster of large capacity rifles, shotguns, firearms and feeding devices, all as defined in section 121, and such weapons referred to in clauses Eighteenth to Twenty-first, inclusive, of section 123.

The secretary shall, not less than three times annually, publish the roster in newspapers of general circulation throughout the commonwealth, and shall send a copy thereof to all dealers licensed in the commonwealth under the provisions of said section 122 of said chapter 140; and further, the licensing authority shall furnish said roster to all cardholders and licensees upon initial issuance and upon every renewal of the same.

The secretary may amend the roster upon his own initiative or with the advice of said board. A person may petition the secretary to place a weapon on, or remove a weapon from, the roster, subject to the provisions of this section. A person who so petitions shall give the reasons why the roster should be so amended.

A petition to amend the roster shall be submitted in writing to the secretary and shall be in the form and manner prescribed by the secretary. Upon receipt of the petition to place a weapon on the roster, the secretary shall, within 45 days of receipt of the petition, either notify the petitioner by certified mail that the petition is denied, or it shall modify the roster. An addition to the roster shall be effective on the date it is included in the next publication in newspapers of general circulation as provided under this section.

The secretary may promulgate rules and regulations relative to the appeal of a decision on a petition to modify the roster and any other regulations consistent with the provisions of this section and section 2SS of chapter 29, sections 11 and 14 of chapter 131, sections 121, 122, 122B, 123, 128, 128A, 128B, 129B, 129C, 129D, 130, 131, 131A, 131E, 131F and 131K of chapter 140 to effectuate the purposes of each said section.

Section 131A: Permits to purchase, rent or lease firearms, or to purchase ammunition; fee; penalties

Section 131A. A licensing authority under section one hundred and thirty-one, upon the application of a person qualified to be granted a license thereunder by such authority, may grant to such a person, other than a minor, a permit to purchase, rent or lease a firearm if it appears that such purchase, rental or lease is for a proper purpose, and may revoke such permit at will. The colonel of the state police or a person authorized by him, upon the application of a person licensed under section one hundred and thirty-one F, may grant to such licensee, other than a minor, a permit to purchase, rent or lease a firearm, rifle or shotgun, or to purchase ammunition therefor, if it appears that such purchase, rental or lease is for a proper purpose, and may revoke such permit at will. Such permits shall be issued on forms furnished by the commissioner of the department of criminal justice information services shall be valid for not more than ten days after issue, and a copy of every such permit so issued shall within one week thereafter be sent to the said executive director. The licensing authority may impose such restrictions relative to the caliber and capacity of the firearm to be purchased, rented or leased as he deems proper. Whoever knowingly issues a permit in violation of this section shall be punished by a fine of not less than five hundred nor more than one thousand dollars and by imprisonment for not less than six months nor more than two years in a jail or house of correction.

The fee for the permits shall be $100, which shall be payable to the licensing authority and shall not be prorated or refunded in case of revocation or denial. The licensing authority shall retain $25 of the fee; $50 of the fee shall be deposited into the general fund of the commonwealth; and $25 of the fee shall be deposited in the Firearms Fingerprint Identity Verification Trust Fund.

Section 131B: Penalty for loan of money secured by weapons

Section 131B. Whoever loans money secured by mortgage, deposit or pledge of a firearm, rifle, shotgun or machine gun shall be punished by a fine of not more than five hundred dollars or by imprisonment for not more than one year, or by both; provided, however that nothing herein shall prohibit a bank or other institutional lender from loaning money secured by a mortgage, deposit, or pledge of a firearm, rifle, shotgun or machine gun to a manufacturer, wholesaler, or dealer of firearms, rifles, or shotguns. The provisions of section one hundred and twenty-three shall not be applicable to any such mortgage, deposit or pledge unless or until the lender takes possession of the collateral upon default or the collateral is removed from the premises of the debtor.

Section 131C: Carrying of firearms in a vehicle

[Text of section effective until January 1, 2021. For text effective January 1, 2021, see below.]

Section 131C. (a) No person carrying a loaded firearm under a Class A license issued under section 131 or 131F shall carry the same in a vehicle unless such firearm while carried therein is under the direct control of such person. Whoever violates the provisions of this subsection shall be punished by a fine of $500.

(b) No person carrying a firearm under a Class B license issued under section 131 or 131F shall possess the same in a vehicle unless such weapon is unloaded and contained within the locked trunk of such vehicle or in a locked case or other secure container. Whoever violates the provisions of this subsection shall be punished by a fine of $500.

(c) No person possessing a large capacity rifle or shotgun under a Class A or Class B license issued under section 131 or 131F shall possess the same in a vehicle unless such weapon is unloaded and contained within the locked trunk of such vehicle or in a locked case or other secure container. Whoever violates the provisions of this subsection shall be punished by a fine of not less than $500 nor more than $5,000.

(d) The provisions of this section shall not apply to (i) any officer, agent or employee of the commonwealth or any state or the United States; (ii) any member of the military or other service of any state or of the United States; (iii) any duly authorized law enforcement officer, agent or employee of any municipality of the commonwealth; provided, however, that any such person described in clauses (i) to (iii), inclusive, is authorized by a competent authority to carry or possess the weapon so carried or possessed and is acting within the scope of his duties.

(e) A conviction of a violation of this section shall be reported forthwith by the court or magistrate to the licensing authority who shall immediately revoke the card or license of the person so convicted. No new such card or license may be issued to any such person until one year after the date of revocation.

Chapter 140: Section 131C. Carrying of firearms in a vehicle

[Text of section as amended by 2014, 284, Sec. 58 effective January 1, 2021. See 2014, 284, Sec. 112. For text effective until January 1, 2021, see above.]

Section 131C. (a) No person carrying a loaded firearm under a license issued pursuant to section 131 or 131F shall carry the loaded firearm in a vehicle unless the loaded firearm while carried in the vehicle is under the direct control of the person. Whoever violates this subsection shall be punished by a fine of $500.

(b) No person possessing a large capacity rifle or shotgun under a license issued pursuant to section 131 or 131F shall possess the large capacity rifle or shotgun in a vehicle unless the large capacity rifle or shotgun is unloaded and contained within the locked trunk of the vehicle or in a locked case or other secure container. Whoever violates this subsection shall be punished by a fine of not less than $500 nor more than $5,000.

(c) This section shall not apply to: (i) an officer, agent or employee of the commonwealth, any state or the United States; (ii) a member of the military or other service of any state or of the United States; (iii) a duly authorized law enforcement officer, agent or employee of a municipality of the commonwealth; provided, however, that a person described in clauses (i) to (iii), inclusive, is authorized by a competent authority to carry or possess the weapon so carried or possessed and is acting within the scope of the person's official duties.

(d) A conviction of a violation of this section shall be reported immediately by the court or magistrate to the licensing authority. The licensing authority shall immediately revoke the firearm identification card or license of the person convicted of a violation of this section. No new firearm identification card or license may be issued to a person convicted of a violation of this section until 1 year after the date of revocation of the firearm identification card or license.

Section 131D: Repealed, 1954, 672, Sec. 7

Section 131E: Purchase by residents; licenses; firearm identification cards; purchase for use of another; penalties; revocation of licenses or cards; reissuance

[Text of section effective until January 1, 2021. For text effective January 1, 2021, see below.]

Section 131E. Any resident of the commonwealth may purchase firearms, rifles, shotguns and ammunition feeding devices from any dealer licensed under section 122, or from such person as shall be qualified under section 128A, or ammunition from a licensee under section 122B, subject to the following conditions and restrictions:

(a) rifles, shotguns and feeding devices therefor may be so purchased only upon presentment of: (i) a valid firearm identification card issued under section 129B; or (ii) a valid Class A or Class B license to carry firearms issued under section 131; or (iii) valid proof of exempt status under section 129C; provided, however, that large capacity rifles and shotguns and large capacity feeding devices therefor may be so purchased only upon presentment of a Class A or Class B license to carry firearms issued under said section 131; and provided further, that no rifle or shotgun or ammunition or ammunition feeding device therefor shall be sold to any person less than 18 years of age; and provided further, that no large capacity rifle or shotgun or large capacity feeding device therefor shall be sold to any person less than 21 years of age;

(b) firearms and feeding devices therefor may be so purchased only upon presentment of: (i) a valid Class A or Class B license to carry firearms issued under section 131; or (ii) a valid firearm identification card issued under section 129B together with a valid permit to purchase a firearm issued under section 131A; or (iii) a valid permit to purchase a firearm issued under section 131A together with valid proof of exempt status under section 129C; provided, however, that large capacity firearms and large capacity feeding devices therefor may be so purchased only upon presentment of: (i) a valid Class A license to carry firearms issued under section 131; or (ii) a valid firearm identification card issued under section 129B together with a valid and proper permit to purchase a firearm issued under section 131A; or (iii) a valid and proper permit to purchase a firearm issued under section 131A together with valid proof of exempt status under section 129C; and provided further, that neither a firearm identification card issued under section 129B, nor proof of exempt status under section 129C, shall be valid for the purpose of purchasing any firearm or ammunition feeding device therefor without being presented together with a valid and proper permit to purchase issued under section 131A; and provided further, that an alien permit to possess a rifle or shotgun shall not be valid for the purpose of purchasing firearms or ammunition or ammunition feeding devices therefor; and provided further, that no firearm or ammunition or ammunition feeding device therefor shall be sold to any person less than 21 years of age. Any person who uses said license to carry firearms or firearm identification card for the purpose of purchasing a firearm, rifle or shotgun for the unlawful use of another, or for resale to or giving to an unlicensed person, shall be punished by a fine of not less than one thousand nor more than fifty thousand dollars, or by imprisonment for not less than two and one-half years nor more than ten years in a state prison, or by both such fine and imprisonment. A conviction of a violation of this section shall be reported forthwith by the court to the licensing authority which issued the license or firearm identification card, which shall immediately revoke the license or firearm identification card of such person. No new license or firearm identification card under section one hundred and twenty-nine B or section one hundred and thirty-one shall be issued to any such person within two years after the date of said revocation.

Chapter 140: Section 131E. Purchase by residents; licenses; firearm identification cards; purchase for use of another; penalties; revocation of licenses or cards

[Text of section as amended by 2014, 284, Sec. 59 effective January 1, 2021. See 2014, 284, Sec. 112. For text effective until January 1, 2021, see above.]

Section 131E. A resident of the commonwealth may purchase firearms, rifles, shotguns and ammunition feeding devices from a dealer licensed pursuant to section 122 or from a person qualified pursuant to section 128A or may purchase ammunition from a licensee under section 122B subject to the following conditions and restrictions:

(a) rifles, shotguns and feeding devices therefor may be so purchased only upon presentment of: (i) a valid firearm identification card issued pursuant to section 129B; (ii) a valid license to carry firearms issued pursuant to section 131; or (iii) valid proof of exempt status under section 129C; provided, however, that large capacity rifles and shotguns and large capacity feeding devices therefor may be so purchased only upon presentment of a license to carry firearms issued pursuant to said section 131; and provided further, that no rifle, shotgun, ammunition or ammunition feeding device therefor shall be sold to a person younger than 18 years of age; and provided further, that no large capacity rifle, shotgun or large capacity feeding device therefor shall be sold to a person younger than 21 years of age; and

(b) firearms and feeding devices therefor, including large capacity firearms and large capacity feeding devices therefor, may be so purchased only upon presentment of: (i) a valid license to carry firearms issued pursuant to section 131; (ii) a valid firearm identification card issued pursuant to section 129B; or (iii) valid proof of exempt status under section 129C; provided, however, that neither a firearm identification card issued pursuant to said section 129B nor proof of exempt status under said section 129C shall be valid to purchase a firearm or ammunition feeding device therefor, including large capacity firearms and large capacity feeding devices therefor, without being presented together with a valid and proper permit to purchase issued under section 131A; and provided further, that an alien permit to possess a rifle or shotgun shall not be valid to purchase firearms, ammunition or ammunition feeding devices therefor; and provided further, that no firearm, ammunition or ammunition feeding device therefor shall be sold to a person younger than 21 years of age.

A firearms collector, licensed pursuant to 18 U.S.C. 923(b), may purchase a rifle, shotgun or firearm that was not previously owned or registered in the commonwealth from a dealer licensed under section 122 if that rifle, shotgun or firearm is a curio or relic as defined in 27 CFR 478.11.

A person who uses a license to carry firearms or a firearm identification card to purchase a firearm, rifle or shotgun for the unlawful use of another or for resale to or giving to an unlicensed person shall be punished by a fine of not less than $1,000 nor more than $50,000 or by imprisonment for not less than 21/2 years nor more than 10 years in a state prison or by both such fine and imprisonment. A conviction of a violation of this section shall be reported immediately by the court to the licensing authority that issued the license or firearm identification card. The licensing authority shall immediately revoke the license or firearm identification card pursuant to said section 129B or said section 131 and no license shall be issued to a person convicted of a violation of this section within 2 years after the date of the revocation of the license or firearm identification card.

Section 131F: Nonresidents or aliens; temporary license to carry firearms or ammunition

Introductory paragraph of first paragraph effective until January 1, 2021. For text effective January 1, 2021, see below.]

Section 131F. A Class A or Class B temporary license to carry firearms or feeding devices or ammunition therefor, within the commonwealth, may be issued by the colonel of state police, or persons authorized by him, to a nonresident or any person not falling within the jurisdiction of a local licensing authority or to an alien that resides outside the commonwealth for purposes of firearms competition and subject to such terms and conditions as said colonel may deem proper; provided, however, that no license shall be issued to a person who:

[Introductory paragraph of first paragraph as amended by 2014, 284, Sec. 60 effective January 1, 2021. See 2014, 284, Sec. 112. For text effective until January 1, 2021, see above.]

A temporary license to carry firearms or feeding devices or ammunition therefor, within the commonwealth, may be issued by the colonel of state police, or persons authorized by him, to a nonresident or any person not falling within the jurisdiction of a local licensing authority or to an alien that resides outside the commonwealth for purposes of firearms competition and subject to such terms and conditions as said colonel may deem proper; provided, however, that no license shall be issued to a person who:

(i) has, in any state or federal jurisdiction, been convicted or adjudicated a youthful offender or delinquent child for the commission of (A) a felony; (B) a misdemeanor punishable by imprisonment for more than 2 years; (C) a violent crime as defined in section 121; (D) a violation of any law regulating the use, possession, ownership, transfer, purchase, sale, lease, rental, receipt or transportation of weapons or ammunition for which a term of imprisonment may be imposed; (E) a violation of any law regulating the use, possession or sale of a controlled substance as defined in section 1 of chapter 94C; or (F) a misdemeanor crime of domestic violence as defined in 18 U.S.C. 921(a)(33);

(ii) has been confined to any hospital or institution for mental illness, unless the applicant submits with his application an affidavit of a registered physician attesting that such physician is familiar with the applicant's mental illness and that in such physician's opinion the applicant is not disabled by such an illness in a manner that should prevent such applicant from possessing a firearm;

(iii) is or has been under treatment for or confinement for drug addiction or habitual drunkenness, unless such applicant is deemed to be cured of such condition by a licensed physician, and such applicant may make application for said license after the expiration of five years from the date of such confinement or treatment and upon presentment of an affidavit issued by such physician stating that such physician knows the applicant's history of treatment and that in such physician's opinion the applicant is deemed cured;

(iv) is currently subject to: (A) an order for suspension or surrender issued pursuant to section 3B or 3C of chapter 209A or a similar order issued by another jurisdiction; or (B) a permanent or temporary protection order issued pursuant to chapter 209A or a similar order issued by another jurisdiction;

(v) is currently the subject of an outstanding arrest warrant in any state or federal jurisdiction;

(vi) has been discharged from the armed forces of the United States under dishonorable conditions;

(vii) is a fugitive from justice;

(viii) having been a citizen of the United States, has renounced that citizenship;

(ix) not being a citizen or national of the United States, is illegally or unlawfully in the United States; or

(x) not being a citizen or national of the United States, has been admitted to the United States under a nonimmigrant visa as defined in 8 U.S.C. 1101(a)(26), unless the person has been admitted to the United States for lawful hunting or sporting purposes or is in possession of a hunting license or permit lawfully issued in the United States or another exception set forth in 18 U.S.C. 922(y)(2) applies.

Such license shall be valid for a period of one year but the colonel may renew such license, if in his discretion, such renewal is necessary.

The colonel may also issue such license, subject to such terms and conditions as he deems proper, to any resident of the commonwealth for the purposes of sports competition.

[Fourth paragraph effective until January 1, 2021. For text effective January 1, 2021, see below.]

A temporary license issued under this section shall be marked "Temporary License to Carry Firearms", shall clearly indicate whether it is Class A or Class B and shall not be used to purchase firearms in the commonwealth as provided under section 131E. Neither a large capacity firearm nor large capacity feeding device therefor may be carried unless such person has been issued a Class A license; provided, however, that the colonel may permit a Class A or Class B licensee to possess large capacity rifles or shotguns or both, and such entitlement shall be clearly indicated on such license. The fee for an application for the license shall be $100, which shall be payable to the licensing authority and shall not be prorated or refunded in case of revocation or denial. The licensing authority shall retain $25 of the fee; $50 of the fee shall be deposited into the general fund of the commonwealth; and $25 of the fee shall be deposited in the Firearms Fingerprint Identity Verification Trust Fund. A license issued under the provisions of this section to a non-resident who is in the employ of a bank, public utility corporation, or a firm engaged in the business of transferring monies, or business of similar nature, or a firm licensed as a private detective under the provisions of chapter one hundred and forty-seven, and whose application is endorsed by his employer, or who is a member of the armed services and is stationed within the territorial boundaries of the commonwealth and has the written consent of his commanding officer, may be issued for any term not to exceed two years, and said licenses shall expire in accordance with the provisions of section one hundred and thirty-one.

[Fourth paragraph as amended by 2014, 284, Sec. 63 effective January 1, 2021. See 2014, 284, Sec. 112. For text effective until January 1, 2021, see above.]

A temporary license issued pursuant to this section shall be clearly marked "Temporary License to Carry Firearms" and shall not be used to purchase firearms in the commonwealth as provided in section 131E. A large capacity firearm and a large capacity feeding device therefor may be carried if the person has been issued a license. The colonel may permit a licensee to possess a large capacity rifle or shotgun or both; provided, however, that this entitlement shall be clearly indicated on the license. The fee for an application for the license shall be $100, which shall be payable to the licensing authority and shall not be prorated or refunded in case of revocation or denial. The licensing authority shall retain $25 of the fee; $50 of the fee shall be deposited into the general fund of the commonwealth; and $25 of the fee shall be deposited in the Firearms Fingerprint Identity Verification Trust Fund. A license issued under the provisions of this section to a non-resident who is in the employ of a bank, public utility corporation, or a firm engaged in the business of transferring monies, or business of similar nature, or a firm licensed as a private detective under the provisions of chapter one hundred and forty-seven, and whose application is endorsed by his employer, or who is a member of the armed services and is stationed within the territorial boundaries of the commonwealth and has the written consent of his commanding officer, may be issued for any term not to exceed two years, and said licenses shall expire in accordance with the provisions of section one hundred and thirty-one.

A license, otherwise in accordance with provisions of this section, may be issued to a nonresident employee, whose application is endorsed by his employer, of a federally licensed Massachusetts manufacturer of machine guns to possess within the commonwealth a machine gun for the purpose of transporting or testing relative to the manufacture of machine guns, and the license shall be marked "temporary license to possess a machine gun" and may be issued for any term not to exceed two years and shall expire in accordance with the provisions of section one hundred and thirty-one.

Section 131F1/2: Theatrical productions; carrying firearms and blank ammunition

Section 131F1/2. Notwithstanding the provisions of subsection (a) of section ten of chapter two hundred and sixty-nine of the General Laws or any other law to the contrary, the carrying or possession of a firearm and blank ammunition therefor, during the course of any television, movie, stage or other similar theatrical production, by a person within such production, shall be authorized; provided, however, that such carrying or possession of such firearm shall be under the immediate supervision of a person licensed to carry firearms.

Section 131G: Carrying of firearms by non-residents; conditions

Section 131G. Any person who is not a resident of the commonwealth may carry a pistol or revolver in or through the commonwealth for the purpose of taking part in a pistol or revolver competition or attending any meeting or exhibition of any organized group of firearm collectors or for the purpose of hunting; provided, that such person is a resident of the United States and has a permit or license to carry firearms issued under the laws of any state, district or territory thereof which has licensing requirements which prohibit the issuance of permits or licenses to persons who have been convicted of a felony or who have been convicted of the unlawful use, possession or sale of narcotic or harmful drugs; provided, further, that in the case of a person traveling in or through the commonwealth for the purpose of hunting, he has on his person a hunting or sporting license issued by the commonwealth or by the state of his destination. Police officers and other peace officers of any state, territory or jurisdiction within the United States duly authorized to possess firearms by the laws thereof shall, for the purposes of this section, be deemed to have a permit or license to carry firearms as described in this section.

Section 131H: Ownership or possession of firearms by aliens; penalties; seizure and disposition

Section 131H. No alien shall own or have in his possession or under his control a firearm except as provided in section one hundred and thirty-one F or a rifle or shotgun except as provided in this section or section one hundred and thirty-one F. The colonel of the state police may, after an investigation, issue a permit to an alien to own or have in his possession or under his control a rifle or shotgun; subject to such terms and conditions as said colonel may deem proper. The fee for the permit shall be $100, which shall be payable to the licensing authority and shall not be prorated or refunded in case of revocation or denial. The licensing authority shall retain $25 of the fee; $50 of the fee shall be deposited into the general fund of the commonwealth; and $25 of the fee shall be deposited in the Firearms Fingerprint Identity Verification Trust Fund. Upon issuing such permit said colonel shall so notify, in writing, the chief of police or the board or officer having control of the police in the city or town in which such alien resides. Each such permit card shall expire at twelve midnight on December thirty-first next succeeding the effective date of said permit, and shall be revocable for cause by said colonel. In case of revocation, the fee for such permit shall not be prorated or refunded. Whenever any such permit is revoked, said colonel shall give notification as hereinbefore provided. The permit issued to an alien under this section shall be subject to sections one hundred and twenty-nine B and one hundred and twenty-nine C except as otherwise provided by this section.

Violation of any provision of this section shall be punished by a fine of not less than five hundred nor more than one thousand dollars, and by imprisonment for not more than six months in a jail or house of correction. If, in any prosecution for violation of this section, the defendant alleges that he has been naturalized, or alleges that he is a citizen of the United States, the burden of proving the same shall be upon him. Any firearm, rifle or shotgun owned by an alien or in his possession or under his control in violation of this section shall be forfeited to the commonwealth. Any such firearm, rifle or shotgun may be the subject of a search warrant as provided in chapter two hundred and seventy-six.

The director of law enforcement of the department of fisheries, wildlife and environmental law enforcement, deputy directors of enforcement, chiefs of enforcement, deputy chiefs of enforcement, environmental police officers and deputy environmental police officers, wardens as defined in section one of chapter one hundred and thirty-one and members of the state police in areas over which they have jurisdiction, and all officers qualified to serve criminal process shall arrest, without a warrant, any person found with a firearm, rifle or shotgun in his possession if they have reason to believe that he is an alien and if he does not have in his possession a valid permit as provided in this section.

Section 131I: Falsifying firearm license or identification card; penalty

Section 131I. Whoever falsely makes, alters, forges or counterfeits or procures or assists another to falsely make, alter, forge or counterfeit a license to carry a firearm or a firearm identification card, or whoever forges or without authority uses the signature, facsimile of the signature, or validating signature stamp of the licensing authority or its designee, or whoever possesses, utters, publishes as true or in any way makes use of a falsely made, altered, forged or counterfeited license to carry a firearm or a firearm identification card, shall be punished by imprisonment in a state prison for not more than five years or in a jail or house of correction for not more than two years, or by a fine of not less than five hundred dollars, or both such fine and imprisonment.

Section 131J: Sale or possession of electrical weapons; penalties

Section 131J. No person shall possess a portable device or weapon from which an electrical current, impulse, wave or beam may be directed, which current, impulse, wave or beam is designed to incapacitate temporarily, injure or kill, except: (1) a federal, state or municipal law enforcement officer, or member of a special reaction team in a state prison or designated special operations or tactical team in a county correctional facility, acting in the discharge of his official duties who has completed a training course approved by the secretary of public safety in the use of such a devise or weapon designed to incapacitate temporarily; or (2) a supplier of such devices or weapons designed to incapacitate temporarily, if possession of the device or weapon is necessary to the supply or sale of the device or weapon within the scope of such sale or supply enterprise. No person shall sell or offer for sale such device or weapon, except to federal, state or municipal law enforcement agencies. A device or weapon sold under this section shall include a mechanism for tracking the number of times the device or weapon has been fired. The secretary of public safety shall adopt regulations governing who may sell or offer to sell such devices or weapons in the commonwealth and governing law enforcement training on the appropriate use of portable electrical weapons.

Whoever violates this section shall be punished by a fine of not less than $500 nor more than $1,000 or by imprisonment in the house of correction for not less than 6 months nor more than 21/2 years, or by both such fine and imprisonment. A law enforcement officer may arrest without a warrant any person whom he has probable cause to believe has violated this section.

Section 131K: Firearms or large capacity weapons without safety devices; liability

Section 131K. Any firearm or large capacity weapon, both as defined in section 121, sold within the commonwealth without a safety device designed to prevent the discharge of such weapon by unauthorized users and approved by the colonel of state police including, but not limited to, mechanical locks or devices designed to recognize and authorize, or otherwise allow the firearm to be discharged only by its owner or authorized user, by solenoid use-limitation devices, key activated or combination trigger or handle locks, radio frequency tags, automated fingerprint identification systems or voice recognition, provided, that such device is commercially available, shall be defective and the sale of such a weapon shall constitute a breach of warranty under section 2?314 of chapter 106 and an unfair or deceptive trade act or practice under section 2 of chapter 93A. Any entity responsible for the manufacture, importation or sale as an inventory item or consumer good, both as defined in section 9?102 of chapter 106, of such a weapon that does not include or incorporate such a device shall be individually and jointly liable to any person who sustains personal injury or property damage resulting from the failure to include or incorporate such a device. If death results from such personal injury, such entities shall be liable in an amount including, but not limited to, that provided under chapter 229. Contributory or comparative negligence shall not be valid defenses to an action brought under this section in conjunction with section 2 of chapter 93A or section 2?314 of chapter 106 or both; provided, however, that nothing herein shall prohibit such liable parties from maintaining an action for indemnification or contribution against each other or against the lawful owner or other authorized user of said weapon. Any disclaimer, limit or waiver of the liability provided under this section shall be void.

No entity responsible for the manufacture, importation or sale of such a weapon shall be liable to any person for injuries caused by the discharge of such weapon that does not include or incorporate a safety device as required under this section if such injuries were: (i) self-inflicted, either intentionally or unintentionally, unless such injuries were self-inflicted by a person less than 18 years of age; (ii) inflicted by the lawful owner or other authorized user of said weapon; (iii) inflicted by any person in the lawful exercise of self-defense; or (iv) inflicted upon a co-conspirator in the commission of a crime.

This section shall not apply to any weapon distributed to an officer of any law enforcement agency or any member of the armed forces of the United States or the organized militia of the commonwealth; provided, however, that such person is authorized to acquire, possess or carry such a weapon for the lawful performance of his official duties; and provided further, that any such weapon so distributed is distributed solely for use in connection with such duties. This section shall not apply to any firearm manufactured in or prior to the year 1899, or to any replica of such a firearm if such replica is not designed or redesigned for using rimfire or conventional centerfire fixed ammunition.

Section 131L: Weapons stored or kept by owner; inoperable by any person other than owner or lawfully authorized user; punishment

Section 131L. (a) It shall be unlawful to store or keep any firearm, rifle or shotgun including, but not limited to, large capacity weapons, or machine gun in any place unless such weapon is secured in a locked container or equipped with a tamper-resistant mechanical lock or other safety device, properly engaged so as to render such weapon inoperable by any person other than the owner or other lawfully authorized user. For purposes of this section, such weapon shall not be deemed stored or kept if carried by or under the control of the owner or other lawfully authorized user.

(b) A violation of this section shall be punished, in the case of a firearm, rifle or shotgun that is not a large capacity weapon, by a fine of not less than $1000 nor more than $7,500 or by imprisonment for not more than 11/2 years or by both such fine and imprisonment and, in the case of a large capacity weapon or machine gun, by a fine of not less than $2,000 nor more than $15,000 or by imprisonment for not less than 11/2 years nor more than 12 years or by both such fine and imprisonment.

(c) A violation of this section shall be punished, in the case of a rifle or shotgun that is not a large capacity weapon and the weapon was stored or kept in a place where a person younger than 18 years of age who does not possess a valid firearm identification card issued under section 129B may have access without committing an unforeseeable trespass, by a fine of not less than $2,500 nor more than $15,000 or by imprisonment for not less than 11/2 years nor more than 12 years or by both such fine and imprisonment.

(d) A violation of this section shall be punished, in the case of a rifle or shotgun that is a large capacity weapon, firearm or machine gun that was stored or kept in a place where a person younger than 18 years of age may have access without committing an unforeseeable trespass, by a fine of not less than $10,000 nor more than $20,000 or by imprisonment for not less than 4 years nor more than 15 years or by both such fine and imprisonment.

(e) A violation of the provisions of this section shall be evidence of wanton or reckless conduct in any criminal or civil proceeding if a person under the age of 18 who was not a trespasser or was a foreseeable trespasser acquired access to a weapon, unless such person possessed a valid firearm identification card issued under section 129B and was permitted by law to possess such weapon, and such access results in the personal injury to or the death of any person.

(f) This section shall not apply to the storage or keeping of any firearm, rifle or shotgun with matchlock, flintlock, percussion cap or similar type of ignition system manufactured in or prior to the year 1899, or to any replica of any such firearm, rifle or shotgun if such replica is not designed or redesigned for using rimfire or conventional centerfire fixed ammunition.

Section 131M: Assault weapon or large capacity feeding device not lawfully possessed on September 13, 1994; sale, transfer or possession; punishment

Section 131M. No person shall sell, offer for sale, transfer or possess an assault weapon or a large capacity feeding device that was not otherwise lawfully possessed on September 13, 1994. Whoever not being licensed under the provisions of section 122 violates the provisions of this section shall be punished, for a first offense, by a fine of not less than $1,000 nor more than $10,000 or by imprisonment for not less than one year nor more than ten years, or by both such fine and imprisonment, and for a second offense, by a fine of not less than $5,000 nor more than $15,000 or by imprisonment for not less than five years nor more than 15 years, or by both such fine and imprisonment.

The provisions of this section shall not apply to: (i) the possession by a law enforcement officer; or (ii) the possession by an individual who is retired from service with a law enforcement agency and is not otherwise prohibited from receiving such a weapon or feeding device from such agency upon retirement.

Section 131N: Covert weapons; sale, transfer or possession; punishment

Section 131N. No person shall sell, offer for sale, transfer or possess any weapon, capable of discharging a bullet or shot, that is: (i) constructed in a shape that does not resemble a handgun, short-barreled rifle or short-barreled shotgun including, but not limited to, covert weapons that resemble key-chains, pens, cigarette-lighters or cigarette-packages; or (ii) not detectable as a weapon or potential weapon by x-ray machines commonly used at airports or walk-through metal detectors. Whoever violates the provisions of this section shall be punished, for a first offense, by a fine of not less than $1,000 nor more than $10,000 or by imprisonment for not less than one year nor more than ten years, or by both such fine and imprisonment, and for a second offense, by a fine of not less than $5,000 nor more than $15,000 or by imprisonment for not less than five years nor more than 15 years, or by both such fine and imprisonment.

Section 131O: Colonel of state police; statewide firearms surrender program

Section 131O. Notwithstanding any general or special law, rule or regulation to the contrary, the colonel of state police, in conjunction with the secretary of the executive office of public safety, shall promulgate rules and regulations implementing a statewide firearms surrender program. In conjunction with this program only, any citizen of the commonwealth who complies with the policies set forth by the colonel shall not be asked for identification and shall be immune from prosecution for possession of such firearm; provided, however, that nothing herein shall prohibit the prosecution of any person for the unlawful possession of a firearm who is not in compliance with the conditions and procedures established by the colonel; and provided further, that nothing herein shall prohibit the prosecution of any person for any other offense committed within the commonwealth.

Any firearm surrendered in accordance with the provisions of this program that is reported stolen shall be returned to its lawful owner; provided, however, that any firearm suspected to be evidence in a crime shall remain in the custody and control of the department of state police in the same manner as any other such firearm lawfully seized by the department of state police. The department of state police may test-fire and preserve any and all firearms voluntarily surrendered. All weapons that have been voluntarily surrendered that are not suspected to be evidence of criminal activity and have not been reported stolen shall be disposed of in accordance with procedures established by the colonel.

Section 131P: Basic firearms safety certificate; instructors; public service announcements

[Subsection (a) effective until January 1, 2021. For text effective January 1, 2021, see below.]

Section 131P. (a) Any person making application for the issuance of a firearms identification card under section 129B, a Class A or Class B license to carry firearms under section 131 or 131F or a permit to purchase under section 131A who was not licensed under the provisions of this chapter on June 1, 1998 shall, in addition to the requirements set forth in said section 129B, 131, 131A or 131F, submit to the licensing authority a basic firearms safety certificate; provided, however, that a certificate issued by the division of law enforcement in the department of fisheries, wildlife and environmental law enforcement pursuant to the provisions of section 14 of chapter 131 evidencing satisfactory completion of a hunter education course shall serve as a valid substitute for a basic firearms safety certificate required under this section. Persons lawfully possessing a firearm identification card or license to carry firearms on June 1, 1998 shall be exempt from the provisions of this section upon expiration of such card or license and when applying for licensure as required under this chapter. No application for the issuance of a firearm identification card or license to carry shall be accepted or processed by the licensing authority without such certificate attached thereto; provided, however, that the provisions of this section shall not apply to (i) any officer, agent or employee of the commonwealth or any state of the United States; (ii) any member of the military or other service of any state or of the United States; (iii) any duly authorized law enforcement officer, agent or employee of any municipality of the commonwealth; provided, however, that any such person described in clauses (i) to (iii), inclusive, is authorized by a competent authority to carry or possess the weapon so carried or possessed and is acting within the scope of his duties.

[Subsection (a) as amended by 2014, 284, Sec. 68 effective January 1, 2021. See 2014, 284, Sec. 112. For text effective until January 1, 2021, see above.]

(a) Any person making application for the issuance of a firearms identification card under section 129B, a license to carry firearms under section 131 or 131F or a permit to purchase under section 131A who was not licensed under the provisions of this chapter on June 1, 1998 shall, in addition to the requirements set forth in said section 129B, 131, 131A or 131F, submit to the licensing authority a basic firearms safety certificate; provided, however, that a certificate issued by the division of law enforcement in the department of fisheries, wildlife and environmental law enforcement pursuant to the provisions of section 14 of chapter 131 evidencing satisfactory completion of a hunter education course shall serve as a valid substitute for a basic firearms safety certificate required under this section. Persons lawfully possessing a firearm identification card or license to carry firearms on June 1, 1998 shall be exempt from the provisions of this section upon expiration of such card or license and when applying for licensure as required under this chapter. No application for the issuance of a firearm identification card or license to carry shall be accepted or processed by the licensing authority without such certificate attached thereto; provided, however, that the provisions of this section shall not apply to (i) any officer, agent or employee of the commonwealth or any state of the United States; (ii) any member of the military or other service of any state or of the United States; (iii) any duly authorized law enforcement officer, agent or employee of any municipality of the commonwealth; provided, however, that any such person described in clauses (i) to (iii), inclusive, is authorized by a competent authority to carry or possess the weapon so carried or possessed and is acting within the scope of his duties.

A current member of the United States military or the Massachusetts National Guard who has not been prohibited under said section 129B from owning a firearm and has received adequate training while serving in the military shall be exempt from being required to submit a basic firearms safety certificate to the licensing authority upon submitting a copy of the member's most current military identification form.

(b) The colonel of state police shall promulgate rules and regulations governing the issuance and form of basic firearms safety certificates required by this section. Said colonel shall certify certain persons as firearms safety instructors and shall certify safety course curriculum. Such certification shall be for a period of ten years, unless sooner revoked by reason of unsuitability, in the discretion of said colonel. The department of state police may impose a fee of $50 for initial issuance of such certification to offset the cost of certifying instructors. The fee for certification renewal shall be $10. Firearms safety instructors shall be any person certified by a nationally recognized organization that fosters safety in firearms, or any other person in the discretion of said colonel, to be competent to give instruction in a basic firearms safety course. Applicants for certification as instructors under the provisions of this section shall not be exempt from the requirements of this chapter or any other law or regulation of the commonwealth or the United States. Upon application to the colonel of state police, said colonel may, in his discretion, certify as a firearms safety instructor any person who operates a firearms safety course or program which provides in its curriculum: (a) the safe use, handling and storage of firearms; (b) methods for securing and childproofing firearms; (c) the applicable laws relating to the possession, transportation and storage of firearms; and (d) knowledge of operation, potential dangers and basic competency in the ownership and usage of firearms.

[Subsection (c) effective until January 1, 2021. For text effective January 1, 2021, see below.]

(c) Any firearms safety instructor certified under the provisions of this section may, in his discretion, issue a basic firearms safety certificate to any person who successfully completes the requirements of a basic firearms safety course approved by the colonel. No firearms safety instructor shall issue or cause to be issued any basic firearms safety certificate to any person who fails to meet minimum requirements of the prescribed course of study including, but not limited to, demonstrated competency in the use of firearms. Instructors certified under the provisions of this section shall forward to the department of state police the names of those persons who have received basic firearms safety certificates. Local licensing authorities, as defined in section 121, shall, upon receipt of an application for a firearm identification card or a Class A or Class B license to carry firearms, make inquiry to the department of state police to confirm the issuance to the applicant of a basic firearms safety certificate.

[Subsection (c) as amended by 2014, 284, Sec. 68 effective January 1, 2021. See 2014, 284, Sec. 112. For text effective until January 1, 2021, see above.]

(c) Any firearms safety instructor certified under the provisions of this section may, in his discretion, issue a basic firearms safety certificate to any person who successfully completes the requirements of a basic firearms safety course approved by the colonel. No firearms safety instructor shall issue or cause to be issued any basic firearms safety certificate to any person who fails to meet minimum requirements of the prescribed course of study including, but not limited to, demonstrated competency in the use of firearms. Instructors certified under the provisions of this section shall forward to the department of state police the names of those persons who have received basic firearms safety certificates. Local licensing authorities, as defined in section 121, shall, upon receipt of an application for a firearm identification card or a license to carry firearms, make inquiry to the department of state police to confirm the issuance to the applicant of a basic firearms safety certificate.

(d) Any person applying for licensure under the provisions of this chapter who knowingly files or submits a basic firearms safety certificate to a licensing authority which contains false information shall be punished by a fine of not less that $1,000 nor more than $5,000 or by imprisonment for not more than two years in a house of correction, or by both such fine and imprisonment.

(e) Any firearms safety instructor who knowingly issues a basic firearms safety certificate to a person who has not successfully completed a firearms safety course approved by the colonel shall be punished by a fine of not less than $5,000 nor more than $10,000 or by imprisonment for not more than two years in a house of correction, or by both such fine and imprisonment.

(f) The colonel of state police shall produce and distribute public service announcements to encourage and educate the general public about: (i) safe storage and transportation of weapons pursuant to sections 131C and 131L; and (ii) importance of firearms safety education and training, including information on places and classes that a person may attend to obtain firearms safety education and training.

Section 131Q: Tracing by licensing authority of firearm, rifle or shotgun, large capacity weapon, machine gun or assault weapon used to carry out criminal act; statistical data; annual report

Section 131Q. A firearm, rifle or shotgun, large capacity weapon, machine gun or assault weapon used to carry out a criminal act shall be traced by the licensing authority for the city or town in which the crime took place. The licensing authority shall report statistical data, when the data is readily available as determined by the chief of police, including, but not limited to: (i) the make, model, serial number and caliber of the weapon used; (ii) the type of crime committed; (iii) whether an arrest or conviction was made; (iv) whether fingerprint evidence was found on the firearm; (v) whether ballistic evidence was retrieved from the crime scene; (vi) whether the criminal use of the firearm was related to known gang activity; (vii) whether the weapon was obtained illegally; (viii) whether the weapon was lost or stolen; and (ix) whether the person using the weapon was otherwise a prohibited person.

The data shall be reported to the commonwealth fusion center or the criminal firearms and trafficking unit within the division of investigation and intelligence in the department of state police established pursuant to section 6 of chapter 22C. The colonel of state police shall produce an annual report by December 31 of each year regarding crimes committed in the commonwealth using firearms, rifles or shotguns, large capacity weapons, machine guns or assault weapons, including all of the categories of data contained in this section, and shall submit a copy of the report to the joint committee on public safety and homeland security, the clerks of the house of representatives and the senate and, upon request, to criminology, public policy and public health researchers and other law enforcement agencies.

APPENDIX E - Code of Massachusetts Regulations (C.M.R.) 527 Chapter 1 Excerpts

1.12.8.39.1.1.4 Permits Not Required.

Permits shall not be required for the following:

(1) For smokeless propellants displayed in commercial establishments intended for sale and not exceeding 25 lbs. and stored in original manufacturer's containers of one lb. maximum capacity.

(2) Small arms ammunition, primers, smokeless propellants and black powder stored in original containers and stored in a locked cabinet, closet or box when not in use as provided in Section 1.12.8.50. Small arms ammunition, as used here, shall mean any shotgun, rifle, or pistol cartridge and any cartridge or propellant actuated devices, excluding military ammunition containing bursting charges or incendiary, tracer, spotting, or pyrotechnic projectiles.

Table 1.12.8.50 Permit and/or License Thresholds

UNOFFICIAL
Massachusetts Amendments to NFPA ®1, 2015

Materials	Quantities	Permit	License
Fuel oil that may be kept for use in a building or other structure.	<10,000 gallons of light or of heavy	yes	no
	≥ 10,000 gallons of light or of heavy	yes	yes
Small arms ammunition of rim fire ammunition [private use]	< 10,000 rounds	no	no
	≥10,000- 30,000 rounds	yes	no
	> 30,000 rounds	no	yes
Small arms ammunition of center fire ammunition. [private use]	< 10,000 rounds	no	no
	≥ 10,000- 50,000 rounds	yes	no
	> 50,000 rounds	no	yes
Small arms ammunition of shotgun ammunition. [private use]	< 5,000 rounds	no	no
	≥ 5,000 rounds- 50,000 rounds	yes	no
	> 50,000 rounds	no	yes
Small arms ammunition primers [private use]	< 10,000 caps or other small arms primers	no	no
	≥ 10,000 caps or other small arms primers	no	yes
Small arms ammunition primers [commercial use]	< 100,000 caps or other small arms primers	yes	no
	≥ 100,000 caps or other small arms primers caps or other small arms primers	no	yes
	< 100,000 caps or other small arms primers	yes	no
Smokeless propellants [private and commercial] Note: Persons under 18 years of age may not keep or store smokeless propellants. Note: Not more than two pounds of such propellant shall be stored in a multiple family dwelling or a building of public access.	< 16 lbs.	no	no
Smokeless propellants [private]	≥16 lbs. through 47-lbs	yes	no
Smokeless propellants [commercial]	> 48 lbs.	no	yes
	≥25 -lbs to < 99 lbs.	yes	no
	≥100 lbs.	no	yes
Black powder [private and commercial] Note Persons under 18 years of age may not keep or store any amount of black powder.	< 2 lbs.	no	no
Black powder [private]	< 5lbs.	yes	no
Black powder [commercial] See Section 1.12.8.39.2.5.1 for permit exemption individual.	≥5 lbs.	no	yes
Special industrial explosive devices	< 50 lbs. net weight of explosives	no	no

About the Author

Originally Mark Shean came from the state of Maine and has been involved with the organized and unorganized shooting sports since 1963 at the age of seven.

In 2000 Shean became a MA State Basic Firearm Safety Course Instructor and overlapping that a certified NRA Law Enforcement firearm instructor, for six years. He is also certified currently in six additional civilian disciplines through the NRA.

Mark joined the US Merchant Marines when he graduated high school. In 1987 he went to work as a Nuclear Security Officer as regulated under the Nuclear Regulatory Commission at the Pilgrim Nuclear Power Station in MA to the present day. His firearm abilities/qualifications are all stringently documented through four varying courses of fire annually, with a minimum score of 80% to pass. Mark's percentage has been a constant 97.3% for 30+ years.

With an LLC business partner, Shean invented and produced a part for a popular shotgun, the (KSG) with a patent pending at shotgunswitch.com.

The course that Shean gives under the State Police guidelines is taken very seriously, this is how his Gun Sense series evolved, it is with the hope that it will help people understand laws surrounding firearm ownership in MA, as well as safety aspects that are relevant no matter where you may live.

His writing style is his own, his passion for the information is genuine and his firearm knowledge comes from many decades of experience that is generational in his family. This is not something new.

It is the hope that you enjoyed *Gun Sense* and pass it on. It could make a good addition in your personal library, hunting camp or anywhere that firearms and citizens are found together.

Mark Shean can be contacted via email at:

mshean1955@yahoo.com

You may also learn more about Mark, his classes and what he is up to at his homepage:

http://mafirearmsafety.com/

Made in the USA
Middletown, DE
06 September 2023

38129744R00191